# AMERICAN
# SOCIALIST

# AMERICAN SOCIALIST

## LAURENCE GRONLUND
### AND THE POWER BEHIND REVOLUTION

Ryan C. McIlhenny

LOUISIANA STATE UNIVERSITY PRESS

BATON ROUGE

Published by Louisiana State University Press
lsupress.org

DESIGNER: Barbara Neely Bourgoyne
TYPEFACES: Minion Pro, text; URW Windsor and Jophey WF, display

A portion of Chapter 4 appeared as "Sacred Socialism: Morality, Humanity, and the Divine in
Laurence Gronlund's *Our Destiny*" in the *Journal for the Study of Radicalism*, vol. 17, no. 1 (2023).

Cover illustration: Sketch of Laurence Gronlund in *The Comrade: An Illustrated Socialist Monthly*,
February 1905, by J. H. E. Partington.

Cataloging-in-Publication Data are available at the Library of Congress.

ISBN 978-0-8071-8351-9 (cloth) | ISBN 978-0-8071-8409-7 (pdf) |
ISBN 978-0-8071-8408-0 (epub)

*To my greatest gifts—Fisher, Canon, Josiah, and Selah—*

*and my greatest love on this side of eternity—Beck.*

# CONTENTS

# ACKNOWLEDGMENTS

It's not uncommon for a historian of slavery and the antislavery movement to enter the world of postemancipation labor. With the continuing contributions provided in the history of capitalism, where scholars have shown the relationship between antebellum slavery and postbellum labor as part of the *longue durée* of American capitalism, the progression only seems natural.

But *American Socialist* is more than just a scholarly exercise for an intellectual community. It is a work born out of conviction, written by someone who finished his PhD a few months before the Great Recession, and who, as a conscious member of an ever-growing intellectual proletariat, continues to navigate the challenges that capitalism has brought to academia. Furthermore, the book is a kind of olive branch, a token offered to heal a divided country. Within the last half-century (though one could easily go back farther), Americans have been warned repeatedly and with increasing intensity of an imminent socialist takeover through government legislation related to social security protections, farm pricing, bank deposit insurance, desegregation, civil rights, healthcare, and climate protections. I was five when Ronald Reagan won the presidency, and for much of my life, I've waited for this harrowing apocalypse to finally manifest itself. While waiting (not so patiently), I've found myself echoing what a frustrated Slavoj Žižek asked of Jordan Peterson in a debate a few years ago: "Where are these Marxists?"

*American Socialist* reconsiders a period of America's socialist past. It does so in the hope of (a) assuaging the unwarranted fears about socialism itself (especially in America), which has continued to exacerbate the country's political and cultural divide, and (b) speaking to those readers concerned over the failures of global capitalism, especially in the aftermath of the Great Recession, and what such failures have produced today. During his life in late-nineteenth-century America, Laurence Gronlund, the central figure of this intellectual biography, offered a clear presentation of how capitalism worked, related centrally to the "fleecing" of value via surplus labor. Even in a postindustrial, information, or gig economy, capitalism continues to function in this way. Can there be capitalism without exploitation? Gronlund's work is relevant for contemporary readers. The average American is working longer hours with less pay, while the wealthiest 1 percent (and less than), both individually and corporately, are raking in record profits. In one sense, we can look to Gronlund as a bridge from the maturing developments of socialism in its golden period in the first quarter of the twentieth century to its revival in the twenty-first. In a world still reeling from the worst economic collapse since the Great Depression—producing historic global inflation, supply-chain issues, a climate crisis, a migrant humanitarian crisis, actual war, a once-in-a-century global pandemic, the rise of fascist authoritarian regimes, a corporate media ecosystem that has intensified an on-the-ground tribalism that spreads like cancer through society—many have asked, as I have, what can be done? The same question was raised by socialist thinkers and thinkers who were sympathetic to socialism (artists, professors, journalists, lawyers, and preachers) for well over a century.

Among the many tired and frustrated are those willing to create a better world. Since 2020, labor activism has been on the rise in the United States. The summer of 2023 alone may soon stand as a critical moment in the history of American labor, becoming a historical equivalent to earlier periods of worker activism. With the growth in labor unrest (autoworkers, writers, actors, scholars, and teachers) and the intensification of neo-fascist politics, I believe this work is important for understanding the contradictions and negative social consequences of contemporary capitalism. Yet more than a critique, this intellectual biography reminds readers of a central feature of American socialism—cooperation.

I am indebted to the handful of experts who patiently offered their time and critical eye to *American Socialist*. I especially want to thank Janine Giordano Drake not only for her observations but also her encouragement regarding the project. And, once again, I am grateful to Rand Dotson for his early endorsement of such a "timely" project. I also want to acknowledge the many workers in a variety of industries in America today who have shown the courage to stand up against corporate greed and exploitation.

# AMERICAN SOCIALIST

# BECAUSE HE WEARS HIS HAIR MUCH LONGER

## An Uncommon American Socialist

In 1895, a journalist for the *Sacramento Bee* attended a lecture delivered by Laurence Gronlund (1844–1899), who was considered by contemporaries to be the "ablest exponent of modern Socialism."[1] The author began his essay by describing Gronlund as someone who looked "like a socialist, because he wears his hair much longer than is the prevailing style."[2] Gronlund was a "quiet, scholarly gentleman," another sympathetic audience member noted, willing to consider the opinions of others, with eyes that grew wider and brighter the more he spoke. He stood with a "good forehead," undoubtedly a phrenological reference to the quality of his "perceptive faculties."[3] As was often the case after a long night of speaking, however, this dynamic figure would go out "penniless and hungry to find a bed in some public park."[4] He would settle into a night's rest "under the steps of the hall," Helen Sumner observed, where he had recently stirred "the hearts and minds of an attentive audience."[5] With his "scraggly whiskers," "mustache" and apparel "so plain as to be almost shabby," as two other writers observed, Gronlund's arguments for a new society based on the principles of collective cooperation, which he had delivered numerous times and in numerous places across the United States, were electrifying.[6] As a passionate radical committed to confronting the moral bankruptcy of a society built upon unrestrained capitalism, Gronlund was certainly out of place, a gentle though committed activist living as a kind of intellectual wayfarer whose principles ran much deeper than shallow bourgeois appearances.

Gronlund was born in Denmark in 1844. Not much is known about his early education, but he did go on to study law at the University of Copenhagen. He later served in the Danish-German War of 1864 (the Second Schleswig War) before relocating to the United States in 1867, where, for a short time, he taught German in a Milwaukee school. He then began a legal career in Illinois in 1869.[7] Gronlund became a citizen of a country reborn—a postbellum nation rapidly transformed by a densely interconnected railroad system, heavy industry, innovative corporate strategies for profit maximization, a growing urban sector that brought greater social and cultural pluralism, and an extensive professional bureaucracy.[8] These were the conditions that would propel America into becoming a global economic and political powerhouse.[9] If this represented the side of "progress," there was a flipside—one that included devastating natural disasters, crowded cities, labor exploitation, social dislocation, a renewed commitment to white supremacy, and the palpable withering of democracy. Such symptoms of American industrial capitalism weighed heavily on the minds of many who found socialism a powerful ideological agent for positive change. Increasingly unsettled by the consequences of this Second Industrial Revolution and growing, according to Stow Persons, "understandably estranged from a profession so largely concerned with the adjudication of conflicting property interests," Gronlund gave up practicing law in 1879 to establish "a less remunerative but more congenial career" as a journalist and lecturer, communicating with evangelical fervor America's imminent transformation into a collectivist commonwealth.[10] Despite its inevitability, the future socialist commonwealth required careful preparation. Gronlund understood the immensity of such a herculean task, given, he admitted in 1880, that the number of socialists in America could be counted on one hand.[11] Yet the new age required only a handful of capable "world-historical figures," to use a Hegelian term, to lead the country into the new era.

In 1884, he published the *Co-operative Commonwealth in Its Outlines: An Exposition of Modern Socialism,* an American adaptation of Marxian socialism, the first of its kind in the United States. Gronlund's unique brand of socialism as laid out in *Commonwealth* had a tremendous impact on several reformers and radicals in the late nineteenth and early twentieth centuries. These, among others, included Edward Bellamy, Julius Augustus Wayland, Frances Willard, Washington Gladden, and, Gronlund's "most eminent disciple," Eugene V. Debs.[12] Writer William Dean Howells considered Gronlund "a man to be read with respect [and] by anyone who wishes to acquaint himself with the hopes and motives of a very intelligent body of men."[13] Popular novelist Edward Bellamy expressed confidence that "school children of the future would be taught to revere the name of Lawrence Gronlund [*sic*]."[14] And his influence stretched across the Atlantic. After writing *Commonwealth,* Gronlund spent a couple of years interacting with a handful of socialists and progressive thinkers in England and France.[15] In England, he was introduced to the British Socialist League and later elected to its council.[16] He was a favorite among the British Fabians, especially, for a time, author and playwright George Bernard Shaw. British novelist William H. Mallock described Gronlund as "the fairest-minded of all our modern Socialists."[17] In France, he was a guest of Jules Guedes and Paul LaFargue, leaders of the French Left. Charles Gide, Professor of Political Economy at the University of Montpellier, referred to Gronlund as "one of the most thoughtful and well-informed social philosophers of our time."[18] Gronlund began a lifelong correspondence with Gide when the two met at a conference in Lyon. Also in France, Gronlund spent a few months at the *Familieriste* cooperative created by Jean Francois Godin. Although initially impressed, he soon became disillusioned with Godin's community. During his stay in Europe, Gronlund wrote *Ça Ira, or Danton in the French Revolution,* not only a history but a philosophy of history. The book was published in Boston in 1886, a year after his return to the United States.

Shortly thereafter, Gronlund joined the Socialist Labor Party, founded in 1876. By the early 1880s, the SLP, made up of "a heterogeneous collection of anarchists, trade unionists, and political actionists," reached a membership of about 1,500. At one point, Gronlund served on the executive committee.[19] Although valuing the work of the party and supporting it in terms of its ideals, he eventually left the group not only because of its overuse of the German language in the meetings, which, in his mind, would have alienated English speakers (similar to what Engels said about the Forty-Eighter German immigrants), but more so, he confessed, because of the drinking bouts that went on afterwards.[20] Politically active throughout his life, the one experience that garnered much public attention was his engagement with the reform efforts of Henry George. Around the time of George's 1886 bid for mayor of New York, Gronlund had written a couple of pamphlets critical of George's single-tax philosophy, a central tenet of George's United Labor Party. Gronlund was quickly identified as one of George's most aggressive critics; indeed, George blamed Gronlund and the socialists for his failed mayoral campaign.[21] Gronlund's tone was stirred in part by George's own harsh and demeaning words against socialism, which included charges that socialists not only lacked a truly radical strategy for change but also (and more importantly) because of their divisiveness in agitating for ideological purity. Gronlund's main criticism, in turn, was that George ultimately failed to grasp the problem of wealth and poverty, especially as it related to the core elements of historic capitalism—namely, labor exploitation. George's tax on the value of land, in Gronlund's judgment, would have done little to alleviate the suffering of workers under capitalism.

Gronlund's interaction with George revealed an important element in his strategy for radical change. Although unwavering in his principles, Gronlund knew when to be pragmatic (at least early in his life) when it came to building political coalitions; that is, while he disagreed with a handful of fellow reformers and their corresponding agencies—George and his United Labor Party, Edward Bellamy's social blueprint in *Equality*, and the Populists of the early 1890s—he nonetheless was willing to work with each, though he did express serious dismay over the popular support for William Jennings Bryan and free-silver.[22] Gronlund did all this while crisscrossing the nation, lecturing at a variety of conferences, churches, and universities. In 1893, he spoke at the Labor Congress at the World's Fair Columbian Exposition in Chicago—organized, according to Shelton Stromquist, to address the "problems of labor and capital, industrial advancement, and the need for labor legislation." Members of the Labor Congress sought a "peaceful solution" to the labor question, holding that a war between labor and capital would be "suicidal." Attendees included Henry Demarest Lloyd, Clarence Darrow, Richard T. Ely, Washington Gladden, George McNeill, Florence Kelley, Samuel Gompers, Henry George, Henry Adams, and William Dwight Porter Bliss.[23] Gronlund was also quick to travel wherever labor activism was most intense, as in the tragic unrest among the "starving miners" (Gronlund's words) of Spring Valley, Illinois in 1895, where he offered instruction in the ways of socialist cooperation in confronting the power "exercised by capital."[24] Sadly, as was frequently the case, Gronlund ignored the serious racial dynamics interwoven into the conflicts between labor and capital, especially in the Spring Valley conflict. Toward the end of his life, Gronlund seemed to become increasingly impatient with reform. Nonetheless, he believed that such nonradical efforts would move society closer to collectivism. What tempered such frustration was his additional belief that despite how effective such programs might be, history would continue along its course. The collective commonwealth would come regardless of impediments, whether from the staunch opposition of capitalists or the half-measures of reformers.

In a letter to Richard Ely in 1891, Gronlund, frustrated with ineffective political activity, wrote of his intentions to establish a socialist fraternity in the Fabian tradition. Membership in the new society, Gronlund proposed, would include "a disposition to welcome the extension of the functions of government" and exclude, as one twentieth-century writer noted, "the followers of [Henry] George and Herbert Spencer."[25] Such specific qualifications, however, were quickly ignored by organizers. He and Bliss became the "leading spirits" in founding the American Fabian Society (AFS) along with its main mouthpiece *The American Fabian* in 1895.[26] The goal of the society was "to unite social reformers and lead the way to a conception of Socialism, broad enough, free enough, practical enough to include all that is of value, no matter when it comes, and replace jealousy between reformers by cooperation for the general good."[27] American Fabians "emphasized eclecticism of thought" and elevated education over political partisanship.[28] And like the Knights of Labor, they pursued the creation of an organization that would align with the machinery of republican democracy. Disillusioned if not wholly frustrated with the Democratic Party in 1896, Gronlund compelled political leaders to "become conscious" that the country was "standing on the threshold of the greatest of all centuries." If the Democratic Party refused to change, doubling down on its ultimately ineffective reforms, or if it failed to confront Republicans' loyalty to the plutocracy, then the country would have to say goodbye "to the many noble hopes which lovers of their kind in this country have connected with the coming twentieth century." By 1899, Gronlund called for a simpler agenda for a new Democratic Party—namely, "to take care of the interests of the poor." With such a focus, "What," he asked, "does it matter if the party be denounced as 'socialistic'?"[29]

After the release of *Commonwealth*, as Henry F. May argued, Gronlund "moved toward a definitely religious emphasis."[30] He found a strong alliance with religious intellectuals—touring with Kingdom Movement founder George Herron and working with Christian socialists like W. D. P. Bliss to establish Fabian-friendly religious agencies throughout the country. He was an occasional speaker at Bliss's Church of the Carpenter in Boston, a favorite meeting place for reformers and radicals, including members of the Society of Christian Socialists. He would go on to serve "as vice-president of the Social Reform Union," organized by Bliss in the 1890s.[31] Although far from a traditionalist when it came to Christian dogma, Gronlund's beliefs influenced leaders of the Social Gospel movement, including Washington Gladden and Walter Rauschenbusch. According to Christopher Evans, the "socialist language of solidarity with the poor, its indictment of wealth, and its vision of a just society paralleled many of the social gospel visions of the kingdom of God as an earthly ideal."[32] In his 2020 biography of Christian Socialist, author, and politician J. Stitt Wilson, Stephen Barton writes that much of socialism's "analysis blended easily with the moral and religious claims from which it was largely derived—the workers are entitled to the product of their labor, the land belongs to all God's children, the wealth of the nation is a product of society, and no individual has a right to take a disproportionate share of it. These were basic elements of the Cooperative Commonwealth, another name for socialism."[33] In her examination of the late-nineteenth-century religious Left, contemporary historian Janine Giordano Drake distinguishes between the "minster-led Social Gospel movement" from the "much broader cacophony of religious visionaries." The latter group utilized religious rhetoric against "modern industrial capitalism on the twin bases of Jesus' historic life and ministry, and the Church's professed principles of cooperative ownership and exchange."[34] Gronlund fit within this more eclectic religious category. With the rising influence of the Social Gospel movement, Gronlund sought to address the relationship between religion and morality within socialism.

While working to construct a national collective that fit the American character, Gronlund faced several personal challenges throughout his life. The death of his first wife in 1892 dealt a heavy blow to his heart and health.[35] Despite his immense sadness (contemplating suicide on more than one occasion) and his steep physical and mental decline, he continued to write and lecture. He found, according to one journalist, that "there was nothing in life left that was worth living for, save the good of his fellow man, and he devoted himself to the propaganda of Collectivism."[36] He soon found love again when he met and married Beulah Alice Carey, an artist and art teacher, on December 24, 1895. He would carry "his wife's photograph with him wherever he went, and often when writing would stand it up before him so that the sweet, blue eyes might inspire and console him in his work."[37] Immediately into the following year, Gronlund moved with his new wife to Seattle, where Beulah organized the Seattle Humane Society, focusing on the prohibition of cruelty to animals.[38] By 1898, Gronlund fell into what today might be considered a serious bout of depression, no doubt exacerbated by his dismal financial situation. He worked through the melancholy with financial assistance from a few reformers, including Jane Addams and Henry Demarest Lloyd, and in writing his final book, *The New Economy*, published in the same year that the U.S. went to war against Spain.[39] *New Economy* offered practical guidance (e.g., creating new democratic agencies to reform existing institutions) on how to move the country closer to the cooperative commonwealth.[40] On October 18, 1899, after writing one of his final pieces on the economic benefits of the sugar beet industry, Gronlund, that "sad gentle-faced dreamer," died suddenly in his room at the Trenton Hotel in New York at the age of 55.[41] Caring little for himself, Gronlund worked tirelessly, wrote A. B. Edler, "to make the world a garden and life a song for the human race."[42]

A considerable challenge in understanding the mind of Laurence Gronlund relates to his journey toward and final embrace of socialism. It is unlikely that it came from his experiences in Copenhagen. In *Strengths and Weaknesses of Socialism*, Richard Ely wrote that the European countries of Scandinavia, Denmark, and Sweden especially, hardly "displayed any considerable socialistic activity." The life of socialism in Gronlund's home country had, at its beginning, "the sicknesses of childhood," according to Gustav Bang.[43] Nonetheless, socialism grew slowly in these parts of Europe. But how strong was the presence of socialism in Gronlund's adopted country, the United States? Although introduced to a favorable audience in the early 1820s, socialism received its highest reception in the postbellum era.[44] Indeed, Gronlund admitted that 1877, a critical year for labor, "fixed the date" for the appearance of modern socialism in America, marking "the entrance of the working class into the political arena."[45] The year 1877 was not only a significant marker for the history of labor in America, but it also launched Gronlund's collectivist career. In St. Louis, a city that some had identified as America's Paris Commune, Gronlund, under the name Peter Lofgreen, helped to rally the frustrations of depressed rail workers. For the capitalist class, labor's takeover of the city represented the "dangers of a conscious working class" intent on overthrowing "existing governments."[46] Gronlund was eventually arrested and charged, according to a writer for the St. Louis *Daily Journal,* with being a "notorious Communist, spiritualist, and general demoralizer."[47] The case against Gronlund and his fellow leaders was flimsy, and the charges were eventually dropped.

It is difficult to know exactly what the unrest of 1877 had on Gronlund's socialism. Certainly, it must have influenced the writing of his first major work (now lost) in 1878, *The Coming Revolution?* One can only wonder why he waited until 1879 to identify as a full-fledged socialist.[48] In 1890, he wrote about his 1879 conversion.[49] Although nothing is mentioned about his activism in 1877, his turn to socialism was something that he could not resist. "I could not help myself," he admitted.[50] Whatever he may have thought about his experience in St. Louis as Lofgreen, Gronlund's conversion was motivated by his own private study. He was a voracious reader. In his mind, books dispelled ignorance by providing useful knowledge for the reader. This included the ways in which they acted "as mirrors," he said, whereby individuals would be confronted with completely new ideas or latent ones that needed to be drawn out. Gronlund was one among many moved by leftist literature. "The printed word," writes Jason Martineck, "was 'mental dynamite,' razing ignorance and opening the mind to the Cooperative Commonwealth."[51] The popularity of socialism in America between the 1880s and 1920 coincided with the "golden age" of books. Socialists took full advantage of the changes occurring in American society, including an increase in literacy, by the turn of the twentieth century.[52]

Interestingly, the one book (strangely absent from his 1890 testimonial) that moved Gronlund, by his own admission, to embrace socialism was Blaise Pascal's *Pensées:* "I really started on the road to Socialism in 1876 by reading Pascal's *Pensees,* and formed gradually a scheme of my own, which in 1879 I found out was plain Socialism."[53] This raises the obvious question as to how. Pascal's "terrible illustration" of the "world as a slaughterhouse," Gronlund confessed, led him "to become a collectivist, a preacher of national co-operation."[54] Beyond this admission, Gronlund is silent, but it would be enlightening to probe a bit more. One might consider how Pascal influenced Gronlund's socialism by exploring the mind of an actual Pascalian Marxist— the twentieth-century philosopher Lucien Goldmann (1913–1970). First, an element in Goldmann's philosophy that certainly shared an affinity with Gronlund's was the emphasis on Pascal's view of the ego as "detestable"; this helped to formulate Goldmann's antagonism toward individualism, a major tenet of the American character. Second, Goldmann, following Pascal, believed that the self was something created in the dynamics of community: "The ontological basis of history is the relation of men with other men, the fact that the individual 'I' exists only against the background of the community."[55] What Pascal and Marx, writes Michael Löwy, "have in common is the refusal of pure individualism . . . and the belief in trans-individual values—God for religion, the human community for socialism."[56] Gronlund, too, as demonstrated consistently through his works, despised individualism and argued that there was no isolated "self" that existed without others. Third, cooperating with others was not only the means to understand the individual self but also to come nearer to God: complete consciousness of humanity was at the same time consciousness of the divine. Consequently, both Goldmann and Gronlund acknowledge that faith was the engine of radical change. Pascal's wager rested on a faith in the liberation of humanity via the existence of God; Marx's wager rested on the liberation of humanity *by* humanity. "Marxist faith," Goldmann argued in *Hidden God,* "is a faith in the future which men make themselves in and through history. Or, more accurately, in the future that we must make for ourselves by what we do, so that this faith becomes a 'wager' which we make that our actions will, in fact, be successful. The transcendental element present in this faith is not supernatural and does not take us outside or beyond history, it merely takes us beyond the individual."[57] Faith, Goldmann intimates, is based not on a critical evaluation or a judgment of facts, but on a wager—a choice weighed in light of not-yet-realized outcomes.[58] What Pascal and Marx shared in terms of faith was a risk of failure mixed with a very real hope of success. Faith could be defined as confidence that a better world is possible. Gronlund certainly exhibited such a faith, placing him in the category of a philosophical theologian more than a socialist agitator.

The second reason Gronlund gave for his turn to socialism revolved around his historical perspective. Socialism was not a static system, but a philosophy of history: "It discloses to us a clear-cut plan running like a reed through human affairs since the dawn of history. It shows us that each period of the long and weary past was a necessary, preparatory step to each succeeding stage, and that the present is but a transition period to the golden age ahead on whose threshold we stand."[59] Playwright and Gronlund admirer

George Bernard Shaw, who published Gronlund's *Co-operative Common-wealth* for a London audience, expressed skepticism of "abstract economics," arguing that no economic theory was "to be trusted unless it can be experien-tially verified by tracing its expression in history."[60] Even as one contemporary scholar noted, capitalism cannot be fully understood if viewed as anything other than historical.[61] Gronlund learned from Marx that history depended on the variations in the modes of production over time, which determined, as Marx wrote in *Contribution to the Critique of Political Economy*, the "gen-eral character of the social, political, and spiritual processes of life."[62] For orthodox Marxists, writes John Judis, history was divided into "distinct stages defined by relations of production (classes) and forces of production (tech-nology) and punctuated by revolutionary upheavals."[63] Gronlund agreed with Marx that history advanced through the succession of modes of production—slavery, serfdom, and wagedom—although Gronlund placed greater weight on the moving power of ideas. Modes of production would begin, develop, and then eventually come to an end, followed by a new mode of production that would go through a similar cycle until there was nothing left to over-come. Ideas would either lead to new modes of production or be shaped in and through such material changes. And each period of production likewise would create new social power relationships—aristocratic masters, feudal lords, and the bourgeoisie. With the cessation of a form of production, social relations would be altered and give rise to a new power elite.

Each material stage had within it the seeds of its own destruction, a kind of entelechy of capitalism.[64] The capitalists of Gronlund's day believed that competition was the lifeblood of the entire system, for it incentivized work-ers. Without it, production would decline and eventually come to a complete halt. But capitalism has never sought to preserve competition; its *telos* is precisely the opposite. Expanding capitalism demands the removal of obsta-cles in the way of its goal: monopoly. In the late nineteenth century, capital-ists publicly, not to mention hypocritically, commended competition while transgressing it privately (though never privately enough). "The industrial capitalist of today [1899] is a collective person," Rosa Luxemburg once wrote: "it has become *socialized*."[65] The robber barons of the Gilded Age recog-nized how cooperation—i.e., cooperation among like-minded capitalists—consolidated production to maximize private wealth.[66] Cooperation could be utilized to defeat competition. John D. Rockefeller, for instance, placed several companies under the control of a governing board with himself as the chairman, giving birth to the modern corporate board. Such companies would be placed under the "trust" of upper-level (and unseen) corporate managers.[67] Gronlund repeatedly wrote about how the trust represented the most developed stage of capitalism. He defined this form of business organization as "a combination of interests, by various corporations in a given line of business, to stop competition between themselves and thus regulate production."[68] The trust was essentially cooperative. As corporations came to realize the monetary benefits of cooperation ("for the benefit of capitalists"), more trusts would be created by different industries.[69] Yet because it was inherently cooperative—and hence socialistic—the trust was not simply a portent but the very source of capitalism's demise.[70] This was why Gronlund believed that the first successful socialist country would be the United States. Once workers came to embrace the benefits of cooperation, they too would harness its effectiveness for their own mutual benefit and break the stranglehold of monopolistic capitalism. If the trust was successful for the plutocratic few, how much more of a benefit would it be for the democratic many? Eventually, the wealthy elite would be unable to control the trust and use it for their own competitive purposes. Cooperation would break through and become the guiding function of society.

In *Looking Backward*, Edward Bellamy echoed Gronlund's understanding of the trust as a form of cooperation; therefore, Gronlund and others believed that Bellamy simply fictionalized Gronlund's *Cooperative Commonwealth*. Consider, for instance, the "Great Trust" in Chapter 5 of *Looking Backward*:

Early in the last century the evolution was completed by the final consolidation of the entire capital of the nation. The industry and commerce of the country, ceasing to be conducted by a set of irresponsible corporations and syndicates of private persons at their caprice and for their profit, were entrusted to a single syndicate representing the people, to be conducted in the common interest for the common profit. The nation, that is to say, organized as the one great business corporation in which all other corporations were absorbed; it became the one capitalist in the place of all other capitalists, the sole employer, the final monopoly in which all previous and lesser monopolies were swallowed up, a monopoly in the profits and economies of which all citizens shared. The epoch of the trusts had ended in The Great Trust. In a word, the people of the United States concluded to assume the conduct of their own business, just as one hundred odd years before they had assumed the conduct of their own government, organizing now for industrial purposes on precisely the same grounds that they had then organized for political purposes. At last, strangely late in the world's history, the obvious fact was perceived that no business is so essentially the public business as the industry and commerce on which the people's livelihood depends, and that to entrust it to private persons to be managed for private profit is a folly similar in kind, though vastly greater in magnitude, to that of surrendering the functions of political government to kings and nobles to be conducted for their personal glorification.[71]

The "advent of the Trust," Bellamy wrote in "Plutocracy or Nationalism," marked the "beginning of the end of the competitive system in industry."[72] Plenty of others recognized a similar reality. Imogen Fales, architect of the Cooperative Congress, believed that "co-operation" represented the "natural tendency of organic life"; it was the "next stage of social development."[73] The Farmers' Alliance encouraged farmers to employ the "same scheme" as corporate monopolists; otherwise, there would be "nothing but serfdom for the industrial classes in the future."[74] By the 1890s, cooperatives of the Knights of Labor and the Farmers' Alliance echoed Gronlund: "there is only one successful way to fight [corporate monopolies], and that is to fight them with a Trust."[75] A writer for *The New Nation* expressed his position that labor could in fact accomplish such a task: "[If] capitalists can manage [oil and rail] for their own selfish ends, then we, the people, can just as well manage them for our own use and benefit."[76]

The trust for Gronlund was more than simply a pragmatic strategy for capitalists to protect their wealth or for workers to protect themselves. It was an inevitable development of the law of history. Gronlund's philosophy of history incorporated the work not only of Marx but also Herbert Spencer and Georg Wilhelm Friedrich Hegel. The United States had become a "Darwinian country," given the ways in which such a paradigm, contemporary historian Jonathan Levy writes, "gripped the imagination of the U.S. bourgeoisie."[77] Spencer likewise captured the interests of socialists. Marx expressed his own enthusiasm for Darwin's *Origin of Species*, realizing, as he communicated to his partner Friedrich Engels, that it was the "book which contains the natural-historical foundation of our outlook."[78] Yet socialists had to separate Spencer's organism from his individualism—a liberal individualism unfriendly to collectivism. Gronlund, according to Richard Hofstadter, "used Spencer's idea of the social organism to refute Spencer's individualism."[79] Gronlund certainly gave credit to Spencer "for his profound speculations on the Social Organism," admitting that he successfully "laid the foundation for constructive Socialism," but he had to separate the organicist side of Spencer from the more popular individualistic side.[80] Yet he was critical of Spencer's individualism (symptomatic of his liberalism)—namely, that the individual, the only real entity in society, had a right to do whatever he pleased so long as his actions did not infringe the rights of others.[81] This "first principle," in Gronlund's words, ignored the responsibility the individual had toward the commonwealth, a notably republican virtue, and the motivation behind the individual competition enabled the social devastation that Gronlund abhorred. Competition derived from the "struggle for life," which "Herbert Spencer glorifies" and that Gronlund later identified as nothing more than "the enthronement of a *lie!*"[82] The only thing that Spencer could justify as "real," from Gronlund's reading, was the individual; society was an abstraction. Gronlund corrected Spencer, so to speak, by reversing the order: "society is the real, and the individual the abstract."[83] It should be noted that many who read Spencer, whether apologists or opponents of capitalism, did so quite selectively, ignoring part of his argument that "egoism" would turn into "altruism," eventually "bringing voluntary cooperation and industrial peace."[84] He was "by no means," Geoffrey Hawthorne has written, "an unqualified apologist for unrestrained competition."[85] Indeed, Spencer was horrified by the conditions at a Carnegie steelworks plant when visiting the U.S. in 1882. "Six months' stay here," he concluded, "would justify suicide."[86]

Spencer defined evolution as a "change from an indefinite, incoherent homogeneity, to a definite, coherent heterogeneity; through continuous differentiations and integrations."[87] What Spencer meant by an "incoherent homogenization" was the attraction and drawing together of disparate things, which would then give way to a unified differentiation, as in the case of the interdependent unity of differing organs in the human body, what Spencer also called "coherent heterogeneity." The process of the "relative indefinite [and] incoherent homogeneity to a relatively definite, coherent heterogeneity" included a concomitant "dissipation of motion." Driving the phenomena of evolution was, Spencer claimed, the "Persistence of Force" tying the indestructibility of matter with the continuity of motion until reaching equilibrium.[88] While it was compelling on purely naturalistic grounds, many, including Gronlund, felt that more was needed. Undergirding his evolutionary perspective and modified Marxism, Gronlund believed that a divine force, what he repeatedly referred to as the "Power behind evolution," guided history.[89] It was not merely the mechanics of the trust, for instance, that would lead to socialism. Rather, it was the divine power using the trust to reach the end of capitalism (history); nothing was strong enough to thwart this invisible hand of socialism. Capitalists (unwittingly, of course) conceded to practical socialism (via the trust), not because they would come to accept the idea of socialism but because they could not help but comply with the direction of the divine order.[90] Furthermore, efforts to destroy the trust, Gronlund warned, were "radically wrong." As Hegel reasoned in his philosophy of right, which galvanized Gronlund's socialism, whatever "is," that is whatever exists in terms of immediate being and experience, is so because it is a necessary part of the historical development toward absolute freedom. As a uniquely "American phenomenon," Gronlund stated, the trust would swiftly lead society to its "predestined goal."[91]

By the 1890s, convinced that the socialist revolution had to be grasped by the "very highest moral and religious truths," Gronlund began to distance himself from the strict naturalism of Spencer.[92] His social philosophy increasingly fell under the scope of an idealism close to that of Hegel's. A writer for the London-based *Pall Mall Gazette* stated that Gronlund "learned from the Hegelians something of the philosophy of history."[93] We should also note that in his final years, Gronlund himself began to associate with Hegel. In 1895, he admitted to a journalist that his version of socialism was "based upon" the investigations "made by Hegel and Karl Marx."[94] There is more than a hint of Hegel's cosmic philosophical theology in Gronlund's later work, especially the notion that the organic development of humanity was also the progress of God reaching full consciousness.[95] For instance, humanity and the divine, intertwined in the process of self-becoming through active cooperation, would attain their liberating unity in the organism of the State. For Henry Schneider, Gronlund's "idealistic theory of the state," presented in *Cooperative Commonwealth,* was "derived largely from Hegel," whose ethical order (*sittlichkeit*), the social interdependence of moral life, also reached its realization in the state organism.[96] The United States was quickly approaching a Hegelian-like collective moment—a "rational socialism," Gronlund observed.[97] Ushered in by "devoutly religious minds," who recognized the "mysteries of God" acting through history, the commonwealth would be identified with the Kingdom of God on earth.[98] Gronlund's *Our Destiny*, published in 1891, represented not only the most mature articulation of his socialism, but also the highest point of his religious perspective and thus his overall philosophy. The post-1890 revisions of the *Cooperative Commonwealth* reflected these developments.

The final reason as to why Gronlund became a full-fledged socialist rested on the moral awakening "palpably taking place," he said, in the minds of Americans generally. He recognized the growing discontent among citizens, especially among workers—workers who experienced the social devastation caused by capitalism. This moral awakening was due, he argued, not so much to declining conditions (American workers being better off than their counterparts in Europe), but a general "increase in unhappiness."[99] Americans realized that they did not share in the material gains brought about by capitalism. The massive amount of wealth created by industrial workers and commercial farm laborers went to the plutocratic few, who, in turn, controlled the levers of power to protect their ever-growing wealth and suppress the will of the people. Such prosperity did not erase, in Gronlund's mind, the spiritual "poverty" of the reigning plutocrats.[100] More and more Americans came to understand that their unhappiness was intensified by the way the ideology of wealth perverted morality itself. Competitive individualism, reinforced by the individualism of Spencer and serving the interests of mammon, was the idol of the late nineteenth century. It led to abandoning that which was at the core of morality—a concern for the well-being of others. Americans were led to believe that true happiness meant getting the edge over their fellow citizen.

The idea of socialism appeared in America as early as the 1820s and generally referred to a vision of a healthy society based on cooperation.[101] With the publication of Daniel Raymond's *Thoughts on Political Economy* (1820), a kind of proto-progressive study on the nature of economic democracy, and Robert Owen's presentation of socialism before both houses of Congress in 1823 where he argued in favor of "union and cooperation" over that of "individual interest" (i.e., competition), reformers had been exploring the importance of cooperation around the time that the United States was going through its own market revolution.[102] "In its loosest usage," according to

Jacob Dorn, socialism "could mean little more than unselfishness, or social cooperation, the opposite of 'individualism.'"[103] A handful of cooperative associations appeared in America throughout much of the nineteenth century. America, Friedrich Engels wrote, was ahead of most countries in moving toward socialism: "Communism, social existence and activity based on community of goods, is not only possible but has already been realized in many communities in America."[104] Gronlund provided a definition of his own brand of socialism in the opening chapter of his *Co-operative Commonwealth* (1884): "The co-operative commonwealth is that future social order—the natural heir of the present one in which all important instruments of production have been taken under collective control; in which the citizens are consciously public functionaries, and in which their labors are rewarded according to results."[105] The ownership of the means of production, arguably the highest form of cooperation, was a shared feature running through the variations of socialism. In *Socialism in Theory and Practice*, Morris Hillquit wrote that socialism "advocates the transfer of ownership in the social tools of production—the land, factories, machinery, railroads, mines, etc.—from the individual capitalists to the people, to be operated for the benefit of all."[106] For Adolph Wagner, Werner Sombart's professor at the University of Berlin and early member of the Christian Social Party, socialists demanded that "the material means of production, that is, land and capital, should not be . . . the private property of single private members . . . but . . . the collective property of society itself."[107] Thomas Kirkup agreed. Industry should "be carried on by associated laborers jointly owning the means of production (land and capital)" and that this "collective capital" should have in view an "equitable system of distribution."[108] More recently, John Judis wrote that American socialism has always been "paired against individualism; cooperation against competition; altruism against selfishness."[109]

But how would workers take back the means of production? Some believed that laborers had little choice but to regain their sovereignty through violence. Gronlund was not among this camp. Indeed, his opposition to class violence was meant to distinguish European socialism from the kind forged in America—socialism with American characteristics.[110] Such warfare fell under the category of competition, which Gronlund identified as a serious detriment to the health of society and the movement toward the commonwealth. Instead, he believed that the best means of reclaiming ownership of production would come through peaceful modes of fraternal cooperation. For Samuel Calvin Tait Dodd, modern society depended on "the evolution of co-operation," not on forms of violence.[111] Christian socialist W. D. P. Bliss argued that socialism, as "the principle of Association," was nothing more than "brotherhood."[112] In his *Forging of American Socialism,* Howard Quint said that Gronlund's socialism "emphasized social solidarity as opposed to class antagonism, compromise and pragmatic give-and-take rather than unbending doctrinaire revolutionary determinism, and individual freedom of choice and dissent instead of dictation from arbitrary authoritarian leadership."[113] And cooperation was not something restricted to labor advocates. Everyone involved in the American economy in the late nineteenth century was compelled to cooperate in some form or another.[114] All Americans "turned to cooperatives as a measure of security."[115] Capitalists utilized cooperation to maximize profit. Workers formed cooperatives to protect themselves from capitalism. The Knights of Labor, the Populist movement, the Farmers' Alliance, and the Grange were all supportive of worker-owned cooperatives, especially related to worker insurance and worker-run grocery exchanges.[116] One member of the Knights of Labor envisioned cooperatives as "a great industrial union, possessing sufficient natural resources and so industrially organized that its members shall, through their own labors, supply themselves with all those things necessary to the comfort of their lives."[117]

Very little has been written on Laurence Gronlund. In *Social Darwinism in American Thought,* Richard Hofstadter wrote that Gronlund was soon forgotten after his death in 1899.[118] By the early 1960s, however, Gronlund was recovered from the dustbin of history. P. E. Maher wrote about him in 1962. His *Science & Society* essay, "Laurence Gronlund: Contributions to American Socialism," provides an overview of three of Gronlund's most important works: *Cooperative Commonwealth* (1884), *Our Destiny* (1891), and *New Economy* (1898). The importance of Gronlund's American socialism, according to Maher, revolved around how he made Marxism acceptable in the American context, influenced Edward Bellamy, and became one of the foremost critics of Henry George's single tax strategy. Solomon Gemorah wrote the first and most comprehensive biography of Gronlund in his 1965 PhD dissertation from New York University.[119] The thesis of Gemorah's dissertation, which never became a separate monograph, appeared in his essay, "Laurence Gronlund—Utopian or Reformer," published two years later in *Science &*

*Society.* For Gemorah, Gronlund's engagement with German scientific socialism was not as significant as his efforts to reconcile "the alternatives of Utopianism or reform."[120] In 1968, sociologist Chushichi Tsuzuki moved in a direction different from that of Gemorah, who situated Gronlund on the side of reform. According to Tsuzuki, Gronlund created a "new economic radicalism" by adapting socialism, essentially a European transplant that had been nurtured by the new immigrants coming into the US, to the American setting.[121] Mark Pittenger devoted an entire chapter to Gronlund in *American Socialists and Evolutionary Thought, 1870–1920.* Gronlund, Pittenger says, "got Marx into the American movement," but what became of his evolutionary collectivism, drawn from Spencer, was more "a progressive rather than a reactionary critique of capitalism."[122]

Scholars have for the most part downplayed the role of religion in Gronlund's commonwealth, ostensibly showing how his religious commitments appeared later in his intellectual development.[123] The current project seeks to reconceptualize Gronlund as a religious and philosophical thinker, or at least to suggest that his belief in a divine agent guiding history, as he himself believed, had always been part of his social philosophy—albeit maturing over time.[124] Gronlund's religious position makes sense in light of a few of his most important beliefs: (1) that a divine agent directed evolution; (2) that humanity partnered with this "Will" in preparing for the commonwealth; and (3) that the United States was destined by such a "Presence" to be the model of collective socialism for other countries. The alliance of the divine with the human in creating that which was predestined for America was a recuring theme in his major works. Humanity and the divine were so intertwined in their own self-becoming that a line separating the two was nearly impossible to draw. The progress of one, as in the case of humanity in its material and philosophical development over time, was the progress of the other. History was the "intelligence behind evolution" that worked through laborers not only by raising awareness of capitalism's contradictions but also by advancing history through stages of cooperation. As workers came to an increasing awareness of the modes of production, the contradictions endemic to capitalism, and the true source of injustices, they would recognize the divine power guiding their lives and the life of society as a whole—a liberating force realized through the collective cooperation. Identifying the interconnectedness of society and the ascendancy of a universal consciousness was, at the same time, the realization of society's God-consciousness, a coming into the being of collective humanity and God. Gronlund believed strongly in this divine agent working through evolution, moving within the consciousness of American society to one day achieve the cooperative collective. Despite the continued efforts of those on the religious right to associate socialism with godlessness, modern scholarship has acknowledged the galvanizing nature of faith, especially Christianity, among socialists, notwithstanding the sharp differences they may have had over issues of political engagement, social strategies, or the application of philosophical and scientific theories.[125] There had to be a powerful motivator to create what Gronlund envisioned as a properly running collective society. An active and intelligent providence interwoven into the evolution of a socialist commonwealth fit that role.

Gronlund could not deny his "latent religious impulses," to use the words of Stow Persons. In the first edition of *Commonwealth,* Gronlund wrote, "I could not get a firm basis for a sound philosophy [related to] the meaning of this life . . . without assuming an intelligence behind evolution whose work we have to do here."[126] Positing a divine agent, however loosely conceived in his mind, made sense to him, for without such a governing agent, chaos and disorder would reign.[127] Perhaps such a position likewise came from his reading of Pascal, who thought that life without God (or belief in God) would have been irredeemably tragic. Chaos was indicative of the plan-lessness of capitalism, and capitalists forged a conflicting morality in the face of such liberality—a morality that could not be justified. Such an ethic resulted in widespread human misery. And the existence of misery, Gronlund believed, was contrary to the divine order of things. Those who sought to curb the chaos of capitalism reflected a connection with the direction of the cosmos. But humans did not always interpret the developments of history correctly. The "Will of the Universe" (another name he used) and the will of humanity, though inextricably tied, were not always in harmony. The latter would often pull away from the former and slow the process of evolution. In other cases, the human agent was not always aware of how to obey the will of the divine.

Gronlund's focus on the divine and his gradual turn away from Spencer and Marx by the 1890s did not weaken his involvement in preparing American society for a cooperative collective. His religious philosophy did not diminish his radical praxis. Establishing the commonwealth required "a series of experiments"—especially with "the socialization of public utilities." "Let us strive," he charged, "for the nationalization of telegraphs, or of railroads, or of the banks, and for helping the unemployed and the poor of our state by municipal and state employment, and find out if that will not work as well as our national post-office departments or the national telegraph systems in Great Britain have done."[128] These experiments, he believed, kept the radical from becoming too dogmatic about the timing or the results of the revolution. Here, he found inspiration in the "liberal socialism" of John Stuart Mill. Mill advocated for, in his words, "experimental modes of socialism," working via piecemeal transitions in building socialism. What is more, such experimentation was to be done "on a moderate scale," with "no risk, either personal or pecuniary, to any except those who try them."[129] The activist had to be open to the dynamics of reality and not force reality to the human will. This seems to fit the posture of the postmodern Marxist, who expresses—though is not frozen by—an incredulity toward metanarratives. In other words, no matter how well-prepared in advance, Gronlund believed, activists would never be able to predict nor control every eventuality that arose from within a revolutionary movement. Nonetheless, the Marxist should always be ready to act. But the idea that humans could force the revolution and ignore the "Order of the Universe" (another of Gronlund's monikers related to God) was the height of arrogance. This was an important part of Gronlund's attitude toward the Georgists, anarchists, and communists. Humans could only discern the will of the divine and prepare the groundwork for the coming revolution. Time and again, Gronlund repeated what he wrote in one of his final essays, "Socializing a State": "It is possible to convert a state of our Union—not into a fully Socialistic Commonwealth, but into a body that decidedly will be an approach to it." Radicals could only "bring a State to the threshold of Socialism, and this may be of immense benefit to our cause, to our nation, and to the world."[130] The "Power behind evolution" would usher in the end of days by the mind of the laborer with the mind of the divine (Chapter 4).[131]

Chapter 1 begins with Gronlund's most popular and influential work, *The Co-operative Commonwealth in Its Outlines: An Exposition of Modern Socialism* (1884). His intent in the book was to subject German Socialism to a kind of "winnowing process, separating that which is distinctively German from what is universally true" in order to make socialism accessible to the "main current of English thought."[132] *Commonwealth* was completed just a few years before the English translation of *Capital,* which means that Gronlund obviously worked from the German. Although not an exhaustive analysis of *Capital,* Gronlund succeeds in noting the basic workings of capitalism, specifically "surplus value," labor exploitation, and the central importance of the labor theory of value. Admittedly, the chapter is intentionally summative for the purpose of not only presenting Gronlund's view of socialism but also to articulate the basic meaning of capitalism, which, I believe, is immensely valuable even for contemporary readers.

My intent is for readers to keep a couple conceptual items in mind as they work through the chapter. First, for those interested in understanding the very nature and meaning of capitalism, *Commonwealth* provides a basic definition. Gronlund does not deal so much with the origins of capitalism (i.e., primitive accumulation in the taking of the commons, the origins of commercialization, or the origins of slavery), but rather in how it is sustained, which, at the same time, reveals its leading tenet. The life of capitalism revolves around the appropriation of surplus value created by workers. This surplus is taken and used by non-producers (the capitalist class) not only to strengthen the conditions that would lead to additional surplus, which inevitably requires the efforts of the state, but also the inequitable power relations of capital over labor (also protected by the state).

Second, chapter 1 introduces readers to Gronlund's view of the divine in history, even though it was significantly muted in the first edition. The only mention of anything related to a "Power behind Evolution" was the "great mystery," which appears toward the end of the book. The intimation of a metaphysical presence functioned to justify an orderly cosmos: "*some* theory of life is needed to give harmony, purpose and vigor to active life, and they will certainly agree on such a theory as will explain the mystery to *them* and satisfy their highest intelligence."[133] Gronlund was writing *Commonwealth* at a time when American citizens recognized how radically free and uncertain the world had become after the Civil War, a world that increasingly displaced a sense of an active Providence for an impersonal naturalism.[134] Moved by Gronlund's work, British author George Bernard Shaw edited the 1884 version for a London publisher. In it, he added "will of the universe" and changed "Great Mystery" to "supreme will" and "Providence."[135] Gronlund accepted the stronger version of the divine, incorporating "God," "Power behind evolution," and "Will of the Universe" (now capitalized) in subsequent editions of *Commonwealth.*[136] It is also possible that these additions came from Gronlund's interactions with the Social Gospel movement beginning in the late nineteenth-century.[137]

Third, this chapter presents *Commonwealth* in the context of what was already developing in late-nineteenth-century America. Members of the Knights of Labor, founded by Uriah Stephens in 1869, capitalized on the importance of cooperation to address the issues of labor in the postbellum era. The goal, according to Stephens, was to create "one universal brotherhood, guided by the same rules, working by the same methods, practicing the same forms for accomplishing the same ends."[138] And the Knights sought to align their efforts at cooperation with America's republican ideology. American workers felt that capitalist economic relations under the wage system reinforced another kind of slavery. The wage system revealed that the war failed to abolish the degrees of dependency that descended into new modes of enslavement. The Knights grappled directly with this dilemma, a paradox, astutely identified by Alex Gourevitch, of reconciling classical republicanism, the notion that freedom required subjugated dependents, with universal equality. By fighting for ownership of their own labor as well as the means of production, the Knights reconstituted republican ideology. Whether or not they were card-carrying Marxists—many, of course, were—members of the Knights "understood their core ideas to be a natural extension of an inherited republican tradition."[139] In presenting a scaled-down Marxism for an American audience, Gronlund added his own international voice to this emerging culture of republican cooperation, which was already nurtured by the Knights. It is not surprising then, given this ideological allegiance, for the Knights to embrace Gronlund's work, encouraging members to study the *Co-operative Commonwealth*, what editors in an 1884 edition of the *Journal of United Labor Party*, the mouthpiece of the Knights, called "one of the best recent publications."[140] Gronlund simply added his voice to the labor republicanism initiated by the Knights.[141]

Chapter 2 considers Gronlund's *Ça Ira, or Danton and the French Revolution* (1886), written during his stint in Europe. Like Marx's *Eighteenth Brumaire*, *Ça Ira* demonstrated the author's philosophy through concrete historical events. Relying on the work of François Victor Alphonse Aulard, the first chair of the History of the French Revolution at the Sorbonne, Gronlund anticipated the Marxist school of historiography, summed up nicely by contemporary historian Gary Kates: "The French Revolution was essentially a class struggle in which one class was destroyed (the nobility), one class was awakened (the sans-culottes), and one class won control of the state (the bourgeoisie)."[142] Yet Aulard, who restricted much of his analysis of the revolution to the realm of politics, believed strongly in the "thinking agent as a basic unit of change," to use the words of Joseph Tendler.[143] Gronlund concurred. The progress of history required wise, intelligent, and courageous actors to recognize and obey the "Power behind evolution." In the case of the French Revolution, Georges Jacques Danton was such a figure. A consensus among historians on the character, role, and impact of Danton vis-à-vis the revolution has been difficult to come by.[144] "The positivists," wrote Gronlund, elevated Danton to the status of a hero, "even a saint." Aulard described the "exalted Danton" as "a truly modern man, an empiricist in politics and an heir of the eighteenth century scientific spirit."[145] Marxist historian Albert Mathiez viewed Danton as "an unprincipled politico."[146] Others, like J. F. E. Robinet, presented him as a politically savvy centrist, "neither a die-hard nor a dogmatist."[147] Biographer Norman Hampson suggests that when it came to the "enigmatic" Danton, there was "always a 'but.'"[148] For Gronlund, Danton became the first to appreciate what the "Revolution afforded for mass politics."[149] More importantly, Danton understood the French Revolution as a major push of the divine will toward humanity's full consciousness. Those who attempted to impede the march of history, bourgeois property owners (although they played an essential role in the revolution), were suppressed—and even sought to turn back—the ongoing developments of the "Will of the Universe." These duplicitous plutocrats were responsible for the revolution's most tragic moment: the Terror. Even some radicals (e.g., Robespierre) succumbed to the dogmatic position that the revolution could go no further; they, too, ignored the "Power behind Evolution." From the toppling of the king and the rising authority of the bourgeoisie, the revolution inaugurated the expansion of democratic consciousness. But the key to the revolution was the spread of democracy beyond traditional authorities to the French people as a whole. This was radical democracy, the kind that Danton was careful to nurture. Danton's greatness fit the concept of the "heroic" figure, as articulated by Sidney Hook, who acted according to a "predetermined pattern laid up in heaven." Agents like Danton were, from a Hegelian perspective, "an expression of 'the spirit,'" a soul of culture, a world-historical figure.[150]

Ça Ira was written with America's future in mind. The memory of the

French Revolution and Danton would, according to Gronlund, prepare the United States for its own impending revolution. Revolutionary events and their consequences beginning in France and eventually extending to most of Europe, parts of the West Indies (especially the Haitian Revolution), and Central and South America influenced the political, economic, social, and cultural developments in the United States throughout much of the nineteenth century. American workers involved in the Great Strike of 1877, especially those in St. Louis, believed that their struggle was akin to the Paris Commune a few years earlier, which many understood to have its origin in the French Revolution. Supporters of the Great Strike believed it to be a watershed moment for the rights of labor in the country; opponents highlighted the bloodshed that seemed to be inevitable in any revolution. While a considerable distance separated the release of *Ça Ira* with the events of the Paris Commune and the St. Louis Commune, Gronlund provided a lens to understand the nature of historical developments and, consequently, prepare American society for its own coming revolution—a revolution that did not require violence but only a few committed individuals guided by the Power behind evolution to usher society toward its revolutionary destiny. "The only thing that can then save us and our children from horrors ten-fold worse than those of the French Revolution, or from such a scourge as Napoleon," Gronlund wrote at the beginning of *Commonwealth,* was the "activity of a minority acting as the brains of the Revolution. For while there will be a revolution, it need not and it had better not, be one marked by blood."[151] America needed leaders in the spirit of Danton. In fact, the collective revolution would never come without them.

While in Europe, Gronlund meditated on a few of the popular reforms proposed to ease the serious unrest caused by unbridled capitalism. Chapter 3 looks at Gronlund's interaction with Henry George's single-tax plan. George, like other reformers, sought to understand (and ameliorate) how America's new industrial economy could produce vast amounts of wealth while concurrently producing greater poverty. His solution was a single tax on the unearned increment on the value of land, the source of wealth, according to George. The imposition of this single tax would eliminate the need for all other taxes, including tariffs. It was also a non-revolutionary solution that would preserve capitalism and the ethic of competition. Gronlund believed that George's solution did not go far enough. Land was certainly a source of wealth, but so was surplus value, which Gronlund explained in *Common-wealth*. A tax on land would not keep capitalists from fleecing the value created by workers. Ultimately, however, George failed to read and understand, Gronlund wrote in *Ça Ira*, "God's mysterious text." George was unable to accept the advancement of capitalism in the U.S. as preparatory for the coming of socialism, the penultimate stage before the consummation of the commonwealth. Gronlund wrote two pamphlets—*The Insufficiency of George's Single Tax Plan* (1887) and *Socialism vs. Tax Reform* (1887)—critical not only of George's plan but also of George's castigations against socialists. George believed that the socialists were not radical enough to make any substantial change to society. But their partisanship, their concern for ideological purity, was much more of a danger since it threatened George's United Labor Party. The relationship between George and Gronlund was irreparably damaged after the 1886 mayoral election. In reflecting on Sombart's discussion about the failure of socialism in America—notwithstanding the problematic nature of the question itself, as Eric Foner and others have noted—it would be easy to see how the Gronlund-George debate weakened the political strength of American socialism.[152]

The next chapter (Chapter 4) deals with *Our Destiny: The Influence of Socialism on Morals and Religion: An Essay in Ethics* (1891), Gronlund's detailed account of the relationship between religious belief, morality, and socialism. An episcopal minister in St. Louis, a "Dr. Short," said that *Our Destiny* was "the best" of all Gronlund's books, "full of meat and very suggestive." Another minister from Mississippi believed that the book would "set half the world on fire."[153] *Commonwealth* uncovered the internal contradictions of capitalism as well as the practices derived from capitalism that led to the collective. *Ça Ira* moved from theory to practice, demonstrating the evolution of capitalism within a significant moment in history. And in showing the historical process—changes in the modes of production and the power of ideas to move from a dying mode to a new mode of production—in actual time (via the Revolution), *Ça Ira* reconciled the slow process of evolution with immediate revolution. *Our Destiny*, Gronlund's most religious and philosophical work, takes a further step above the perspectives of *Commonwealth* and *Ça Ira* to explore the entanglements of the divine and human in evolution.

The competitive individualism that shaped American capitalism grew out of Protestant theology. Socialism was the "inveterate foe" of traditional orthodoxy.[154] Such a theology ignored the communal and focused solely on the individual. But the Will of the Universe would compel citizens to leave this theology behind and with it the "satanic element" of "selfness." Gronlund's collectivism would shift the emphasis away from "a narrow personal concern between the individual and his maker" and toward "a social concern between humanity and its destiny."[155] Evolution would lead society naturally toward a higher plane of being. This new revival would come once humans learned to work together, to cooperate. True religion was a matter of reconnecting individuals to the human community and humanity to God. Utopian writers like Edward Bellamy, Edward Carpenter, and Charlotte Perkins Gilman followed the path carved out by Gronlund as they articulated the central belief that the "self was an illusion, that everyone was united in an inclusive divine spirit, and that humanity was destined to realize its oneness."[156] Cooperation would "inculcate a belief in a Will of the Universe" and unite the one, universal soul of humanity with the divine "One," the "Power behind evolution": "The Supreme will is providence for humanity [as a community]; it enters into vital relations with the individual only through humanity as the mediator; it commands the interdependence of mankind, and our duty is to obey, for there is no other thing that we can do."[157]

At the close of the nineteenth century, America was rapidly rising as a global economic powerhouse—an empire. Plenty of socialists were quick to note the logical connection between capitalism and imperialism. Indeed, for Vladimir Illich Lenin, imperialism represented the highest stage of capitalism.[158] America's massive capitalist boom, its railroad infrastructure and the big businesses fueled by it (mining, meatpacking, oil, and banking), extended beyond its geopolitical borders. Far from the conclusions drawn by Lenin regarding imperialism, Gronlund was concerned that the urgency in forging an international socialism would ignore the priority of creating national collectivism. The economic extension outside a nation's geopolitical borders, Gronlund intimated, was a potential liability to the health of the domestic state. The problem was not expansion per se, which included massive investments in large infrastructural works abroad, as in the case of the Nicaraguan Canal, which Gronlund supported; rather, imperial growth had the potential to slow the progress of collectivism at home. This reflected the Fabian influence of Gronlund's socialism.[159] International socialism would not be successful without the initial success of domestic socialism. Of course,

Gronlund's interest in creating an American socialism was never separated from economic expansion nor an international outlook. But one needed to come before the other. Once a modern nation established itself as a collective commonwealth (or one very close to it), it would stand as an example to the rest of the world. Gronlund had faith that the United States would be the leader, the first, in establishing a truly cooperative society. What is more, a nation created along the lines of a practical and well-working collective commonwealth would eliminate the capitalist empire. While America was fighting its war against Spain in 1898, Gronlund was busy writing his final work, *The New Economy: A Peaceable Solution to the Social Problem*, an elaboration of practical proposals for American citizens who wished to reclaim their country from the destructive forces of capitalism. Gronlund's *New Economy* is the subject of Chapter 5.

Socialist Carl Schurz once highlighted the danger of writing biographies— namely, the temptation to "idealize" the object of study, which tended toward "a state of mind very unfavorable to sober, critical judgment."[160] This intellectual biography does not lionize its subject. It does not shy away from the euphemistic label of "complicated" or "problematic" when speaking of its central character. There is no denying that Gronlund was such a figure. There continues to be much in his intellectual life that needs reconciling, especially if the writer and his audience together focus on what Gronlund might offer to the modern world. First, he appreciated but did not always reconcile the symbiosis between ideology and material dialectics as forces of change.[161] Second, is it possible to consider Gronlund as both radical and reformer? These terms need not be mutually exclusive. A reformer is one who addresses the negative consequences of a system yet leaves it fundamentally intact. A radical, on the other hand, seeks to uproot the system (as *radix* means "root"), but there is an array of opinions as to how to get there. Gronlund, as we will see later in the book, supported reformist efforts (the eight-hour day, single-tax, and Free Silver), but not as ends in themselves. Competition, wage-slavery, and surplus value were—and continue to be—not only essential to the very meaning of capitalism but were also—and continue to be—the cause of so much suffering in the modern world. Unless for the purpose of radically transforming society, these reforms would be nothing more than ephemeral panaceas. Third, the contemporary mind would be quite discouraged by Gronlund's views on the status of women and African Americans, given the number of more egalitarian minded intellectuals in his circle. His relegation of minority rights to focus on the roots of discrimination was part of his overall historical outlook. Labor was constrained by its "patriarchal and white-supremacist structures of Gilded Age American society."[162] Gronlund was not ignorant of this or the discrimination against women and minorities. He may have betrayed his more liberal approach by considering as mutually exclusive the drive to get at the roots of the system while at the same time confronting the immediate cultural manifestations of it. Yet he frequently reminded his readers and listeners to focus their energy on the causes of social inequality: exploitative capitalism. He was not completely off in this way. The link between capitalism and forms of discrimination remains relevant for the contemporary world. How effective would the battle against discrimination be if we ignored the source of that discrimination, which includes not only attitudes and ideologies but material conditions as well? Fourth, Gronlund was a proponent of democracy, but in a way that was largely elitist (prefiguring the kind of party-driven communism found in the USSR and the PRC). He assumed that a small group of intellectuals who discerned the place of evolution and simply aided it would lead citizens toward consciousness of their power as a democratic source in creating the organism of the State.[163] Yet these intellectuals remained independent, never tied to party organizing. Finally, Gronlund's socialism was shaped and motivated by a religious ideology that posited not just a divine agent moving evolution but also the fact that the advancement of human cooperation was the realization of the consciousness of God. Those who could discern the "Power behind evolution" accelerated the progress of history. Gronlund's Hegelian-like idealism might alienate the contemporary reader. But part of the reason why I wish to draw attention to this aspect of his thought is to dispel the notion that religion and socialism are inherently antithetical to one another. The legacies of the Kingdom Movement, Social Gospel, and Liberation Theology throughout late-nineteenth and twentieth centuries have demonstrated this.

This book is written for a world in crisis—a world still reeling from a global recession, a world facing wars and rumors of wars, a world harassed by neo-fascism, and a world in the throes of climate crisis. It attempts to show that a reconsideration of just one element of America's socialist past—the mind of Laurence Gronlund—can inspire citizens toward a peaceful restructuring of American society. This might be dismissed as too lofty a goal. The

United States, some may say, is irreversibly divided. But social renewal can begin with cooperative care for the lives of citizens and the world they inhabit. It is neither quixotic nor utopian to adopt an attitude of "cooperation" over that of competition in establishing a healthy commonwealth. History can help heal the deep divisions in America today. Reviving the memory of Gronlund is a healthy step in that direction. While aspects of his Americanized socialism may have been a bit romantic (e.g., the State as an organism), concerning (e.g., administrative governance), and downright reprehensible (e.g., discrimination against African Americans, immigrants, and women), Gronlund offers an inspiring objective for a healthy commonwealth— cooperation. Eugene V. Debs once praised Gronlund's "unrelaxing energy" in the battle against exploitative capitalism. His works, Debs continued, stand as "eternal monuments."[164] Sadly, however, the managerial authoritarianism and "inverted totalitarianism" symptomatic of contemporary neoliberal corporate capitalism continues to suppress the memory of socialism in America.[165] For those interested in a reclamation of democracy and healthy cooperation in the pursuit of a stronger commonwealth, figures like Gronlund can be a helpful guide, reminding contemporary citizens that they can be that "Power behind evolution."

# CHAPTER ONE

# NO ORDINARY BOOK

A Critique of American Capitalism

In his testimony before the U.S. Strike Commission in the aftermath of the 1894 Pullman Strike, Eugene V. Debs identified himself as an advocate of the "cooperative commonwealth."[1] While in prison for defying a court-ordered injunction to end the strike, Debs read, among two other important works, Gronlund's *Co-operative Commonwealth.* He found himself aligning with the collectivist "principles laid down by Laurence Gronlund."[2] Gronlund's specific brand of cooperative socialism, introduced a decade before the unrest at Pullman, was immensely popular among leading progressive writers and prominent labor activists. W. D. P. Bliss admitted that Gronlund's *Co-operative Commonwealth* was "the first full statement of modern socialism published" in the United States.[3] A reviewer for the *New York Sun* wrote that the book explicated "with admirable conciseness and distinctness all the leading tenets of the socialistic philosophy and political economy."[4] England's *Christian Socialist* called *Commonwealth* "one of the best contributions to contemporary literature on socialism."[5] Thomas Harris Lake recognized it as the "Euclid of social mathematics," written with "the ripe wisdom of the scholar in his specialty."[6] When J. A. Wayland, editor of *Appeal to Reason,* moved to Colorado, he became convinced of socialism after reading Gronlund's *Commonwealth.* Through Gronlund, Wayland "saw new light," he said, "and found what I never knew existed. I closed up my real estate business and devoted my whole energies to the work of trying to get my neighbors to grasp the truths I had learned."[7] In a letter to Friedrich Sorge, the spearheading organizer of the Socialist Labor Party of America, Friedrich Engels admitted that Gronlund's *Commonwealth* had made a "strongly speculative impression" on him. But by 1888, Engels changed his tone, concluding that

Gronlund had "not astonished" him much at all.[8] Closest among the circle of Marxists, Edward Aveling, Marx's son-in-law, noted that next to *Capital* there was "scarcely any better work."[9] For French socialist deputy and journalist Gustave Rouanet, the "remarkable" *Commonwealth* was "tempered with a warm humanism" that distinguished it from the works of other Marxists.[10] According to historian Howard Quint, Gronlund's *Commonwealth* "was no ordinary book, since it was the first attempt by an American socialist to write in English a comprehensive yet simplified analysis of Marxism for the man in the streets."[11] Frederic Faires Heath agreed, recognizing *Commonwealth* as "the first book to place the new theory" of cooperative socialism "before American readers in a popular way."[12]

Not even Gronlund could ignore the impact of this important work. In later editions, he wrote that *Commonwealth* "led indirectly and probably unconsciously, to Mr. Bellamy's *Looking Backward,* the novel which without doubt," he continued, "inoculated thousands of Americans with socialism."[13] Novelist and fellow utopian William Dean Howells said that Bellamy's immensely popular utopian novel was "constructed almost exactly upon the lines of Mr. [Laurence] Gronlund's Cooperative government's acquisition of the vast trusts and monopolies, just as the collectivist author teaches."[14] Robert L. Shurter stated that *Looking Backward* was indeed a "fictionalized version of *The Co-operative Commonwealth,* and little more."[15] In 1952, Daniel Bell questioned the uniqueness of Bellamy's novel given the fact that Gronlund had already "outlined a society based on cooperation rather than competition."[16] The general consensus among scholars is that Gronlund did in fact influence Bellamy. The view to the contrary is the minority position.[17] Of course, a contemporary Leftist may certainly entertain the question as to who came first, Gronlund or Bellamy, yet that same Leftist would be remiss if when thinking about Bellamy he or she failed to think about Gronlund. Both radicals imagined, says author Claire Goldstene, "a moral, peaceful, and cooperative future built on an expectation of linear progress."[18]

All "progressive countries," Gronlund argued, were inevitably moving toward collective commonwealths.[19] In an effort to aid such movement, he sought to sift out from socialism that which was "distinctively German," including "any vindictive feelings" against persons or classes, from what was "universally true" about the system.[20] He did this to discover what precisely each nation had to undergo. First, a nation had to move through the stages of capitalist development—industrialization, commercial production, and the ascendancy of the bourgeoisie via capital accumulation. And the United States was further along than any other country in this regard. Second, such an economic trajectory would eventually reach a crisis point in social and political relations—between the powerful elites who hoarded and enjoyed the lion's share of the country's wealth and the laboring classes who created such wealth. What came to be an irrevocable truth by the late-nineteenth century was that liberty and democracy would necessarily shrink as capitalism expanded. As Gronlund's friend Henry Demarest Lloyd wrote in *Wealth Against Commonwealth*, "Liberty produces wealth, and wealth destroys liberty."[21] Yet the majority of citizens in Gilded Age America seemed unable (unfree, really) to counter the strength of the capitalist plutocracy in exercising their social and political rights. Unregulated capitalism was antagonistic to American freedom. The increasing control of the nation by corporate robber barons threatened a government that had been created by and for the people. For Gronlund, the way to regain American democracy was not through violence but by forging ways to work together.[22]

Cooperation was at the heart of Gronlund's socialism, but it was not something that he alone introduced in America. The Knights of Labor, for instance, not only placed a high value on cooperation, but also sought to align it with a key feature of America's political culture: republican ideology.[23] To solve the problem of wealth and poverty, some called for a return to a republic of the small farmer, but this would not have worked in the context of the Gilded Age. The reason why had to do with what Alex Gourevitch, author of *From Slavery to the Cooperative Commonwealth*, highlights as the paradox of traditional republican ideology. Classical republicanism assumed a class of independents, whose liberty was inextricably tied to property, and a class of dependents, the propertyless masses who were dependent on the former. Yet the relation between independents and dependents through property (i.e., republicanism) clashed with equality, which rested on the inalienable rights rhetoric enshrined in the *Declaration*. Both slavery and wage-labor (or "wage-slavery" for many) created dependent classes, neither of which contradicted republican ideology, at least not in a logically *necessary* manner. Universal equality, however, did. The Civil War and the end of slavery, undermining an important part of classical republicanism, did not lead to full equality. As Terence Powderly wrote in 1880, "the method by which we hope to regain our independence [is] by embarking in a system of COOPERATION which will eventually make every man his own master—every man his own employer."[24] Resolving the paradox between republican liberty and universal equality, Gourevitch ingeniously argues, came only through cooperation—specifically, "cooperative ownership and control of productive property" by labor itself.[25] This did not seem to threaten America's republican heritage. While plenty of the Knights did not identify with Marx, they did recognize that their shared labor commitments, as Gourevitch saw it, were part of "an inherited republican tradition."[26] Gronlund was drawn to the Knights because of the organization's goal of abolishing the wage system and in establishing "a national cooperative system."[27] Likewise, the Knights enthusiastically embraced Gronlund, encouraging members to read *Commonwealth*.

From Gronlund's perspective, the exhaustion of capitalism and the social stress that it caused were necessary historical developments, harbingers of the coming commonwealth.[28] And the key to understanding such development was to look past mere phenomena to identify the divine providence above it. The presence of such a metaphysical power was presented in a rather opaque way in the first edition of the *Commonwealth*. As mentioned in the introduction, the idea in Gronlund's mind of a conscious providence carving out the path toward the commonwealth matured in subsequent revisions of the *Commonwealth*, where he emphasized the "Reason in the Universe"—the divine architect behind the new social order. This dynamic force came into sharper relief in the London edition of *Commonwealth* in 1884, edited by George Bernard Shaw. The theists, Gronlund said, referred to this Power behind evolution as "God"; the atheists, the "The laws of Life," and the Spencerians, "The Unknowable."[29] Gronlund preferred to call it the "Will of the Universe."[30] The "coming change" in the American nation to a socialist collective, was, he said, "God's will." Those who came to recognize the inevitability of a coming collective would, at the same time, realize that humanity was "co-operating with the Power behind Evolution"—"fighting on the side of God."[31] There was, then, a unity in the mind of God and humanity. As cooperation allowed individuals to identify with others, forming a larger mind, cooperation was also an identification with the Will of the Universe. His thoughts on religion took on a more salient form with *Ça Ira* (Chapter 2), written a couple years after *Commonwealth*, but reached a fuller development six years later in *Our Destiny* (Chapter 4).

With this supreme intelligence central to his theory of evolution, Gronlund began *Commonwealth* by detailing the workings of capitalism. Modern capitalism, he believed, must be understood as a large and interconnected whole. It could not be defined solely as a matter of innovation, the production of marketable products, laws of supply and demand, or the creation of wage-based employment. These, of course, are necessary but not sufficient. The use of labor to produce goods for a distant market long predated historic capitalism itself. Likewise, the goal of capitalism was not to be restricted to turning a cash profit—again, necessary but not sufficient. Rather, capitalism had always been (a) the process by which wealth accumulation came through a circulation of exchangeable commodities (producing and circulating commodities) that (b) created specific and inherently inequitable socioeconomic relations. But we still need to ask the question as to the origins of *a* and *b*. More importantly, how did the evolution of the two come to make and sustain capitalism?

This gets us to the central defining feature of capitalism—namely, the creation and control (i.e., distribution) of surplus value. In examining the relationship between the growth in production with that of wages in America between 1850 and 1880, Gronlund noticed that workers produced far more than what they were paid. "How," Gronlund asked, did "this surplus originate?" It started with individuals becoming rich from a variety of "superfluities," including inheritance, bank loans, interest, and, though Gronlund does not mention this, the primitive accumulation from human chattel bondage. Once this "little amount of wealth" went into commercial enterprises, capitalism—the cultivation of surplus value—would come into being. The profits from such commercial endeavors revealed the real value generated by labor and how that value was distributed. A portion of the overall profit was reinvested in materials, overhead, and operational costs. Another was divided among a handful of other non-producers: "landowners, bankers, and other 'gentlemen at large.'"[32] Even after such distribution, a significant amount of value (i.e., extra labor) would be left over and taken by the owner without the consent of those who created the surplus. It is true that workers receive only a small portion of the value that they produced in the form of wages—wages, it should be noted, determined by the owner. There would have been no way for workers to retain the full value produced by their labor, otherwise there would be no profits. But workers produced far more than what they were actually paid. Gronlund estimated that the wages laborers received in the late 1880s were equivalent to roughly half (or less than half) of the total hours of labor in each day.[33] So, for instance, a laborer's work might meet his or her predetermined contractual wages after 4 or 5 hours of labor a day.[34] But, of course, they continued to work beyond what they satisfactorily produced. The capitalist, because he purchased "the value of a day's labor-power," as Marx put it in volume one of *Capital,* was able to squeeze out even more labor from workers: "On the one hand the daily sustenance of labor-power costs only half a day's labor, while on the other hand the very same labor-power can remain effective, can work, during a whole day and consequently the value which its use during one day creates is double what he pays for that use; this circumstance is a piece of good luck for the buyer." Indeed, the surplus retains "all the charms of something created out of nothing," which was precisely why the capitalist could take it for himself—taking without making.[35] Capitalism depends on this "sum of surplus values," what Gronlund referred to as "fleecings." By the time of Marx and Engels, capitalism created a social situation in which the private few pilfered that which was created by the public many—hence, the inherently exploitative nature of the system. For Gronlund, the "mark of the age," the Gilded Age, was that this economic reality was happening "in all industries, manufacturing, mining, agricultural and commercial."[36]

This economic arrangement perpetuated not just "capital," but the "capitalist"—the one "who possesses wealth" without doing any of the work. The money that the capitalist invested from fleecing allowed for an augmentation of the system's operation as well as the power of those who managed it. While this would produce more capital, it would provide no necessary increase in wages. Surplus value maintained the iron law of wages, where workers were paid at or just below subsistence levels. An increase in wages would mean a deficit in the capitalist's profits. The workers would get "just enough to keep up life and strength" and, to the benefit of the capitalist, "bring up a new generation of laborers." Gronlund affirmed that capitalists would do *some* work, but what they earned far exceeded what they produced. He knew that the system was rigged in favor of the "non-producers": no valuable work on their part was necessary for them to become wealthy. This represented the magic of capitalism as well as the source of capitalist hegemony. Consequently, the small class of wealthy capitalists in Gronlund's day (as it is today) had the ability to utilize a variety of social institutions, especially that of the government, to enforce their will on citizens: "those who by the control of the instruments of labor have acquired the more advantageous position [and] are now our masters, the dominant power, who by laws and usages enacted by themselves have made this advantageous position of theirs a permanent one."[37]

Labor represented the true source of value. Some located value in the law of supply and demand, what consumers were willing to pay for a product on the market.[38] Gronlund challenged this notion. Such a law was, he said, "simply the effect of making [products'] prices (that is, their value expressed in money—in gold and silver) vibrate, now a little above, now a little below."[39] Others placed an item's value in relation to its usefulness (e.g., a hammer efficiently and successfully hitting a nail). This is known as "use-value." But "usefulness," Gronlund responded, was relative: "a loaf of bread is 'worth' infinitely more to a man who has not eaten anything for forty-eight hours than to one just risen from a hearty dinner; yet the former can buy the loaf just as cheaply as the latter." A serious challenge in this regard came when different values collided in the exchange of goods. "In what respect," Gronlund wondered, would items be similar other than in their utility, "which we have found to be incommensurable, and therefore incomparable."[40] Overcoming this problem required a common medium for exchange. How much cotton, Gronlund used as an example, had to be produced and given as an equivalent for another item? A hundred bales of cotton might be exchanged for five pairs of shoes. The person that received the cotton would use a small portion of the cotton to make clothes. But what was to be done with the remaining quantity? Perhaps it could be exchanged for another equitable item, an item with comparable value. But this was impractical. There needed to be a neutral means to exchange disparate materials and values. This is where money, the driver of the process, came into the capitalist equation. Money was used to exchange items. A more valuable item would have its equivalent in the quantity of monetary notes, so that the person receiving cotton would not be burdened with having to exchange cotton for another bartered item, the full value of which they may not have needed. Money permitted the direct purchase of what a consumer needed, eliminating the complications of value in relation to the accumulation of material things.

Yet money could easily mask the true source of value (labor). As Marx argued in Volume I, Chapter 1 of *Capital:* "As use values, commodities are, above all, of different qualities, but as exchange values they are different quantities, and consequently do not contain an atom of use value."[41] Not only would use value be separated from a commodity, but virtually any value, including an artificial one, could be stamped onto an item, and thus no discernible difference concerning "use" would remain. Exchange value was merely, according to Marx, a "mode of expression," a "form of appearance": "With the disappearance of the useful character of the *products* of labor, the useful character of the *kinds* of labor embodied in them also disappears; this in turn entails the disappearance of the different concrete forms of labor. They can no longer be distinguished, but are all together reduced to the same kind of labor."[42] "Money, with all its colorlessness and indifference," wrote George Simmel in *Metropolis and Mental Life* (1903), "becomes the common denominator of all values; irreparably it hollows out the core of things, their individuality, their specific value, and their in-comparability."[43] Money erases the differences and values between things exchanged. Gronlund concurred: "Money obscures the transaction of all buying and selling; it serves as a mask, which this change [the coming of the commonwealth] will tear off."[44] As contemporary Marxist Hadas Thier writes in *A People's Guide to Capitalism*, "Money conceals the true nature of value, so that when you go to the supermarket, you don't think you're trading an equivalent amount of your 'congealed mass of labor,' with someone else's."[45]

Although not addressed by Gronlund, this foreignness illuminates another important aspect of capitalism—namely, the "commodity fetish." This is, I believe, important to mention. Commodities are always presented to consumers as being immaculately conceived, abounding in what Marx called "metaphysical subtleties and theological niceties."[46] An item in the market is separated from the labor that goes into producing it, divorced from its history (i.e., the labor that went into making it), the true source of its meaning. Thus, the commodity comes to be something that magically falls from heaven *sui generis*. Consequently, any origin myth can be attached to the product (enter the world of advertising), including, for instances, narratives that extol the ingenuity and generosity of the capitalist, while disparaging or outright negating the true creators—the workers. The capitalist need not retain the true history of what is produced, suggesting that capitalism is not only motivated by profit but also deception. Modern advertising helps in this regard. Consumer items are placed within a compelling narrative—a bucolic country setting, a family reunion, and sex.[47] In each case, the consumer is enticed by a foreign discourse impressed onto an object—a discourse that is deeply intimate, liberating, and spiritually fulfilling. The capitalist willingly expends resources to hide the true reality behind mass production, covering up the exploitative core of capitalism. When becoming conscious of these false narratives, labor can and occasionally does expose the capitalist's penchant for fetishizing commodities. Yet the power of labor is precisely what capitalists fear and subsequently seek to suppress. Marxist thinkers have never tired of emphasizing this point.

Common to both use-value and exchange-value was labor.[48] Every product had a mixture of both nature and labor. Gronlund wrote, "*Labour is* [a product's] *father and Nature* [its] *mother,*" and labor alone created "all real values."[49] Value, in turn, represented "the amount of labor," multiplied by time, "crystallized in an article."[50] This was a position held by classical economists as well as the earliest utopian visionary Robert Owen. As Owen argued, the standard of value is, "in principle, human labor, or the combined manual and mental powers of men called into action."[51] Labor stood as, Gronlund surmised, "a far more appropriate, constant, and convenient measure" than something like supply and demand.[52] And such labor could be calculated through a medium of exchange. In Gronlund's commonwealth, exchange would be "carried on" not through money but through "labor-checks"— "notes, tickets issued by authority."[53] Each note or ticket would represent different amounts of labor. Instead of inquiry about the value of a coat in so many dollars, "we shall in the New Commonwealth discard all mystery and call it worth so much work." Monetary notes would gage the amount of "one day's labor or [a] fractional part thereof." The base measure would be the basic or common labor of a "day's work"; skilled or professional labor would become "nothing but multiplied common, or unskilled, work."[54] Hence, money, as understood in Gronlund's day, would "become entirely useless in the coming Commonwealth."[55]

Opponents of socialism, ignoring these fundamental aspects of capitalism, concerned themselves with how capitalism might generate more private wealth. Some advised creating wealth through committed saving habits. The implication of which was that if workers saved their meager wages, which many did, they would eventually find themselves to be wealthy. Gronlund knew better. The wage earner, if he were to save his wages, during the time

Gronlund was writing, would have taken "more than 3,000 [years] to accumulate $200,000."[56] This was not enough time to enjoy let alone realize such wealth. Besides, saving wages said nothing about the *modus operandi* of capitalism, which, as we have seen, centered on surplus value. The only one who would benefit from saving was the capitalist. And remember that when speaking of the capitalist, we are speaking of someone already in a system. At any rate, saving, in the mind of the capitalist, meant accumulating: saving that which had already been saved. "Accumulate, accumulate," Marx cried, "'Industry furnishes the material which saving accumulates.' Therefore, save, save, i.e., convert the greatest possible portion of surplus value or surplus-product into capital!"[57]

Nor, as Gronlund's critics suggested, did one become wealthy by investing or borrowing. "In former times when people borrowed money," Gronlund noted, "they generally did it because they were in distress, and it was, very naturally, deemed disgraceful to take advantage of another's misfortune."[58] The borrower would become for a time dependent on a lender which received a portion of the overall profits. If the profits from the borrowing business were generated from surplus value and fleecing (if a business were to be successful in doing so), the initial borrower could eventually become independent. Profits would be reinvested to generate more capital, which would transition the investor from a dependent borrower to an independent capitalist (a borrower that breaks even, so to speak, or fails completely would remain in a dependent status). Either way, the borrower and the lender would continue to enable the production of a surplus. Yet the now-independent capitalist would paradoxically enter a new mode of dependency. Capital would become dependent on labor in a kind of master-slave dilemma. Independence was as illusory for the capitalist as it was for workers—though the former had a much greater material cushion than the latter.

Yet this kind of capitalist saving would not continue forever. Unfettered capitalism, socialists argued, would eventually lead to crisis—specifically the crisis of overproduction, where unregulated production that surpassed market equilibrium would inaugurate a decline in the price of products. The extent of overproduction—how far "over"—determined how steep the decline in value. And a steep decline in price could threaten not only businesses but whole markets. Gronlund admitted, as Marx and Engels did before him, that the "evil workings of unrestricted 'private enterprise'" had "performed wonders": "But we contend that it now has done nearly all the good that it can, that the evils which now flow from individualism far outweigh the benefits it confers."[59] While the consequences of overproduction hurt society as a whole, it hurt the laborer far more than the capitalist. Cycles of overproduction would continue under the capitalist order. And the response among those who wanted to save capitalism was to return to the same conditions that created crises in the first place. A capitalist society, Gronlund reminded his readers, "commences to recover slowly, but only to repeat the old story": ignore the precarity inherent to capitalism, produce more, generate more profit, and repeat the crisis.[60] Knights of Labor member Paul Ehrman acknowledged this in an essay he wrote for the *Journal of United Labor*: "As long as the present mode of capitalistic production prevails, financial panics and crises [will] return in regular intervals about every ten years . . . and thousands of small producers [will be] swept away entirely by each of these periodic storms."[61]

Individual capitalists looked for ways to shield themselves and their industries from such crises, doing so without disrupting their profits or the vital organs of the system. Ironically, they avoided crisis by abandoning the very thing that they believed stimulated economic growth: competition. The robber-barons of the late nineteenth century, while singing the praises of competition and the liberalization of the economy, hardly abided by it themselves. They knew that cooperation was the best means to augment wealth, allowing therefore a kind of socialism for the wealthy. America's plutocrats understood that while competition could just as easily be used "against their weaker rivals," Gronlund wrote, combination was far more beneficial.[62] Railroad men, for instance, made alliances with "bonanza farmers to crush out the small farms." Owners of the Erie and Pennsylvania Railroads and railway-tycoon Cornelius Vanderbilt brought their interests together with Standard Oil, transporting oil "at much lower rates than the oils of other companies." Cooperative practices would "give other combinations of capitalists the control of the lumber, cotton, iron, and coal of the United States." Groups of wealthy businessmen made "enormous combinations of capital to 'corner' the market, locking upon millions of bushels of wheat, and maintain famine prices in the midst of plenty."[63] Such strategies shielded cooperative corporations from larger economic downturns.

There was no higher form of capitalist cooperation than the trust. Yet such a scheme was not simply a new and artificial means to harness wealth.

The motive behind capitalist cooperation was proof of the "Power behind Evolution." The trust demonstrated how both socialism and capitalism, the former growing out of the latter, were part of a larger historical process of becoming. If one were to use the term "natural," it would be here. The trust was a development out of the necessity of natural evolution. Consequently, efforts to destroy the trust through progressive legislation or violence were, for Gronlund, retrogressive and foolish. Capitalism—and all that came with it, including the ethic of individualism—had to run its course. In a dialectical fashion, every historical epoch retained the seeds of its own demise. The awareness of capitalism's contradictions, beginning with the intellectual few chosen by the Will of the Universe, was, at the same time, the awakening of social consciousness. At this penultimate stage of history, with the establishment of the trust, all would see the benefit of cooperation. Once the trust moved from "private control" to "national control," Gronlund wrote in 1898, it would "totally revolutionize our whole civilization."[64] Laborers would eventually understand the nature of the cooperative trust and use it to their advantage. Writing in the Knights' *Journal of United Labor,* Imogen Fales encouraged readers to accept cooperation as a "natural tendency of organic life." Fales agreed with Gronlund that the trust would be useful in the course of labor's ascendancy: "The system by which a *few* combine to enrich themselves at the expense of the many, is the very system by which the *many* can protect themselves against the few and secure an independence and happiness now unknown."[65]

Understanding the trust and harnessing its effectiveness required a knowledge of history. Examining the stages of the "onward march" toward socialism would allow intellectuals "to infer the next advance," Gronlund wrote, "in the van of progress."[66] The primary way to identify a critical stage of history was to track the changes in the conditions of workers—all workers throughout history, from slaves to wage earners. These material changes were structured by the opposite sides of cooperation—coercion and voluntarism. Each advance in the stage of history would be a move closer toward social liberation since the voluntary aspect of cooperation would increasingly overtake its coercive counterpart, eliminating all forms of coercion in the commonwealth at the end of history.[67] Slavery (Roman slavery, in Gronlund's mind) was the first stage; serfdom, the second; "wagedom" the third; and the commonwealth, the fourth. "Slavery was, to our race, the first division of labour;

it was the first form of co-operation"—coercive co-operation, keep in mind.[68] Slaves were forced to cooperate with each other as they lived under the power of Roman aristocrats. Their "cooperation" (we might say subjugation) within the slave system was the source of the master's authority. To undermine the source of such authority was for the laborer to regain a portion of owner-ship over his production. Ex-slaves, those no longer under Roman authority (after the Empire's collapse), would then be able to work together, but they would immediately face the power of those (chieftains) who held more land. This brought the period of serfdom, which arrived around the same time as Christianity. Although tied to land and "protected" by a lord, laborers under serfdom were "invested with the most elementary right of all: that of creating a family for themselves." What is more, the rights of peasants were secured by the "ruling principle" of "Custom," which included access to the commons and fixing "the amount of work due to [the peasants'] lord for the use of the soil."[69] There was a modicum of voluntary cooperation as both landlords and peasants abided by such habits. In other words, serfs or peasants swung closer to the side of voluntary cooperation in contrast to slaves, who had been situated further on the side of coercive cooperation.

Changes in production always impacted social relations. For millennia, the cultivation of the human environment created divisions of labor. This was an historical constant. But the specific form of those social-material re-lations (e.g., hunter-gather, feudalism, or capitalism) were not. Though de-pendent on fundamental aspects of previous systems, capitalism was com-pletely unknown in the classical and pre-modern periods. By the time of the Renaissance, innovations in commerce, global discoveries (especially that of America) which helped to create modern slavery, the printing press, and the steam engine helped to "nourish Capital," which broke the "iron bands of Custom" in the "closing years of the Middle Ages."[70] This opened the door to the next historical phase: industrialization and the wage system. Once again, there was further movement away from coercive cooperation (peasants forced to work the manor) and progress in voluntary cooperation—hence, an increase in liberation. Gronlund located the beginning of the wage system around the time of the French Revolution, when, he argued, the bourgeoisie reconstituted society, bringing the rhetoric of liberty, fraternity, and equality together with the practical ethics of individualism, competition, and prop-erty. The supporters of this modern socioeconomic arrangement extolled its virtue in part by saying that it was far removed from the barbaric system of slavery and serfdom. Citizens were free to compete. True, industrial laborers were no longer under the yoke of the landlord; they were free to find jobs in the cities and do with their meager wages as they saw fit.

And just like the previous ages (the Roman aristocracy and later, the nobility, church, and monarchy during the age of serfdom), new forms of coercion would appear, develop, and then lead to the next stage of cooperative development. An aspect of a previous system would remain in the latter. Wage earners, under the illusion of independence, entered the world of capitalist dependency, which for many became a form of slavery under a different name. Gronlund pondered the similarities between slavery and the wage system: "True, a master could whip his slave; but our employer can discharge his employees whenever it takes his fancy, which often has worse consequences for the latter than a whipping would have."[71] Once alienated from the work of their hands, laborers would fall under the whim of employers. They had no say in how the goods they produced would be distributed, nor in what percentage of that value would return to them in the form of wages. Receiving little to nothing in return, workers would be subjected to the tyranny of the plutocratic elite. An important part of what kept workers in a dependent cycle was the only thing that they could sell: their own labor. But like other commodities, labor was purchased and thereby owned by the capitalists. In doing so, the capitalist stole the value and hence the identity of the laborer, who, in short, lacked the freedom to own himself, the fundamental mode of production. This was, for many Americans, nothing more than slavery under a different name. The capitalist system turned the bodies and souls of workers into the property of another that could be exchanged on the market. Labor became "shamefully dependent on the will and whim of an individual employer."[72] The Knights made a similar observation: "When a man is placed in a position where he is compelled to give the benefit of his labor to another, he is in a condition of slavery, whether the slave is held in chattel bondage or in wage bondage, he is equally a slave."[73] "Co-operation," a member of the Knights wrote in the *Journal of United Labor,* was "the antithesis of slavery."[74] New England labor leader George McNeill saw this selling of labor commodity which perpetuated a system of dependency as contrary to America's liberal tradition: "There can be no liberty until man has restored his right and power to sell the product of his time, skill, and endurance."[75]

Eventually, like earlier systems of production, capitalism would exhaust itself. The final stage came when workers recognized the contradictions of capitalism (overproduction and the creation of the trust). They would rapidly repossess land, take for themselves the tools of production, and administer the distribution of wages, reaching thereby the socialist collective. Such an economic arrangement would irreversibly transform the moral ethos of a society. There would be no going back to forms of coercive production because citizens would secure cooperation. Cooperation would be absolute and thus final. These developments in civilization formed "a long weary road," Gronlund wrote, a necessary "link in the chain of progress" and a "preparatory step to each succeeding stage."[76]

While modes of production played an important role in history, it would be inaccurate to conclude that Gronlund was a material reductionist. American socialists like Gronlund demonstrated, Pittenger argued, "an unwavering belief in the power of ideas."[77] Solomon Gemorah argued that Gronlund "placed great significance on the role of ideas rather than impersonal forces in historical change."[78] Ideas did not simply explain the workings of the world, they galvanized humans to act. They prepared members of society for the transition from one mode of production to another. History would raise up certain individuals to articulate and apply such ideas in order to lead society toward the next stage in human development. Such figures had a special insight as to the course of humanity: they could identify the working of that Power behind evolution, regardless of whether they could identify it by a specific name.[79] The first ideological step in the progress of humanity (next to modes of production), according to Gronlund, came in what was essentially the religious democratization brought about by the Reformation, a period that "introduced individualism." Note that the Reformation, for Gronlund, came out of the economic period of serfdom; he does not account for the shift from ancient slavery to serfdom, other than a passing reference to the role of Christianity in making the transition. The work of Protestant reformers allowed the common people to read and understand the spiritual world on their own, unaided by authorities in the church.[80] This gave the average person a higher sense of their own self-worth. It also instilled a greater sense of sovereignty in how they directed their lives, especially their religious lives. This new sense was supported by material changes. The printing press provided the means for individuals to think for themselves, placing western civilization on a trajectory toward greater enlightenment. The naturalistic mind of Enlightenment thinkers challenged the whims of kings, nobles, and church leaders. The ideas cultivated during the age of science and the Enlightenment produced the democratic revolutions of the late seventh and eighteenth centuries—most importantly, England's Glorious Revolution of 1688, the American Revolution of 1776, and the French Revolution of 1789. Together, these revolutions inaugurated the "third stage" in the development of civilization: "the Wage-System and Individualism."[81] Each revolution, through the power of philosophical ideas, expanded political sovereignty and compelled individuals to cooperate to create a new society.

As in the case when new socioeconomic arrangements both advanced and stalled emancipation, new liberating ideologies would do the same. An idea could easily be turned on its head. For instance, the individualism born of universal language that would potentially apply to all (e.g., the doctrine of the "priesthood of all believers," that "all men are created equal," or the motto "liberty, fraternity, and equality") could be manipulated by an elite group hell-bent on hoarding power for themselves. Late-eighteenth-century French bourgeois revolutionaries who dismantled the monarchy and crushed the power of the nobility and the clergy elevated themselves to a place of dominance. The cherished ideals of the revolutionary era—individualism, property, representation, equality, and fraternity—certainly moved its way through all classes of society and cultivated cooperation on a larger social scale, but the property-owning plutocracy grabbed the apparatus of power (government) to secure the blessings of liberty for their own class, denying to the general population the blessing of social democracy. Liberty, fraternity, and equality, which undoubtedly appealed to a vast number of people, certainly motivated the working classes but only benefitted the "fleecing classes." By the turn of the nineteenth century, the bourgeoisie exploited the language of liberty, property, and self-reliance to calcify what would become the central ideological drive of capitalism—individualism. In doing so, they arrested the march of history. More will be said about this in the next chapter.

By the 1880s, the ideology of individualism legitimized the material forces and social power behind capitalism, bringing society to its knees. The privileged classes used revolutionary language to secure their own hegemony while denying it to rest of society. It needed to be confronted and overcome. But how? Gronlund preferred persuasion and electoral politics. Violence was never an option.[82] He opposed class antagonism and revolutionary violence from among the Marxists.[83] This did not mean, however, that Gronlund ignored the reality of class hatred in America, though such classes (bourgeoisie and proletariat), he wrote in 1890, were "only in embryo."[84] The notion that an amicable "natural partnership" between capital and labor in America stood in contrast to Europe was delusional.[85] Capital and labor, Gronlund admitted, existed in "chronic warfare," as evidenced in strikes.[86] There was no harmony between worker—"to whom nothing is coming beyond necessaries and decencies of life; to whom even the most loathsome and irksome labor does not insure subsistence; who is not benefited by his own increased capacity of production; who is far from becoming richer the more he works"—and capitalist, who became wealthier the more workers toiled for him, benefiting "by every increase in productive capacity."[87] Nonetheless, whether it be the bourgeoisie over the proletariat or the other way around, the effort of one class to crush the other was "detrimental to the welfare of the whole social organism."[88] What was keeping Europe from creating a cooperative socialist state was this incessant emphasis on such irrevocable conflict. As he would later write in *New Economy*, his final work, Gronlund described the appeal to class war as the "greatest blunder" of European socialists.[89] A war between classes would fracture a nation and shatter the bonds of cooperation. The goal of the socialist state was to establish a brotherhood, a humanitarian community whereby citizens could not live without one another. Class antagonism was "a deplorable aberration that really should make [classes] dread their success as much as their defeat."[90] In *Commonwealth*, Gronlund argued that the defeat of one class over another (e.g., the proletariat over the bourgeoisie) would never assuage class hostilities. Marx expected that the workers of the world would build a "resolute party," Gronlund said, that would "seize the government of some great country and henceforth control it." And the emancipation of the proletariat was to be initiated and completed by the working class, an injunction that became "law to [Marx's] disciples."[91] But the ascendancy and sovereignty of the proletariat through revolution would only enrage the opposing class, the bourgeoisie, and weaken society. The losing party would harbor resentment against the victorious class. The former, then, would wait for an opening to unleash its pent-up rage. This was precisely what led to the "Terror" during the French Revolution, when counter-revolutionary bourgeois leaders attempted to prevent the full extension of liberty, fraternity, and equality to workers. Class hatred was, therefore, a "sandy foundation on which to construct the new social order."[92] Any nascent class, whether bourgeoisie or proletariat, could not help but to be biased "in favor of their special interests," which would necessarily lead to the collapse of society.

Violence would break out during times of crisis.[93] The cause of a capitalist catastrophe was overproduction. In many ways, such occurrences were unavoidable; it was very difficult to have a birds-eye view over a capitalist economy to predict with certainty when overproduction would lead to a crisis. What is more, overproduction came in degrees; an economic slowdown did not equal an economic depression, for instance. Nonetheless, plans could be implemented to prevent the degree of overproduction, caused by a corresponding degree of "planlessness," that made violence a proximate reality. Thus, the key was to find remedies that would cool social tensions to prevent violence altogether when overproduction came. Gronlund examined a few. He first considered a proposal by William M. Evarts, secretary of State under Rutherford B. Hayes. Evarts argued that the lives of workers would improve, easing thereby class antagonism, if the nation expanded into foreign markets. Gronlund believed, however, that this would only extend the system of capitalist exploitation and expand the reality of unrest to "all capitalist countries." It would, Howard Quint suggested, lead "into conflict with European competitors." Utilizing foreign markets would only multiply competition and intensify hostilities. Economies in China, Japan, and India were in the process of, Gronlund observed, "learning to manufacture for themselves." This meant that the violence of capitalism was already intensifying class antagonism. The plutocratic powers in America would "immolate men, ruin cities, annex or conquer half-civilized countries, shake up by the roar of cannon the sleeping Chinese, encourage the building of railways in Mexico, and incursions into the heart of Africa." Foreign markets would compound the problem of competition and violence. Not only would it lead to competitive individualism within a country it would also contribute to competition and the threat of violence among nations. It's easy to forget that Gronlund's *Commonwealth* was published around the time of the Berlin Conference, called by Otto von Bismarck to partition Africa. Seeking markets abroad, therefore, was nothing more than "grasping at a shadow."[94]

Another remedy came from Irish political economist John Elliott Cairnes. Cairnes, one of the last remaining classical economists, advocated for workers to have an equal share "in the general advantages arising from industrial progress."[95] The way to do this was for laborers to contribute a portion of their wages for "a common fund which they employ as capital and co-operate in turning to profit." Although sympathetic, Gronlund considered this to be unfeasible. First, it was absurd of Cairnes to assume that workers should generate capital through their own production—to compete with capitalists. This was not how the system operated. Second, how could they save but also contribute to a fund when their wages fell far below the ability to provide for the "necessities of life"? What extra cash did workers have to "invest their savings in such risky enterprises"? Third, to compete with capitalists, labor associations would have to become capitalistic themselves. But whose labor value would workers fleece? Cooperation by way of consumption, however, was quite different than worker cooperatives for the purpose of generating capital. In this way, workers—with the support of socialists—would create "co-operative stores and thus get better goods and save the profits otherwise going to the middlemen," a strategy likewise supported by the Knights.[96]

The solutions offered by Evarts and Cairnes failed to deal with the root of capitalism and hence the true reasons for class conflict. However, some reforms confronted capitalism directly without uprooting it. A couple called for trade unions and the legalization of the eight-hour workday, remedies that would have checked the increasing power of the capitalist class. The eight-hour day movement, one of the longest campaigns in U.S. history, evenly divided the day between work, rest, and play and helped to curb the unchecked abuses of capitalism. Trade unions, from Gronlund's perspective, stood as "powerful instruments for educating" citizens for the "coming social order."[97] These would effectively strengthen the power of workers in the country, forcing capitalists to recognize the power of labor. Moreover, the federal government would provide aid by offering trade union workers an advance of "all the capital they may be in need of, at a very low rate of interest, say one percent."[98] This would be done largely for the purpose of surviving potential economic downturns. Such policies could be accomplished within a capitalist society and without having to transform the nation, a small step toward practical socialism.

Implementing a socialistic farming program out west would have been the strongest remedy, Gronlund believed. Agriculture was the one economic sector that would put "the break, so to speak, on the wheel of [capitalist] progress," though it would not ultimately dismantle capitalism.[99] Anticipating the creative frontier thesis of Frederick Jackson Turner, a former student of Richard Ely, Gronlund argued that the extension of useable farmland would relieve the pressures of the urban industrial sectors of the nation. The western frontier was the very soil in which socialism would flourish.[100] Agricultural cooperatives would be immensely successful in leading the nation toward a collectivist society. In fact, in 1893 Gronlund wrote to Kansas Populist G. C. Clemens, expressing his interest in making Topeka the "national headquarters of the Socialist movement in America."[101] J. A. Wayland purchased land in Tennessee and organized the Ruskin Cooperative Association in 1894 with a dozen members, constructing a printing press as the first and central construction of the community.[102] In the 1890 revised and expanded edition of *Cooperative Commonwealth,* Gronlund directed his readers to the "cooperative enterprise in California, called Kaweah," as a perfect example of a successful socialist cooperative.[103] Gronlund identified California as a fitter model commonwealth "than anywhere else in the country" and Kaweah as the "nucleus for the agitation of socialist principles."[104] Christian Socialist George Howard Gibson, who identified Gronlund as "a courageous advocate of socialism," established the "Christian Corporation" colony in Nebraska. Inspired by Gronlund's *Commonwealth,* William C. Damon and Ralph Albertson created the Willard Cooperative Colony in North Carolina.[105] Although supportive of such efforts, Gronlund feared that even the agricultural sectors of the country were in danger of being swallowed-up by capitalists. Cultivated swaths of land in "Minnesota, Dakota, Texas, Kansas, and California," were quickly becoming the private enterprise of "presidents and directors of railways." These so-called "Bonanza Farms" were not appropriated for domestic bliss—"no families, no women, no children, no homes."[106] Such communal farms were created for labor and commercial production and sustained the kind of competitive individualism that socialists opposed.

Trade-unions, the eight-hour workday, government aid to workers, and cooperative farming collectives, while helpful in the short run, were ultimately "impotent to counteract the workings of individualism."[107] These economic reforms certainly slowed the accumulation of capital, which was partially good, but more importantly, they softened the blow of capitalist crises that citizens would unavoidably face. The goals of such reforms would be temporal at best so "long as the Established Order" remained.[108] Yet Gronlund was wary of imposing any remedy, however effective in the long-term, without a proper understanding of the developments of history. That is, policy impositions needed to fit in with the direction of evolution. There was no doubt that capitalism needed to be pulled up by the roots, but it also needed to reach its culmination, what Gronlund had called its "darkest hour"—the crisis of "overproduction."[109] The solutions may not have led directly to the dismantling of capitalism, but that really was not his issue in this part of his discussion. Gronlund's concern centered on how citizens might survive crises. Although socially unfortunate, capitalist crises were historical necessities. This did not make him a fatalist, however. Crises moved history along, but this did not mean that no efforts were to be made to ease such troubling periods. The above-mentioned reforms, again, would stave off crisis, but citizens needed to find ways to keep these crises from recurring. Devising schemes to soften the blow of such crises did not necessarily impede the march of history. In another sense, however, economic catastrophes were necessary to produce a moral awakening in the minds of Americans, an awakening to the necessary contradictions and periodic failures of capitalism and the need to reconstitute society along cooperative lines.

The best way to protect society from violent outbreaks caused by economic crises was to expand the powers of the state. When the symptoms of overproduction could no longer be ignored and reforms failed, the levers of power would be taken from America's autocrats and given to the "impersonal power" of the state. No other social institution was as singularly focused on managing the wellbeing of the commonwealth than the state.[110] But this was a difficult pill to swallow for many Americans, especially those from among the Spencerian faction, who held that government interference was a detriment to a flourishing economy. Spencer and his followers had, Gronlund claimed, "a morbid aversion to all State activity" and sought to reduce its influence.[111] Those who used Spencer to justify competitive individualism viewed the state solely as a policeman; they opposed governmental interference as a violation of the dictates of nature—even when nature allowed the "stronger to kill and eat the weaker, and for the weaker to be killed and eaten."[112] This turned the idea of freedom into a farce. No one had the right to enslave someone, whether by individual force or by systemic structures within a given society, and keep them from working, eating, or learning. Liberty had to be proactive: "A man who is ignorant is not free. A man who is a tramp is not free."[113] Liberty as pure negation was not liberty in Gronlund's estimation. A man who could not ameliorate the suffering of a wife or starving child was not free: "freedom is not alone bread, but leisure, absence of cares, self-determination, ability and means to do the right thing."[114] The cooperative commonwealth recognized freedom as that which is conferred, rights guaranteed, onto its citizens. Freedom was more than simply the absence of obstacles; it included positive efforts to confront those obstacles that restricted an individual's freedom. To accomplish this, citizens needed to work together. Fighting for one's own freedom meant fighting for the freedom of all. This kind of freedom, Gronlund believed, represented the "highest ideal of Collectivists."[115]

The primary job of the government was to protect its citizens and allow them the freedom to flourish on their own accord. This included protecting citizens from one another, as when the freedoms of one or a few inhibited or cancelled out the freedoms of others. Even more so, the state was charged with protecting the most sacred of American rights—private property, the source of life and liberty. If the state threatened an individual's right to property, then it violated the social contract and forfeited its reason for existing. But what was the state to do with the "liberty" of capitalists in eliminating workers' freedom by exploitative fleecing? Was the state responsible for protecting the property of the capitalist when that "property" was essentially a human wage-laborer? The way around this problem was to deny it. Capitalists did not believe that the life and liberty of workers were violated. Indeed, many believed then, as they do now, that capitalism was best suited to maximize individual freedom. The fact that workers could choose not to work meant that they were not owned—hence, pure freedom. But could workers freely choose *not* to participate in a capitalist system? It was "a paltry evasion," Gronlund reasoned, "to say that the workers are free to consent or to refuse the terms of the employer."[116] The capitalist failed to see how few could freely decide to leave an economy without serious consequences. Either the laborer sold his labor and forfeited his sovereignty or was punished for failing to do so. What is more, submission to the disciplinary demands of the employing class was not consent to those demands.[117] Workers would lose if they refused work; they would also lose if they did work, since they would never be able to escape the fleecing practices of the capitalists. Where was the freedom to choose? To survive, laborers had to yield to the exploitative conditions of the capitalist. This was the extent of their freedom, which was little to no freedom at all. And matters worsened the moment workers signed their labor contracts. The capitalist would subsequently control the price of commodities, the pace of production, and the wages of the worker; he also maintained strict control over workers while they worked, creating thereby "ox-eyed, docile wage-workers, restrained by arbitrary shop rules prescribed by their lord—rules that forbid them to talk to each other, or even to laugh—who not for a moment bear comparison with the merry families of master and men of the despised middle age."[118] The laborer was "forced" against his will to become an item of property.

The issue of the government's job to protect both citizens and private property could often create a serious dilemma, however. How was the government to protect private property when that property itself violated the life and liberty of supposedly "free" citizens? One answer was that the state could step in when property, however compliant it might have been with Lockean ideology, threatened the public good. Of course, we should note that the government regularly interferes in an economy—doing so on behalf of wealth, not labor. In line with other socialists, Gronlund provided a response that reconceptualized property as public, not private. Both labor and the products of labor were constituted by society itself, not by any one individual. It was absurd for one group, especially capitalists who had no hand in production, to claim proprietorship over even a small portion of property. This would be stealing from society. The state did not exist to protect private interests; its responsibility revolved around the wellbeing of the whole. Ownership would be extended to those who produced and used property, depending on how much labor was put into that which became property. Property derived from mixing individual labor with that which was common to all—the natural environment. Distribution of a common resource should not be in the hands of private ownership. The State, as the organic collective of all citizens, owns the land and was, Gronlund said, "the sole landlord."[119] All the land in America, especially the huge patches of it in the west, belonged to all citizens in common. No railroad, steel, or oil tycoon could claim as his own that which was given to all equally, otherwise the people (the State) would move—move democratically—against the schemes of wealth, whose greed threatened the commons. Baltimore lawyer Daniel Raymond identified a similar notion in his *Thoughts on Political Economy* (1820). There was no private property, according to Raymond, in "derogation of the public weal." Individual claims of private property were fine, but they did not supersede the "title of the whole," since there was no private property, no production drawn from the natural world, apart from the public. The private, including the material items within its realm, derived from the public; that is, it was the public that determined the limits of what could be private. Moreover, the government was the only legitimate institution to regulate property "which the public interest may require."[120] From a Marxist perspective, commodities produced by an army of laborers would become "government property to dispose of"—not for profit but for the benefit of those who created such products.[121] The state would simply facilitate the equitable distribution of goods. The best way to properly recognize the ownership of items produced by society was through representation, whether by the workers themselves through trade unions or labor bureaus made up of workers and run by them or state and federal legislators. Those who contributed to society, especially workers, would elect governing representatives to distribute the goods of the industries that they were part of.

It was never Gronlund's intent for the government to stand above the sovereignty of the people. He believed wholeheartedly that governing power derived from the consent of the governed. But in Gilded Age America that consent seemed to be restricted to the captains of industry, those who took captive both society and politics. America's governing institutions at both the state and federal levels were nestled deep in the pockets of the country's richest oligarchs. Radicals and reformers sought to sever the enticements of mammon from the function of the State, desiring greater accountability from their governing officials. This required an expansion of democratic activity in the procedures of governing, leading to things like the referendum, the initiative, and the recall, as well as the Civil Service Act and the direct election of senators via the Seventeenth Amendment. Gronlund praised "the objectives of the Civil Service Reform Acts," which intended "to secure real merit as the sole ground" for governing appointments.[122] Added to these changes, Gronlund envisioned a state that "would be the employer [and] the people the employed" with "no conflict of interest," for "all would work as a cooperative commonwealth, with a mutual interest."[123] Sadly, however, his vision of democracy did not include ethnic minorities or women (more on this in the following chapters).

Up to this point, Gronlund had been speaking of the state as an administrative institution. But there was more to it than that. The administrative state
was subsumed under the State organism. The State was the general spirit of a
particular people—hence the reason why he capitalized "State."[124] The *state*
(lowercase) referred to practical governance. Drawing on Rousseau and the
German notion of a *volkgeist*, "a spirit which has its life in the national history, which produces specific traits of nationality" beyond the "common traits
of humanity," Gronlund believed that America's own spirit manifested itself in
the opening shots at Fort Sumter.[125] Drawn out from the crucible of Civil War
was the seed of an organic mind intent on moving closer to societal emancipation. "The people themselves *are the State*," a member of the Knights of Labor declared.[126] Gronlund did not mean this in a purely metaphorical sense.
The State—made up of its people, the land, and what is produced in relation
to both—was "literally," he proclaimed, "an organism, personal and territo-
rial."[127] Gronlund's concept of the State as an actual organism echoed not only
the philosophy of Hegel but also the Hegelianism of American Episcopalian
theologian Elisha Mulford. In *The Nation: The Foundations of Civil Order and
Political Life in the United States,* published a few years before Gronlund came
to America, Mumford argued that the members of society, those who formed
an organic whole, existed not as "wheels in mills," but as "members of a living
body . . . a living spirit working through the whole."[128] Kaweah cooperative
community founder Burnette Haskell, directly influenced by Gronlund, and,
in his own words, a "follower of Hegel," likewise shared the view of the State
as an organism, which "developed just as our physical bodies."[129] Economist
Richard Ely came to a similar view. A socialist society was not merely "an
aggregate of individuals, but a living, growing organism, the laws of which
are something different from the laws of individual action."[130] Universalist
clergyman and socialist Charles H. Vail, one of the first organizers of the
Socialist Party of America, drew from Gronlund the notion that socialism,
"as a growing organism," signified "the rejection of selfishness" and the affirmation of altruism "as the principle of social action. It thus recognizes society,
what Gronlund understood as the State, as an organism."[131] Mulford argued
that society, as "a moral organism," moved "toward its realization" through
laws and institutions. Gronlund would have agreed: the work of the state as
administrator was necessary for the development of the State organism. As
an individual cared for "his own well-being," the job of the legislative state

was to care for the good of the public at large by "making all special activities work together for one general end."[132] The state administration was formed to deal with the "miseries" created by competition (e.g., poverty, inequality, plutocracy) and resulting in overproduction. It was to be viewed, therefore, as "man's greatest good" and not a "burden" or "necessary evil."[133] And there was no need to force society to comply with the State as organism or the state as administration. The Will of the Universe working through evolution would guide society to its destiny. What members of society needed to do was simply partner with evolution through labor. The State represented the latest in the advancement of the human spirit—the divine Reason. Gronlund accepted Hegel's proposition that "whatever is, is rational."[134] The rationality of the State was the mind of the "Will of the Universe."

Gronlund knew that speaking of the State in this way would invite confusion. The term "organism," he feared, would have associated the "State" with the utopian ideals of communism and anarchism, which most defenders of capitalism, including "well-informed people," he said, confused with socialism.[135] Gronlund reserved his harshest criticisms for the latter, which he viewed as an extreme form of individualism. In an essay for *The Nationalist* in 1889, he wrote that anarchism was far from "socialistic in spirit"; it was "purely individualistic."[136] Likewise, communism and socialism represented "two radically different systems." He opposed the communist ideal of making "all property common property." Communism would, in Gronlund's mind, "abolish the institution of property," and crush "individuality" (separate from "individualism"). His commonwealth would accomplish just the opposite. Socialism would not seek to distribute property evenly. Instead, it would place the means of production "under collective control." The problem with communism (along with anarchism) was that it did not protect legitimate forms of property. The "essential qualities of propertyship" [sic] rested on an individual's direct labor. Gronlund was not opposed to private ownership, just so long as ownership of an item was attached to the one who labored to produce it. Indeed, so long as property was not acquired through fleecing, private wealth would be, he said, "harmless." Gronlund wanted to make sure that the one who produced received the full recognition in the form of compensation for the value produced. Everyone, including a skilled factory manager, would be "entitled to the full proceeds of his own labor."[137]

Equitable distribution of property and thus a proper account of labor production would extend not just to mechanics or technical workers but to all contributors in a commonwealth—to all citizens. "Brain work," too, would have "its due weight." Such workers included teachers, artists, writers, and accountants. It also included those integral to capitalism—managers. If a new manager, in comparison to a previous one, increased the earnings of a factory, the commonwealth would reward the manager with a slightly higher wage. His concern on this point was to avoid equalizing every form of work, comparing "common labor" with either skilled or professional labor or what he referred to as "multiplied common labor." In a note to the revised edition of *Cooperative Commonwealth,* Gronlund challenged Bellamy's proposal of equal wages, that "every person, whatever his work, his industry, or his needs," would be given the same income at the beginning of every New Year's Day," a proposal that Gronlund believed to be "impracticable and unjust." Along with this, he supported a basic livable wage for all workers regardless of their labor. But who or what body would be entrusted with determining the varying value of labor beyond a basic income, "a delicate and dictatorial function"? Responsibility fell to the elected representatives of the commonwealth, those who demonstrated "the best interests of the whole." Such arbiters would be appointed and removed by the workers of a particular industry. There was not a hint that such elected representatives would be considered infallible. At the end of each year, they would undergo an evaluation of their success, specifically as it related to the well-being of the workers, by those who appointed them.[138] Because they held final authority, workers would retain greater responsibility for themselves and society.

All work would be done on a cooperative basis and coordinated in such a way as to benefit the entirety of society. Small businesses would not have to compete with one another since there would be one "great permanent bazaar, embracing all possible articles of consumption." Workers would plan production to reduce risk and avoid overproduction. Agriculture would move toward collective farming, completing what was already being done in "bonanza farming," but not for private gain. Cooperation would, Gronlund said, "increase the total production of our country at least as much beyond the capability of the present system."[139] Since citizens would be able to engage in work that they enjoyed, more work would be done—not for the purposes of survival or because of fear of discipline but because of the intrinsic good of work itself. This would lead to a reduction of working hours for the blessings of greater leisure.

The challenge came in determining the value for vastly different kinds of work. Gronlund believed that wages would be the measure (not the source) of distinguishing the compensation for different work. Recall that monetary notes would be essentially labor notes. Gronlund suggested the establishment of a board of arbiters to determine compensation. Such a board, for instance, would establish wages well above the level of subsistence and after a year, consider to what degree such wages needed adjustment: "a year's experience will teach them whether they have raised the wages too much, or not high enough." Likewise, those who set compensation rates would come from among those who worked in a particular industry—not from an outside bureau or a non-producing corporate board, as was the case in capitalism. Each "branch of industry," Gronlund reasoned, would "settle that matter of remuneration for themselves." The "watchmaker's labor," he argued, would be "rated above" that of a hod carrier, largely to compensate for the many years of education and apprenticeship.[140] Training to become a watchmaker required remuneration which could be offered in the future by way of a higher salary. A failure to remunerate for training could be construed as a kind of reverse fleecing, forcing someone to produce without paying him. Thus, the value for a teacher, doctor, or lawyer, for instance, would be much higher given the years (i.e., time) necessary not only to become one of these figures but to be retroactively reimbursed for what they have already produced—in this case, a doctor, a lawyer, or a teacher. But they would continue to receive a higher wage because of the weightier work they did for the benefit of society. The point is that workers would determine their own pay.

The increase in production brought about by cooperative labor, however, did not ultimately solve the problem of overproduction. Gronlund did not ignore this. Dealing with the possibility of overproduction demanded the abandonment of a "planless" economy. The nation's economy could not be left alone. According to his plan, citizens would learn to harness the laws of supply and demand, through "proper foresight and abundant statistics," to avoid the contradictions of capitalism and preserve "economic equilibrium." It should be noted that Gronlund did not accept out of hand the idea that governments were unable to properly regulate the economy "as well as private individuals," offering the example of the telegraph, postal services, and railroad management in parts of Europe. America, too, had examples of healthy oversight agencies. The success of "scientific labours" in the "Coastal Survey, Lighthouse Service, Naval Observatory, Signal Service, Patent Office, [and] Geological Surveys" in America proved that the state could, indeed, "direct the work of Society."[141] This was the model for all sectors of the economy. But one needed to remember that overproduction in Gronlund's day was tied to "fleecing"—fleecing that depended on surplus labor. And so, we are reminded that dealing with capitalism required eliminating the structures that generated the additional labor expended by the worker. Even if a surplus continued in the commonwealth, it would be given back to the workers to soften the social consequences that came from overproduction. One thing was certain in Gronlund's mind: overproduction in the commonwealth, if it were to occur, would not be nearly as devastating as overproduction in the capitalist state.

Economic regulations would likewise have a positive impact on land use, including rent. Regulating the production of land and monitoring rent would be two crucial functions of the state. Rents fluctuated as elected laborers from all industries determined the price of goods by monitoring supply and demand. And through regulation, no charity would be needed to aid the exhausted worker. Under capitalism, benevolence was offered not for the well-being of workers but to puff up the pride and bolster the hegemony of condescending capitalists. The state would be able to provide low-rent housing but also public services: "libraries of schools for his children, of hospitals, asylums, [even] assistance in his old age."[142] The commonwealth would also have the authority to protect the environment. Disease, polluted air and water, and other industries "willed with garbage," results of a "planless" economy, would fall to "the control of an energetic administration." As if to anticipate the devastations caused by the Dust Bowl in the 1930s, capitalist destruction of rich agriculture lands by way of bonanza farming, a "mode of farming that impoverishes the soil," Gronlund wrote, would also end. "Every bushel of wheat sent to our large cities or abroad," he argued, "robs the soil of a certain amount of nutriment." Nothing was ever to replenish the land.[143] Here, Gronlund identified the environmental impact of commercial capitalism, a concern that persists today. In the early 1830s, it took about three days to get a bushel of grain to the granary. By 1930, it took about three hours. It

is not hard to see how commercial production can have devastating consequences on natural resources.[144]

The move away from a planless (or semi-planless) economy to a more
regulated one likewise required serious changes in America's political culture. Many feared that socialism would destroy the nation's most cherished
document—the Constitution. Such fears, however, were unfounded. Gronlund did not see the problem with reconceptualizing the Constitution under
the lens of collectivism. A profound error in the American mind was the
assumption that "constitution" meant strictly a legal document. Following
Hegel, Gronlund understood "constitution" as the dynamic development of
a nation's spirit. "A constitution *develops* out of the spirit of a nation," Hegel
once argued: "It is the indwelling spirit and the history of the nation . . . by
which constitutions have been and are made."[145] "Every society was "constituted" by the consciousness of its members.[146] Such a "constitution" was
contingent, subject to historical processes. When the "organic power" of a
nation changed, according to Gronlund, so would its governing document.
He mentioned the Civil War and the end of racial slavery to illustrate how a
nation's "constitution," its social and political culture, could be altered. With
the abolition of slavery, the Constitution's meaning was modified by the Thirteenth, Fourteenth, and Fifteenth Amendments. But this was only because
the general will of the United States, through the trials of war, had itself been
altered. The mere apparatus of governing (i.e., the process of law making)
was never "the substance of society." The nation's "substance," its "constitution," underwent further changes in the years after the war. Gronlund and
other socialists recognized how the American government, at both the state
and federal level, became corrupted because of the powerful influence of the
rich, who twisted the constitution, especially the Fourteenth Amendment,
to achieve their own private ends. The "political machinery," whereby wealth
and influential political bosses held a monopoly on governing power, needed
to be eradicated. Many attempted to roll back this expanding hegemony.
Regulatory legislation like the Sherman Anti-Trust Act were woefully ineffi-
cient. The judicial system, too, played a part in protecting the interests of the
plutocracy. Gronlund proposed a restructuring of American government that
would eliminate representative democracy in favor of direct democracy. The
American republic had become corrupt by legislators who conducted "public
affairs with a view to private and class interests." Not only did he support the

dismantling of the "term-system," following Albert Stickney, author of *A True Republic,* Gronlund suggested that the entire system of representation at all levels of governance was "unfit for a higher civilization." When in the grip of wealth, the representative system destroys true democracy, which Gronlund considered a "form of administration" in which no public offer would be able to direct public affairs for private ends.[147]

Gronlund did not call for the complete scrapping of the Constitution nor for any changes in its basic governing structure. But Americans allowed the mere administrative function of the Constitution to guide the general will. This was backwards. The Constitution had to conform to the dynamics of the general will so that it, too, would align with the dialectical progress of the "Will of the Universe." And such conformity was inevitable. Governing practices would be changed whenever there was a foundational shift in society. The United States did not revolve around a "piece of paper" but the "organic power" of its citizenry. Americans had the power to "shift the center of gravity" and thus alter the meaning of the Constitution, and at times, they did—as demonstrated particularly during and after the Civil War. Modifications in the general will of the people rested on changes in "economic conditions"; otherwise, the political "machinery" would be useless, Gronlund believed. For instance, slavery was interwoven into the American psyche in the antebellum period, but the uprooting of the institution led to a fundamental alteration in the American mind. Emancipation revolutionized the way in which the Constitution was viewed and applied, becoming "a very different" document. "Socialists, then," Gronlund assured his readers, had "no thought whatever of 'laying impious hands' on this glorious paper 'constitution' of the United States."[148] The Constitution would continue to change as the spirit of the American people adapted to the divine power guiding events. Cooperation, empathy, and care that each citizen would show to one another would protect individual rights and compel representatives, heretofore under the manipulations of wealth, to focus even more intently on the needs of the republic.

The American government had become undemocratic and thus "unfit to furnish a good administration of the people's affairs." As the "organic power of Society" that made the United States what it was, labor was the highest legitimate governing authority. Political power within a capitalist system, Gronlund wrote, was "nothing but the organized power of classes, or men, or sets of men, to 'govern' others," to dictate how citizens were to live. The material forces that created the hierarchy of classes would not exist in the Commonwealth (though divisions of labor would); hence, the new social order, according to Gronlund, would be truly "classless." Consequently, there would be no cohort of men above the nation. A more democratic society would come by way of changes in economic conditions, and such changes would be made by workers from a variety of industries. Every citizen would perform their "appropriate share of the administration." Specific governors, "competent and qualified functionaries," would be appointed "from below." This was what Gronlund meant by democratic government: "Administration by the Competent." America's "chief industries" would elect representatives from among their ranks. The commonwealth would create an abundance of local and democratically controlled markets, "permanent bazaars, embracing all possible articles of consumption." The transportation infrastructure would fall "under collective control." No longer would land and the railroads be dominated for the purposes of private gain. Newspapers would be freed from moneyed interest, eliminating the practice of "bribing newspapers for puffs" or using "lying labels" to "sell adulterated goods." Those who elected such officials would do so because they would have "a knowledge of the capacity of the candidate for a given office, and a knowledge of what the duties of that office are." Every economic sector, from "mechanical and agricultural and mining pursuits" as well as for teachers and physicians would choose a "chief." These chiefs would compose a "national board of administration."[149]

Gronlund was never free from criticism, especially from among the plutocratic elite in the country. Some argued that his commonwealth would quickly descend into "unbearable omnipotent centralization." More directly, however, the expansion of the state would lead to an expansion of corruption: "If corruption is now everywhere cropping up in the American civil service, how will it be when the service shall be increased a thousand fold?"[150] Gronlund first pointed out that Gilded Age America was already under the thumb of a large centralized administration—bank-presidents, merchants, and superintendents: "Is there not an immense number of men now occupying private positions intent only on their interests or the interest of their employers, and yet to all intents and purposes, officials of Society?"[151] Likewise, the country was already corrupted by an overbearing bureaucracy in the form of organized capitalism. John McArthur of the Farmers' Alliance would later note that the American economy was already "in the clutches" of the railroads. America's entire economic system, wrote Bellamy, was "administered by great capitalists"—not the people's elected representatives.[152] If Gronlund's critics were concerned about bureaucratic corruption, they needed to look no further than the "centralization of power" in their own industries. There was really nothing to fear in "centralization," Gronlund believed. In fact, he simply wanted to shift the center of power—from one that was driven by greed and self-interest to another focused on altruism and social benevolence. The State reflected each individual: "Every healthy man is an instance of the most perfect centralization in his own person. Indeed, the moment that perfect centralization ceases, suffering is the result. And as with the human organism, so with the social organism."[153] The real fear among antisocialists revolved around the executive function of governance. But even this was overblown, since there would only be three limited functions of the State-organism in the *Commonwealth:* Chief Superintendent, Chief Statistician, and Arbitrator.[154] The assumption that a reduction in corruption corresponded to a reduction in the number of bureaucrats and bureaucratic agencies was fundamentally misguided. Corruption, for Gronlund, came from a lack of oversight for those few in power, individuals (capitalists) not elected by the American people.

The absence of democratic accountability was fertile ground for political scandals at all levels of government. The way to reduce corruption was to make sure that elected officials worked under the watchful eye of "the public conscience." The tenure of service for a legislator in the commonwealth would be determined by the will of voters and good behavior, which Gronlund defined as efficiency in relation to the expertise of the one elected. Officials, which Gronlund restricted to men, would be held responsible "if the work was not done well." Evaluations would be conducted by those under him. If an elected official did his job well, he would continue in his position as long as he chose to stay and based upon the review of those under him. This would eliminate the dangers of a corrupt bureaucracy. It would also ensure that the best individual would be elected. When it came to evaluating candidates for administration positions, Gronlund emphasized experience and expertise: "Is a physician a bureaucrat? When a patient has found a good physician, he keeps him and follows his directions; and yet we should say, that that patient's power over this physician is not nugatory, though he does not direct what medicines shall be administered."[155] A patient had the freedom to choose an expert, but the patient did not have the right (because they did not have the knowledge) to make decisions as how the expert might fulfill his responsibilities. A board of doctors, train conductors, masons, or journalists would recognize the value of their own workers, choose from among them, and govern their own sector.

The commonwealth would implement practices to check the actions of elected administrators. For instance, electors would have access to the "referendum," defined as "the submitting [of] all bills of a general nature to the people they are intended to affect, before they have the validity of laws."[156] While proposals would be drafted by the "wisest and most competent" experts, citizens would make the final decision as to whether such proposals would be implemented as law for society. This extended the democratic decision-making process for citizens: "when the voters have measures before them . . . to discuss, and then to ratify or reject, it may fairly be expected that they will take a considerable and increasing interest in public affairs."[157] Next came the recall. Elective administrators could be removed from office if they failed in their responsibilities to the public. In the same way that citizens could vote someone into office, they could just as easily vote them out by a decision of the majority. Immediate elections would be held for new directors. The one qualification in Gronlund's plan different from his own time was that a worker removed from a position of administration would not be left without work. Unlike his own day, a dismissed worker/official would be "put back among the rank and file, until elevated by a new election." This was the "remedy by which society could protect itself against any rebellious or negligent worker." The final means by which to hold officials accountable would be "through the public journals." Journalists were, in Gronlund's sense, the conscience of the people. Unlike Congress, they were "in constant session," faithfully watching events as "public criers" for the benefit of the commonwealth. Wealth would no longer direct the information given to the public—information that would inevitably protect the interests of the wealthy. Thus, there would be "little space for editorials." Unencumbered by corporate oversight, commonwealth newspapers would not compete with one another for subscribers, which would inevitably tempt editors to either embellish or fabricate stories. They would become "collective institution," not the private tool of profit mongers. As a result, journalists would no longer be intimidated by officious plutocratic overlords. Even if there were editorials, they would be written with the wider public in mind. The collectivization of media would also widen the opportunities for citizens to share their opinions: "Anyone—whatever unpopular opinions he may entertain, however hostile to the administrators he may be—will be entitled to have anything decent printed."[158]

Gronlund was not so naïve to think that his commonwealth would be an idealistic and impractical utopia. He anticipated social conflicts and juridical disputes. Most social conflicts derived from competition in pursuit of wealth. By eliminating the ideology of competition, enabled by money interest, and by reconceptualize labor, few conflicts would arise. Likewise, legal clashes would be few, since the main cause of litigation, again, the protection of wealth and property, would be abolished. As one familiar with the legal profession, Gronlund had a particular bone to pick with attorneys. The juridical class in late-nineteenth-century America—and Gronlund himself would have known—represented "the most mischievous of all classes, the one that most clogs the wheels of progress." Lawyers perpetuated an unjust system—a system set toward protecting private wealth. But in the Gronlund's commonwealth, legal cases, if they were to arise at all, would be decided in accordance with the laws that the people sanctioned. And since the people sanctioned the law, judges would not have the authority to nullify them unless otherwise directed by the people. Only "competent and qualified judges" would be appointed by other judges. Gronlund favored the "judicial functions" of the Danish model, where if two judges could not decide on a case, then a third would enter so that the majority could decide. In a society where the people established the law, there would no longer be a need for a large "tribe of lawyers" motivated by financial gain.[159] Appellate courts would be done away with (as cases would be determined by established law), and those bringing a suit to court would pay nothing.

Such fundamental changes to governance had to be preceded by altering the material conditions of workers, which began with an examination of the plight of workers. The progress of human civilization demanded the democratization of the labor force, a widening of worker prerogatives. Yet he accepted the fact that this would be gradual. In the later portions of the *Commonwealth,* Gronlund focused particularly on the labor and status of women to identify the stage of civilization in evolution. He expected that with the elimination of competition and the advent of cooperation, women would be placed on an "equal footing with man." The commonwealth would give women "the power of earning" her own "living at pleasure," of making decisions for the direction of her own life. Gronlund, like other American social-ists, retained a middle-class vision of gender. This equality, again, was not a matter of likeness, making men exactly like women and vice versa but equal-ity that recognized and appreciated "natural" differences. Upon this ostensi-bly "natural" difference, Gronlund assumed, women would retain their own "physiology." In this line of thinking, he contended for "special vocations" between the sexes, since the two "walk in different pathways." There were specific jobs, he said, that could (and should) be done primarily by women, like becoming medical doctors: "Why should not our women insist on having female physicians" as opposed to nursing strictly?[160] At any rate, Gronlund did not delineate all possible work for women. His focus was on incremen-tally dismantling the economic dependency of women upon men.[161]

Many of Gronlund's contemporaries believed that women would achieve greater independence once granted the right to vote.[162] Gronlund was skep-tical of this, however. First, voting was not a private right, but a "public trust."[163] Second, expanding the right to vote would not *necessarily* lead to an alteration of economic conditions, the true source of discrimination. Voting, regardless of who held the right to exercise it, was ineffective so long as the conditions that entrenched and exasperated inequity remained: "the ballot would not bring strength to the lightless eye or the thin hand of the needle-woman of this age of competition."[164] Capitalism was the source of injustice in America, not the absence of an individual's opportunity to participate in electoral politics. Besides, the majority of women in late-nineteenth-century America, Gronlund assumed, had little motivation to confront exploitative capitalism; thus, an extension of the vote to women had the potential of strengthening capitalist power. If granted the opportunity to vote, women would not effectively deal with the capitalist conditions that oppressed them in the first place. Women were far more traditional and thus conservative. But he nonetheless gave—in a way that may seem patronizing to contemporary readers—"credit to these persistent 'women's rights'" advocates for confront-ing patriarchal hegemony.[165]

On the topic of women's liberation, Gronlund's enemies pushed the ab-surd notion that socialists, because they advocated for the economic inde-pendence of women, intended to destroy the family.[166] This did not follow either. Commonwealth socialists, far from "free lovers," were challenging the reasons behind seeking marriage.[167] Women, for instance, pursued marriage not out of a deep sense of love but for the purpose of ameliorating economic pressures. Of course, he says nothing about a man's marital endeavors for similar reasons. Gronlund sought the removal of the "causes which now make woman prefer almost any marriage to working for a living." Sadly, however, these marriages turned women into items of property—dependents, whose lives were ostensibly owned and directed by their husbands. Socialism, he wrote, would "enable every healthy adult man and woman to marry whenever they feel so inclined"; it would do away with the notion that a wife is nothing more than "the husband's property." The commonwealth would end the commodification of marriage and significantly reduce the number of women who entered loveless marriages or who chose prostitution to supplement their income. What is more, a socialistic marriage, a union created out of mutual respect and love, would decrease the number of divorces, induced, much like everything else in Gronlund's day, from economic pressures.[168]

Gronlund's final and what he believed to be his most important proposal for changing the conditions of labor revolved around restructuring America's educational system. Education in late-nineteenth-century America was little more than preparation for a child's placement in the grinding individualism of competitive capitalism: "The ideal, the end of education now sought to be attained, is to enable the individual to achieve success in life, to get the better of his fellow-men in the struggle for the good things of this world. That is the meaning of individualism."[169] Federal acts like the Morrill-Land Grants created an array of public universities across the country. Late-nineteenth-century private universities endowed by wealthy elites—such as Vanderbilt (1873), Stanford (1885), Chicago (1890)—sprang up around the country.[170] The priority among these schools was to advance industry and business, to create an army of competitive individuals, not necessarily to nurture humanity. Besides, this type of capitalist education catered to those who could afford it. Working-class children had to toil for the pittance that barely contributed to a family's income and survival; the minimum education provided in Gronlund's day was woefully inadequate. Since there was no equity in America's educational system, few had the opportunity for an advanced education. Gronlund proposed the removal of the obstacles in the way of a child's intellectual development—to "relieve children from the task of being breadwinners."[171] Every member of society would have equal access to education: "As the boys will be really educated, so the girls will be." The "first object of education" in the commonwealth would be to "establish in the minds of the children an indissoluble association between their individual happiness and the good of all." This would require a curriculum focused on the "harmonious and balanced cultivation of all the faculties." To do this, he believed, schools needed to invest in the arts, which members of society in large measure were deprived of. The "comfortable classes" established "expensive theatres," where they would "idle away their time" and by doing so drive a wedge within society. Art allowed young people, according to Gronlund, to critically examine the world and creatively contribute to its flourishing. It stood as the true social means by which to elevate humanity. In the commonwealth, art would "once more belong in the midst of the people, because of its eminently educational importance. He who has learned to appreciate the beautiful will never after have a taste for the low."[172]

The state would take up the task of providing universal public education. Of the three social pillars that held up a modern nation—the family, the church, and the state—only the state was qualified to provide such a common education. The church could not, since it had become a pro-capitalist "institution to darken men's minds." The church was "incompetent," Gronlund cynically quipped, because it knew "nothing worth knowing." He could have said the same about the capitalist state, but he hoped that the democratic reformation of this institution (mentioned above) would be much more effective in implementing an egalitarian commonwealth. Moreover, religion was interested more in the inner and private than the outer public. Similarly, the family, though not on the same level as religious organizations, could only provide a modicum of education. But since public schooling was a matter of "scientific labor," society could entrust education to a body of qualified experts. Parents were not specialists in any one academic discipline. The state was able to raise up a cadre of individuals to educate the nation's next generation. The family needed to become subordinate to the collective State: "A social spirit—i.e., the spirit of all being members of one organism—must be substituted for family spirit."[173] By extension every individual of the family was part of the State. Thus, in a very real sense, children "do not belong to their parents; they belong to society."[174] Gronlund qualified his remarks by saying that he was not making "war on the family." Indeed, he valued the right of a "healthy man and woman to form a family."[175] What he opposed was "exclusiveness," whereby wealthier families (or family that could afford it) would educate their children, removing them from the state and intensifying the individualistic competition for the purpose of gaining an advantage over others. Every family belonged to the commonwealth since every member contributed to it.

Gronlund ended *Commonwealth* with a brief discussion of the relationship between socialism and morality. Morality was, for Gronlund, not grounded in traditional doctrine but in society—ethics derived from social experience. He rejected theological dogma not so much because it was difficult to give credence to anything that "cannot be touched or handled," cultivating thereby "sickly spiritual hallucinations," but more so because dogma was in part the source of social division. Society had to be raised "to a higher plane of thought"—"elevated," he urged, "from being a narrow personal concern between the individual and his maker into a social concern between humanity and its destiny"[176] As society moved closer to the commonwealth, American citizens would gradually "leave theology behind." The moral vices plaguing the American population—theft, gambling, drunkenness, prostitution—had been enabled by this theological individualism, which traditional religion never overcame.[177] In other words, such vices would persist if capitalism remained. Because it created isolated individuals, removing them from the communities necessary to cultivate individual morality, capitalism enabled immorality. Paying exorbitant salaries to a company's executive officer, issuing high interest loans, selling shoddy products, manipulating prices, and speculating on stocks were, for Gronlund, serious moral crimes against society. In its essence, capitalism was theft. The highest evil was how every millionaire took what did not belong to him by way of fleecing the value produced by workers. In his desire to correct such a moral situation, Gronlund asked his readers how American society came to such a "low level of integrity": "Why do people steal, and rob, and embezzle, and in other ways take more than their share out of the common stock?" The great moral crime of Gronlund's day related to how capitalism legitimized exploitation. "Every millionaire," he wrote, "takes what does not belong to him."[178]

Traditional religion was individualistic at its core. This was to its detriment, thought Gronlund, for it ignored the place (and meaning) of the self in relation to others, to society. Restoring the individual self—the goal of redemption (returning the self to its true state before God)—could not be accomplished without others. Full or complete salvation demanded social redemption. Sadly, however, traditional religion lost sight of the community. Individualism was a prominent feature in America's myriad moral reform campaigns—campaigns, again, that dealt with the symptoms not the sources of immorality. But a focus on individual salvation would not solve the problems of individualism. Anything that harmed the human collective harmed the individual human and was therefore immoral. "Right," Gronlund reasoned, "is every conduct which tends to the true welfare of society; 'wrong' what obstructs that welfare." Criminal activity was in essence the "neglected responsibilities" toward others. Gambling, for instance, was immoral "not because it tends to ruin the gambler, but because [the gambler] cannot win unless somebody loses." Drunkenness would be reduced because once the commonwealth took charge of the traffic in liquor, there would no longer be an interest in the quantity sold. Sexual immorality came from the desire of individuals to satisfy their own lusts. It also stemmed from women who would sell themselves in a desperate effort to supplement their meager incomes. The economic habits of the Gilded Age produced the "frauds, dishonesties, and this hypocrisy" characteristic of American society. And such evils would persist so long as the system continued. Competitive self-interest served as "the foundation, the prime motor, the mainspring" of the country's moral state.[179]

Anticipating the social gospel, Gronlund's concern for a renewed morality had less to do with changing human nature than in reforming the social lives of men and women—"their surroundings, the constitution of society, the mold in which their lives, thoughts, and feelings are cast." Instead of the selfish pursuit of wealth, members of the State would be guided by greater sympathy, not pity. Pity, the bad-faith piety of the wealthy, was really a way of viewing others as inferior. The rich conspicuously contribute to charity as a way to show their superiority over those they exploit. Wealthy elites, who in truth lacked "all moral value," hid their immorality through charity. The goal of morality was for all to take advantage of their best work and "to make it natural for men to love their neighbors as themselves." This required changes in material relations. Gronlund's discussion of morality revealed his radicalism. He was less concerned about dealing with the immediate manifestation of what may be considered immoral. Instead, he examined the root cause of immorality, derived from material conditions. Christ himself, Gronlund argued, would not stop at "denouncing sin as merely spiritual evil"; rather he would have drilled down to the roots, destroying the flower of competition "by cutting at the roots—poverty and ignorance." The best way to end prostitution, drunkenness, and even gambling was not through the reformation of individual habits but by uprooting the conditions that feed such activities. The obsession with domination over others through competition and exploitation was the single most challenging obstacle in the way of sympathy: "Sympathy requires equality; pity regards the object not only as suffering, but as weak, hence as inferior . . . It is just because the occasional so-called 'charities' of the wealthy have their motive in pity and not in sympathy, that they lack all moral value."[180]

Debs confessed to the Strike Commission of 1894 that Gronlund's *Cooperative Commonwealth* was the most "rational solution" to the "whole [labor] question."[181] Such a widely read work moved Debs closer to embracing socialism, which he did officially after the presidential election of 1896. "I am for Socialism," he said, "because I am for humanity." The reign of capital, of "gold" and "money," constituted, Debs continued, "no proper basis of civilization. The time has come to regenerate society." High civilization and the health of society demanded the creation of a cooperative commonwealth.[182] Gronlund was confident that every modern society would necessarily move toward social democracy. And while he believed socialism could not be stopped in any final sense, he warned against passivity. Citizens needed to help build the commonwealth: progress demanded cooperation. Socialists, those who cared "not a jot about reforms," were the true revolutionaries. Half-measure reforms were "just as unscientific and stupid as bleeding for a fever in olden times," since they only suppressed the symptoms of the problem. "How can anyone 'reform' away abuses that are inherent in the system?"[183] A new revolution in America was near—a revolution not of "destruction and violence" but of cooperation and an enlightened conscience. This coming revolution, far from destroying "an atom of what is really good," would be society's redemption.[184]

# CHAPTER TWO

# OH, IT GOES . . . GOD WILLS IT

## A Model for Revolution

The "Power behind evolution" moved history irreversibly toward its end in socialism. A key part of such development included how this divine force selected a handful of gifted humans who were able to discern the progress of history, as God communicated it to them, and thus take up the responsibility to guide society toward its destiny. Such world leaders came to the fore at times of immense historical change. They were true revolutionary figures—creations and creators of history. Gronlund defined a revolution as "a complete change, [a] vigorous adaptation of all social elements to new conditions, most orderly, but effecting vast and permanent alterations."[1] But such radical moments did not appear *ex nihilo*. They were an essential part of the progress of natural evolution. In fact, there was no revolution without evolution first. Gronlund agreed with Spencer that evolution, as a "normal condition of the race," was "uniform, gradual, regular"—even slow. Though slow at first, history would then move to revolution "with the speed of a railroad [and] accomplished in the twinkling of an eye."[2] The participation of humanity was the key to this acceleration. Gronlund was critical of Spencer for downplaying the important role of human actors, especially the way evolution gained speed by those who had become conscious of the movement of the divine, inaugurating thereby the collective revolution.[3] A revolution was the "decisive point of evolution," when humanity took control of its historical affairs.[4] When, through the tutelage of historical leaders, humanity became conscious of the actions of the divine and hence conscious of their own identity, the movement of evolution jolted forward into its revolutionary stage. As

pregnancy was to the birth of a child, for Gronlund, so evolution was to revolution: "The birth of a child is a revolutionary event: it is the decisive point
between its evolution in the mother's womb, and that in the outside world."[5]
And here we see the influence of Hegel on Gronlund. In *Phenomenology of
Spirit*, Hegel, reflecting on the French Revolution in a way similar to that of
Gronlund, likewise used the metaphor of pregnancy and birth to describe
his own philosophy of history:

> Just as the first breath drawn by a child after its long, quiet nourishment
> breaks the gradualness of merely quantitative growth—there is a quali-
> tative leap, and the child is born—so likewise the Spirit in its formation
> matures slowly and quietly into its new shape, dissolving bit by bit the
> structure of its previous world, whose tottering state is only hinted at by
> isolated symptoms. The frivolity and boredom which unsettle the estab-
> lished order, the vague foreboding of something unknown, these are the
> heralds of approaching change. The gradual crumbling that left unaltered
> the face of the whole is cut short by a sunburst which, in one flash, illumi-
> nates the features of the new world.[6]

In formulating his view of history, Gronlund combined an older continental
idealism with a younger evolutionary theory.

After the publication of *Commonwealth*, Gronlund traveled to Europe,
staying there for a few years to write *Ça Ira, or Danton in the French Revolution*, which began as a lecture at the Social Reform Society at Edinburgh
University entitled "What 1789 can Teach 1889." It was not reported what
Gronlund anticipated in the year 1889.[7] This was also, as mentioned earlier,
the time when Gronlund publicly discussed his form of cooperative socialism
and its relationship to religion and morality. Gronlund said that among his
other works, this one was "decidedly my favorite." If sales were indicative of
popularity, however, *Ça Ira* was the least, since it "sold worst."[8] There is no
information as to why it was a commercial flop, but in terms of understanding Gronlund's philosophy of history—a synthesis of the work of the divine
in evolution that produced revolutionary moments through the agency of
select intellectuals—*Ça Ira* is, indeed, a very important work. *Commonwealth*
provided a historical critique of capitalism and an initial blueprint for the
future collectivist society. *Ça' Ira*, conversely, addressed the dynamics of his-

tory.[9] Said differently, the former focused on the inner workings of capitalism, including the source of its own demise, the latter on the developments within history that led to the rise of the capitalist order, and both books on the overall outworking of the mind of God with the aid of humanity. With *Ça' Ira*, Gronlund moved from economic theory to historical reality, discussing the cooperative work of the infinite with the finite as represented in the French Revolution and Georges Jacques Danton. One reviewer recognized the book as a "valuable contribution to political ethics" and one of the best studies of the French Revolution produced in America. Another wrote of *Ça Ira* as a "literary event of considerable interest."[10]

Among the world-altering social and political revolutions in western civilization, arguably none was as impactful—both in the immediate and long term—as the one in France in 1789. St. Louis Hegelian William Torrey Harris considered the French Revolution "a gigantic object lesson of the dialectic in human history."[11] America's own foreign policy, expansionism, ideological entanglements with liberalism and nationalism, and tensions between labor and capital, especially in regard to the morality of chattel slavery, drew inspiration from revolutionary events in Europe, Central and South America, and the West Indies in 1789, 1791, the 1820s, 1830, and 1848.[12] The issues that the United States faced after the Civil War—unionism, free silver, the Trust, etc.—were, Harris claimed, "looming up out of the future."[13] The experience of the Paris Commune of 1871, in particular, inspired hope that a socialistic revolution in the United States was more than a possibility. It also stoked fears of violent bloodshed. The Great Strike of 1877, according to Philip Foner, brought the United States "closer to a workers' revolution than at any time in its history."[14] Wendell Phillips, that great polemical orator of the antislavery movement, noted the latent revolutionary sentiment in America ready to manifest itself: "Scratch the surface of New York society, and you will find the Paris Commune."[15] Journalist and Knight supporter John Swinton warned that the alliance of capitalist interests with state violence was well on its way in creating "Bonapartism in America," a "worm-eaten Empire of Napoleon the Third."[16] Some of those involved in the strikes in St. Louis were veterans of the 1848 revolutions and the Paris Commune, who often sang the *Marseillaise* as they marched to the picket line. Workers, likened to the "men who led the Commune" as the "noblest patriots of France," effectively connected "American labor with European revolution."[17] Stirred by this revolutionary spirit of 1877, Gronlund (as Lofgreen) inspired workers in St. Louis: "Why should we allow ourselves to be trodden upon by a few monopolists, who have the reins of government in their hands, are using the organized assassins to crush us?"[18] Thus, the impact and implications of revolution reshaping the Atlantic world remained fresh on Gronlund's mind at the time of his writing *Ça Ira*.

Yet it may seem strange that in the entirety of his new book, Gronlund was silent on the events of 1877. According to Solomon Gemorah, Gronlund's experience in St. Louis in that year compelled him to write *The Coming Revolution*, published in 1878. Unfortunately, however, we have only Gemorah's word on this, since *Coming Revolution* is no longer available. Yet it is unavoidable, at least for those wishing to go deeper into Gronlund's mind, to inquire about the relationship between the Great Strike, the French Revolution, and the writing of *Ça Ira*. David Burbank speculates that Gronlund's leadership in the labor unrest in St. Louis may have come from his dismay over the absence of "capable, gifted and cultured" individuals who could raise the collective consciousness of workers for the purpose of bringing about collective change.[19] This reference to capable leaders was certainly in line with Gronlund's activist philosophy. Furthermore, it is "not impossible," Burbank appropriately surmises, "that [Gronlund's] difficulties with the 'violent and course element' in 1877 helped to form his views [about the role of violence]."[20] The violence used by strikers and the violence of the establishment against them did not seem, for Gronlund, to be effective; it only made matters worse. Recollections of the Paris Commune, where socialists who effectively took control of the city for a time yet were later brutally crushed by the French national army during "The Bloody Week" of May 1871, may have also contributed to Gronlund's hostility to class warfare. Adolph Douai, Gronlund's fellow member of the Workingmen's Party of the United States, "the first Marxist political party in North America," encouraged those involved in the strike, especially among those who took control of St. Louis (effectively becoming the "St. Louis Commune"), to "depreciate and shun all violence, all wanton disregard of existing law, how bad so ever they be, and all bloodshed, unless we be provoked and wantonly attacked, and forced to resist."[21] Gronlund knew that America was on the brink of a collectivist revolution, yet he was concerned that violence would delay its coming. It was not up to one particular class, neither the middle class nor the working class, but the intelligent class to prevent such an outbreak.

Gronlund wrote *Ça Ira* with the purpose of providing guidelines for how a true revolution should unfold. And he had America's future at the forefront of his mind. Those sufficiently aroused by inequity and injustice, Gronlund believed, were to follow the lead of influential thinkers (like Danton), who would cultivate the necessary intellectual preparations for the coming revolution.[22] Yet Gronlund found much of the historical literature on the topic deficient, especially among writers who viewed the Revolution's descent into violence, which contributed to the rise of Napoleon, as indicative of its failure. To talk about the failure of an historical event was to presuppose it as self-contained and disconnected from what went before and what would come after. Gemorah suggested that Gronlund viewed the French Revolution as "an important transitional, evolutionary development in the common history of mankind."[23] It prepared the way for the ascendence of the bourgeoisie and the development of capitalism.[24] This was why Gronlund titled his work *Ça Ira,* meaning "Oh, it goes," a phrase used by Benjamin Franklin, an American diplomat in Frances, when asked about the American Revolution. It was later incorporated by the French in one of the first revolutionary songs, "jubilantly changed by all patriots on the anniversary of the taking of the Bastille," Gronlund wrote: "*Ah, Ça ira! Ça ira! Ça ira!*" Gronlund tacitly accepted this "future social order," which he outlined in *Commonwealth.* "I assume the co-operative commonwealth to be, if not the final, at least the next stage in the evolution of human societies," and he argued that the French Revolution was an important step in that direction. The Revolution, then, became "a guide" to prepare American society for its coming revolution and "how to carry it through in an orderly manner."[25] He sought to inspire his younger readers "with a new sense of duty, with the conviction of a call to interfere actively in the molding of events."[26]

Those who, in Gronlund's estimation, properly understood the Revolution came from among the followers of Auguste Comte—in particular, François Aulard.[27] Gronlund largely followed Aulard in writing a "political history of the Revolution from the point of view of the origins and development of Democracy and Republicanism." He did, however, note an aspect of Aulard's work that fit with a later Marxist paradigm: the Revolution as a period in which "the whole political and industrial power" of France would be "lodged in the hands of great chiefs of industry, great capitalists, who, by organized public opinions" would compel citizens to submit to "their power and wealth."[28] In this way, Aulard, according to Gronlund, offered "an hypothesis of the future."[29] The events of 1789 would open the way for the rule of the bourgeoisie—made up of craftsmen, merchants, intellectuals, doctors, lawyers, and governing officials of the Third Estate—and the growth of capitalism, the next stage in human evolutionary development.[30] Capitalism would eventually be consumed under the weight of its own contradictions and replaced by socialism, where human consciousness and democracy would grow to full maturity and hence complete liberation. And in true Marxist fashion, the decline of the bourgeoisie would bring the rise of the proletariat, as Jean Jaures argued: "The French Revolution indirectly prepared for the coming of the proletariat. It brought about the two essential conditions for socialism: democracy and capitalism." But this required, Jaures continued, "the political arrival of the bourgeois class."[31] All socioeconomic conditions that created class warfare would be smoothed over through the expiration and final cessation of material dialectics and the concurrent maturation of Revolutionary ideology. The inherent antagonism between the capitalist class and the working class would disappear; competition would be exchanged for cooperation. The bourgeoisie and the proletariat, evolving into distinct classes, would remain for a time but eventually disappear, since the conditions enabling such an economic divide would likewise disappear.[32]

Unique to this socialist interpretation was that it was not reductively materialistic. The French Revolution, as a major historical event, was part of a larger divine plan. Gronlund placed greater emphasis on the role of this "force" in *Ça Ira* than he did in *Commonwealth*. Evolution progressed in accordance with the "Will of the Universe." To repeat, this "Will" appointed agents, moved by the ideas of the divine, to assist in directing society closer to collective liberation. Gronlund identified Georges Jacques Danton (1759–1794) as such a figure, elevating the French revolutionary to heroic status by disassociating him from the "terrible names" of Jean-Paul Marat and Maximilien Robespierre.[33] Danton was a true revolutionary guided by the "Power behind evolution." Events would never happen randomly, by some "*in*human Providence" but rather through the work of a "helpful Presence in Humanity working by law—the 'sacred torch.'" As the "very embodiment of the Revolution," Danton was the "true instrument in the hands of the Power behind Evolution, and just the *kind of leader [Americans] should encourage*."[34] He

accepted the will of the divine in determining the leadership of the bourgeoisie in directing the Revolution—the bourgeois class cooperating with
providence. Yet he knew to avoid restricting revolutionary thought to his own
class. To do so would be to invite conflict. He understood the need to open
the democratic possibilities of the Revolution.

The "Will of the Universe" relied on the work of public intellectuals like
Danton to guide the "instinctive effort of the common, associated, mind of the
race to come to self-consciousness."[35] The intellectual knew to expand collective freedom through stages of cooperation. The more advanced or complete
the cooperation, the more humanity would become aware of its shared consciousness. No single individual could understand himself or herself without
the other; communal awareness began by recognizing the self in the other.
This required working together—i.e., cooperating. Once individuals realized
their single identity in community, they formed a society, which would be
consolidated in the State, "the guardian of our destiny as a race." At some point
in this entire process, members of society would become "aware of something
animating humanity and directing the margins of the race"—"something
superior" (to themselves) and "superior to society itself." Transitioning from
the "absolutism of the past" (i.e., the King), "through [to] present individualism" in the capitalist state, to a future of appropriate authority in social
cooperation was the "true drama, plotted by that Power." And as someone
faithful to the revolution and its legacy, Danton was "obeying this [divine]
authority"—this "ceaseless efflux of a helpful Presence in Humanity."[36]

Civilization progressed not by leaps, that is by abrupt breaks (as revolution without evolution was implausible in Gronlund's mind), but through
gradual and uniform developments. Gronlund identified two organic periods
in which civilization accrued "a kind of hard, thick shell around itself." The
first concentric stage emanating outward came from the "dawn of history" to
the end of the Roman republic, the second from "the ascendency of Christianity to the Reformation." The student of history would be able to see in these
near-stationary periods the "fruits of struggles and martyrdoms," the flourishing of the "arts and literature" of the West, and the cultivation of "high
ideals, corporate responsibility, and public spirit"—periods in which sacrifice
was offered for the unity of the "common weal as a matter of course."[37] But
how would history advance toward each stage? History, which Gronlund

identified as providence, focused on the "constant growth in co-operation," where individuals became increasingly aware of their "proper acquaintance" with social consciousness through an engagement with the material world.

Three major socioeconomic periods preceded the coming commonwealth: slavery, serfdom, and "wagedom." Each represented a moment whereby humanity would move away from masters toward greater autonomy—the end of which would be complete consciousness and ownership of the social self and what it produced. Said differently, the changes to labor relations came as humans retook ownership of their labor (and hence their freedom). The first long period, from the Greco-Roman society to the high Middle Ages, was dominated by coercive cooperation—i.e., slavery. The second form of compulsory co-operation, more humane than its earlier form, according to Gronlund, was serfdom, introduced in the Middle Ages. Serfdom allowed peasants tied to the land of the nobility a modicum of freedom over their own families. Slaves had no ownership of self, no agency, no family, according to Gronlund; serfs had a little through the ownership of their cooperative families—the primordial collective. Yet they also had freedom in relation to common agricultural lands. The next stage came when serfs recognized that they, like slaves, were much too dependent on the whims of a landlord or manager. Greater independence was achieved for the serfs when traditional sources of medieval authority weakened—when the size of the nobility shrank due to wars of conquest or succession, the division of the Roman Catholic Church, innovative economic schemes regarding land, or epidemiological occurrences like the Black Plague. The period of the Renaissance inspired the invention of new technologies, new—including foreign—lands, and new economic proto-capitalistic relations that in turn cultivated a new kind of individualism. Eventually serfs found alternative economic activities in commercial labor, whether in agriculture or the textiles and craft skills of the growing urban sector, introducing a new system of wage labor. In places like England between the fifteenth and sixteenth century, large swaths of land would be fenced off and placed into private hands—no longer common—for the purpose of setting up commercial agriculture. Gronlund failed to note the ways in which modern race-based slavery began soon after Europeans began discovering new lands in the Atlantic for the purpose of commercial production. But one could fit the emergence of Atlantic slavery within his historical trajectory, since the growth of Atlantic slavery provided, as Marx argued, the primitive accumulation necessary for the birth of industrial capitalism.[38]

The primitive accumulation through commercial agriculture and the perfecting of the Atlantic system prepared the way for capitalism.[39] The privatization and land enclosure forced peasants to either become contract agricultural workers for their landlords or move to the urban centers for factory jobs. The discovery of coal, the making of textile machines, and the use of steam power led to the establishment and growth of factories and thus factory labor for the mass production of commodities. Laborers felt a greater sense of liberation, more so than serfs and slaves previously, because they were able to dispose of their wages as they saw fit. But such liberty was seriously limited by wages. Although milder forms of compulsory co-operation, those under "wagedom," the wage system, were not coerced by slaveowners or feudal lords; they were, however, "by their daily wants," becoming dependent on their capitalist owners. This new stage of "voluntary co-operation" benefited the "well-off middle classes," who sought to freeze the historical moment. The growth of capitalism and the middle class attached individualism to the ideology of competition. Consequently, Gronlund argued, "while hitherto there [had] been systematic unity, now everything"—from the economy to the life of the mind—"[was] planless, orderless; everywhere perfect anarchy reigns—in beliefs, in morals, in politics, in social relations, and, worst of all, in industrial relations.[40] Something had been forgotten: "The bond that hitherto united men—the collective conception of the world [had] been broken." Industrialization created a world of disconnected individuals, severing meaningful social bonds. Progress toward full human consciousness had been interrupted. The changes in material conditions, particular relations of labor and production, produced new masters. At the same time, laborers, especially in the Atlantic world, violently disciplined to lay the ground for capitalism, developed animosity against their masters.[41] This was a crucial phase in evolution—crucial in the sense that although industrialization increased production and capital it disrupted cooperation and inspired revolutionary dissent.

These were the historical circumstances that brought France's middle class to power in 1789. Indeed, the rise of the middle class was the natural course of history, as exemplified, Gronlund noted, in England much earlier. The

English nobility limited the absolutism of the king in the early thirteenth century in the Magna Carta, investing the "plutocracy with political power."[42] By the 16th century, England's wealthy elites "obtained dominion" in the urban centers. Two centuries later "small masters" in the urban center needed political protection against the much richer "clothiers" who oppressed "the weavers by paying less wages than formerly," renting the looms at "unreasonable rents," and "employing unskillful journeymen." During the reign of King Charles I, a series of technological innovations led to the consolidation of manufacturers "into the hands of large capitalists"—a kind of early trust.[43] Manufacturers would then carry their products "to places free from the control of the craft-guilds," which led to the eventual collapse of the guilds. The wealthy in England, despite the King's interference, were able to rise to a position of power over that of the King. The "Long Parliament" set a precedent for France. Simply stated by Gronlund, the King needed money and called on the "rich middle classes for it," which then cleared the "many inconvenient and oppressive feudal burdens" for the benefit of the propertied capitalists. When the English Civil War commenced, the middle classes declared themselves as representatives of the people. By the late seventeenth century, as demonstrated in the events surrounding the Glorious Revolution of 1688, power finally nestled into the laps of the middle class.

It is important to reiterate that the movement of history, for Gronlund, was not solely socioeconomic. In *The German Ideology*, Marx argued that life (material conditions connected to modes of production) produced consciousness (ideas), not the other way around. He said much the same in the preface to his *Contribution to the Critique of Political Economy:* "The changes in the economic foundation lead sooner or later to the transformation of the whole immense superstructure."[44] From this, it may be easy to conclude that Marxists have fallen into the habit of devaluing or wholly dismissing the role of ideas. This is not quite right. Marxists have done well in dismantling ideologies (defined by Marxists as essentially false beliefs), but this does not mean that they completely dismissed the power of ideas. Ideology and ideas should not be confused. Ignoring the material conditions that produce, for instance, a middle-class cultural identity, which rests on the false notion that one can create identity purely through creative hard work, is ideological. It requires dissenting ideas to counter such an ideology.[45] Gronlund followed Marx when he wrote in *Commonwealth* that changes in the social order come first through material forces; from there, the "new superstructure" is "gradually built up."[46] Here too, readers might conclude that the primary causal forces in history were material. But how were they to reconcile this with what he said in *Ça Ira*—namely, that historical movements "are always under the empire of ideas, consciously or unconsciously."[47] It is possible, argues contemporary historian Peter Wirzbicki, for thinkers to "be attentive to the internal logic of abstract ideas," while at the same time asking how such ideas might be "in dialogue with social and economic life."[48] In his intellectual history of revolutions, Enzo Traverso reasons that class struggles "cannot be explained exclusively through economic necessity or the mechanical submission to structural factors."[49] For Gronlund, ideas and material forces formed a kind of symbiosis, mutually moving and reshaping one another.[50] Modes of production certainly reshaped societies, but ideas, Gronlund wrote, cultivated "a ferment in the minds of the people."[51] The role of ideas can be reconciled with Gronlund's understanding of the relationship between natural evolution and revolution, connected furthermore to the divine partnership with the human agent. The individual actor, situated within and prepared by material forces in natural evolution, used the force of ideas to tip society over into the revolution. In short, material forces prepared the ground for revolutions; ideas ignited them.

The events of 1789 were part of a larger historical process that began with Martin Luther and the Protestant Reformation.[52] Thinkers like Luther developed doctrines that not only provided a new sense of individual self-worth, especially among the poorer working classes, but also a greater sense of agency in determining their own destiny. Luther, Gronlund wrote in *Commonwealth*, "introduced individualism."[53] His protest of the very powerful Roman Catholic Church was liberating in the sense that every Christian became his own priest. Individuals were invited to acknowledge their own private and unmediated covenantal relationship with God—a union that did not require an officious priestly class. As serfs slowly became economically liberated from the nobility, the religiously devout became spiritually liberated from the clerical hierarchy. Protestant doctrines like the "priesthood of all believers" allowed individuals to bypass—even ignore—anything in the way of the individual's access to God. Such ideas swept across Europe, essentially breaking the universal power of Rome. The seeds of democratic revolution were planted.

The ideas born of the Reformation, particularly that of nascent individualism, fostered new attitudes about the nature of work. All forms of labor had their equal worth under God. There was no type of labor that was removed from personal piety. Labor was "reformed." No work was distinguished as either sacred or secular. All could be done for the glory of God. Even the most mundane could be elevating. As Luther wrote, "household chores are more to be valued than all the works of monks and nuns."[54] "[W]ashing the dishes and preaching the Word of God," believed William Tyndale, were both "as touching to please God."[55] Consequently, from bricklayers to bakers, bishops to barons, workers could find meaning and thus take proud ownership of their work, since it could be a means to worship God. For the devout, if work was an act of worship, then there would be an increase in both. This does not mean, however, that Protestantism produced capitalism. What it did, as the Weberian thesis suggests, was provide a new attitude—a higher attitude— toward labor, which, in turn, contributed to greater production.

Protestantism likewise "caused the movement in political ideas."[56] God's redemptive covenant with his people could be used as a model for contracts between humans in society. The basis of civil government rested on the consent of those who came together to create a commonwealth. In the *Commonwealth,* Gronlund wrote that Rousseau's Social Contract, "though false," did a "great service to Humanity, by serving as a logical basis for the American and French Revolutions."[57] Gronlund was particularly interested in Rousseau's consideration of the general will, the social organism. But the organism and hence the social contract could be changed based, again, on the will of the people. John Locke had earlier "added the lesson of the right of resistance to bad rulers" in his social contract theory.[58] Resistance and the creation of a new contract were justified when rulers violated what the contract stipulated—most importantly, the protection of life and property. Yet on a more fundamental level, the sovereign erred when ignoring the will of the people, impeding, consequently, the movement of historical consciousness. Indeed, for Gronlund, critical events in history were constituted in the moments of overcoming those who wished to obstruct the advancement of democracy by restricting autonomy to their own interests. The Revolution of 1688 was simply the men of property securing their sovereignty over that of the monarch. Laws were then made to protect ultimately the interests of the propertied classes. France followed a similar course in 1789.

Ideas from the French Enlightenment generated and justified the revolution. For Jonathan Israel "nothing about the French Revolution makes the slightest sense, or can even begin to be provisionally explained," without reference to the Enlightenment.[59] Gronlund would have definitely agreed. Among the contributions of France's philosophers, Gronlund noted that the revolutionaries brought together Montesquieu's theory of the "separation of powers" with Rousseau's "dogma of the sovereignty of the people" in his *Social Contract*, "the mightiest revolutionary instrument for doing what was to be done."[60] Such thinkers expressed a deep love for their fellows, "a steadfast faith in human nature, and firm aspiration [for] justice and progress." Yet the emphasis on property gave rise to a new mode of authority in the middle class. French thinkers who "demanded unlimited freedom in all relations of industrial life," anticipating thereby "all the essential propositions laid down by Adam Smith in his Wealth of Nations, which appeared several years later." The words of Diderot appealed to the middle classes, Gronlund thought: "It is property which makes the citizen. Every man who has possessions in the State is interested in the State; it is by means of his possessions that he acquires a right of having himself represented."[61] The Enlightenment, in Gronlund's mind, sealed the rights of man to the middle class.

France's economic troubles, a good portion of which came from the debts incurred after helping the Americans in their war against Britain, motivated members of the rising middle class, which had not been "sufficiently developed," according to Gronlund, to become "rulers of the new era." They sought to restructure France's government to benefit their own economic interests. Leading the Third Estate, they quickly created the National Assembly, demanded a constitution and the abolishment of serfdom, and the opening of public offices to all (male) citizens. They further worked to reform the judicial system, establish and protect a free press, allow for the free exercise of religion, and, arguably the most important, liberate industry and commerce. The Assembly determined that taxes would not be levied without the consent of the representatives that made up the assembly, abolishing "all feudal burdens that rested on the peasants and on agriculture, as the tithes, the duty of the latter to grind their corn at their landlords' mill, the duty to work on highways, the right to the chase, etc." Yet, as Gronlund pointed out, members violated their own commitment to the sanctity of property by confiscating the "landed property of the Church." These measures certainly benefited some among the peasantry, but only to those "who possessed some land." The early decisions of the Assembly "realized all the economic demands made by the writers of the *Encyclopedie*," particularly, competition and private enterprise, leading to a "steadily growing development" in industry. In the end, these liberalizing measures benefited those who owned raw materials and the means of production. The majority of citizens, however, including the working poor, did not benefit from such changes. The conditions of the laboring masses were secondary for the bourgeoisie. It was only the middle classes "who could sing '*Ça Ira!*' with more unction than ever." Thus, the middle class of France, "being in a clear majority of the National Assembly" became the "supreme power," creating a society where individualism and private property triumphed.[62]

The rise of the bourgeoisie in France was a natural unfolding of evolution (more on this below), and with it "not a blow had been struck, not a particle of violence committed."[63] Gronlund never accepted violence as a necessity in revolution. He nonetheless recognized its reality in the case of France and provided an explanation as to why. The storming of the Bastille, the October Days, the military campaigns against foreign invaders, and ultimately in the Terror were the result of "the frantic efforts of the old powers to overthrow the new *regime*, and bring back the old *regime*." This included, of course, members of the middle class who used revolutionary slogans to undermine the continuation of the revolution. True revolutionaries were not responsible for the violence. Counterrevolutionaries, those of the Old Regime as well as the property elites, opposed the "will of the Intelligence that directs human events," Gronlund wrote. The success of the English Revolution in the 1640s and later in 1688 centered precisely on the aristocracy allying itself with the new sovereigns, "rich manufacturers and merchants," "in a joint empire"—in short, a new and younger class cooperating with an older one. In France, however, the nobility refused to "divide their power" by recognizing and submitting to the authority of the middle class.[64]

To counter Old Regime counterrevolutionaries, the men of property worked to harness the "strength and the brute force" of urban workers and countryside peasants, as these groups appropriated the ideals of the revolution.[65] Not always able to temper the passions of the laboring masses, to mitigate the enthusiasm among workers for full liberty and equality, they miscalculated the power of the people. After the fall of the Bastille, the propertied elite pressured the mayor of Paris to forbid the laboring poor "to wear the patriotic cockade under pain of arrest."[66] This was the initial wedge driven between the middle class and the working class. The fear among property holders toward workers was essentially an unwillingness to abide by the direction of that Power guiding evolution, which was to expand cooperative democracy. Thus, while members of the middle class were responsible for moving humanity toward its destiny of collective consciousness, it was also responsible for slowing that progress. Even after the events of the October Days in 1789, when the people of Paris, defying the counterrevolutionaries, returned the royal family to the Tuileries Palace, the leaders within the assembly "did not and would not labor for the multitude, but for men of property."[67] Having subdued the nobility and the monarchy, the assembly continued its work of securing the sovereignty of property holders—dividing France into communes and departments, making "all magistrates elective," instituting "justices of the peace and juries," reforming the criminal and civil law codes, doing away with torture, suppressing "all religious orders," establishing a unitary monetary system of weights and measures, and nationalizing the army. But "most importantly," Gronlund wrote, the Assembly implemented that which was "absolutely essential to a *capitalist* era"—namely, "*lending money out on interest.*" This final action was the "first legal sanction" for the cultivation of capital and the capitalist state. "Liberty," "fraternity," and "equality" essentially became empty terms, replaced by "Free Competition, Equality before the Law, and the Unity of the State."[68]

Although eager to expose the duplicity of French bourgeois leadership, Gronlund affirmed that their class rightfully came to power, for the divine "Intelligence" of the universe "*willed* it so." Civilization had to be raised up from the medieval period to the higher form of "co-operation, *free co-operation*, where no one was to be dependent for living on any other individual."[69] The feudal system was dismantled by property owners, who utilized land for commercial and industrial production. The "division of labor, machinery, the inventions, which the middle classes" utilized, accelerated production. They created a host of consumer items that satisfied many of the "*social wants*" of society, justifying such production by using the language of "free competition" and "private enterprise." Life certainly improved for all, but these benefits were accompanied by curses, such as reducing workers to consumable (and disposable) "wares." Propertied leaders were not interested in the welfare of the masses, but on their own private interests—on profit. Here again Gronlund used the example of England. The English bourgeoisie, created by early industrialization, cheated the laborer, cutting not only his wages but also his dreams and aspirations: hitching "women and babes to the machinery of production," breaking up families, exposing workers to "perilous and deadly conditions," deforming the "human frame" by damaging the health of workers in the "dust of steel, of lint, of rags, of coal, from vapors of lead, gas, chlorine, acids," and mutilating bodies with "bands, wheels, and unprotected machinery." "The French followed this example," Gronlund argued, and "did even worse": "while the British plutocrats despised their working classes, the French *bourgeoisie* manifested absolute *hatred* for theirs. The English at least passed a poor-law, the French *descended to the lowest crimes.*" One particular action during the Revolution that demonstrated such cruelty centered on the confiscation of property. The land that had been expropriated from the clergy and nobility was not given "to those who had only labor to give" but "to those able to pay cash, and pay quickly." Much of the land was sold "to satisfy bankers and capitalists," but not a cent was "appropriated to the poor." Those who generated private wealth in such land grabs "gave the course of the Revolution as an excuse." After storming the Tuileries Palace (August 10, 1792), leading to the end of the monarchy, two other important "batches of lands," at one point promised to the poor for "redeemable ground-rents," were taken up into private hands: "the communal lands and the estates of the emigrants." Speculation included that which came from the land. "Stock-jobbers," Gronlund pointed out, cornered the market in "corn and other articles of food," creating famines that made it very difficult for the poor to survive. These were the "deeds of the French *bourgeoisie*" when they first stepped "upon the scene as masters."[70]

Georges Jacques Danton was born into the "mental atmosphere" of the French Enlightenment on October 26, 1759. He was, to borrow Spencer's term, a "resultant," an individual created by "a long series of complex influences."[71] Gronlund described him as a loyal son to his mother and stepfather. Having been educated in Champagne and Troyes, Danton, a dedicated student, went on to receive a degree in law in 1784, beginning his practice in Paris in 1787. Often "hot-tempered" yet "easy to conciliate," Danton had always radiated with "intelligence and good humor."[72] This "Hercules" of a man, whose bout of smallpox as a youth left him scared, came of age in the midst of France's pre-revolutionary fiscal troubles. He was 30 when the Revolution began.[73] In 1790, he became a member of the Paris Commune and helped found what later would become the Cordeliers Club and frequented the Jacobin Club. Jean Jaures extolled Danton's political temperament, including his efforts to moderate events to "avoid a terrible crisis."[74] Much of *Ça Ira* recounts the ways Danton tried to keep the Revolution from being torn apart by factions, both internal and external. He held an "overshadowing influence all over France," maintaining, in particular, a "wonderful influence" over the masses, "which he kept to his dying day."[75] One of his means of winsomely guiding society toward the commonwealth was by smoothing out partisanship through persuasion.[76] His effort to accommodate the concerns of others in a spirit of cooperation was indicative of his alignment with the "Will of the Universe," Gronlund believed.

Danton's star rose around the time France was considering what to do about the status of the king. The ruling class believed that protecting their material interests required framing a new government that included a place for the king—a constitutional monarchy that would secure "the middle classes unquestioned dominion" against the masses, "whom they commenced to fear."[77] But the retention of the monarchy was their "great blunder." Danton believed that there was no need for a king in a republican system of government. The United States proved that. He thus waited for an opportunity to rid "France of royalty forever." He strongly doubted whether France's monarchy would consent "to be degraded to a figure-head."[78] After Louis's failed escape on June 21, 1791, Danton intensified his commitment that the king was now "nothing to us, unless he shall become our enemy."[79] Unfortunately for Danton, the Assembly "overlooked Louis' flight" and attempted to turn France into a constitutional monarchy.

This divided Paris into two competing political camps: "republicans—the masses of the people—and royalists, with whom now the official middle-class leaders ranged themselves."[80] The efforts to reestablish the monarchy led to a "bloody skirmish" on July 17, 1791, at the Champ de Mars. The republicans opposed the decision of the Assembly regarding Louis XVI. Citizens came to sign a petition demanding the king's removal and ended up engaging in armed conflict with the National Guard. This was certainly troubling given the fact that the Assembly was close to adopting the Constitution of 1791, which would have set up a constitutional monarchy. Marquis de Lafayette, "the middle-class general," and Jean Sylvain Bailly, "the middle-class mayor," fired on the crowd. Up to 50 people were killed and many others wounded in the massacre. Republican leaders and a few radicals were arrested, though some escaped. The freedom to speak, especially in print, was sharply curbed. Identified as an instigator, Danton fled to London.[81] Notwithstanding the conflict, the Assembly completed its task, compelling the King to swear allegiance to the constitution, dissolving the National Constituent Assembly, and establishing the authority of the Legislative Assembly. Assembly members "left their class in supreme power."[82]

In the final months of 1791 to the beginning of 1793, continued efforts were made by counterrevolutionaries, both in and outside of France, to thwart the progress of the Revolution. The Assembly spent a good portion of its time defending the new regime against enemies outside of France.[83] The Emperor of Austria and the King of Prussia combined forces and moved well-within France's frontiers. The Duke of Brunswick issued a manifesto on July 25, 1792, that threatened retaliatory action against the citizens of Paris if any harm came to the King and his family.[84] These developments, Gronlund believed, justified the insurrection and the assault on the Tuileries palace on August 10, when Danton, "the soul of the movement," and his allies led Parisians to attack it: "'Ça ira!' shook the very vaults of the building." Parisians and the National Guard battled the Swiss Guard who were defending the royal family. This was, Gronlund wrote, the "answer to Brunswick's 'manifesto.'"[85] After the insurrection, the legislature appointed Danton minister of justice.[86] He seemed to be the right person for the position, since he exhibited, according to Condorcet, the confidence of one "who had just overturned the throne; a man who, by his ascendency, could keep in order the many unruly instruments of a Revolution."[87]

Taking up responsibilities related to foreign affairs, the war office, and the ministry of the interior, Danton, Gronlund believed, successfully crushed the counterrevolution in Paris. He expelled the invading enemy and planted "the republic on a secure foundation." Motivated by liberty and a love for France, Danton compelled the assembly to grant municipal authorities to seize any and all conspirators and to search homes for needed arms and munitions. A sentence of death, proclaimed by the Legislature, was pronounced on those who refused to either march or give their arms for defense. On September 2, 1792, a massive convergence of citizens descended upon the Champ de Mars

where citizens raided the prisons and murdered hundreds of suspected counterrevolutionaries. "Danton had no part" in the mob violence, for he was, as
Gronlund said, "the reverse of cruel and bloodthirsty." One significant consequence of this September Massacre was that it turned many citizens toward
Maximilian Robespierre.[88] Those who blamed Danton for both the August 10
insurrection and the September massacres, including Marie-Jeanne Madame
Roland, "have been cruelly unjust," wrote Gronlund.[89] The citizens of Paris
had been thrown into "perfect hysterics" by Brunswick and the invasion of
foreign allies into France.[90] Though attempting to cool the hysteria, Danton
had no power to pacify the mob or secure the prisons. The job of fortifying
the prisons was largely that of the minister of the interior, Roland. The legislative body too was powerless. Gronlund seemed doubtful that Danton had
a strong enough voice to calm the people by bringing them to reason, but
doing so would have turned Danton into a martyr. He would have been torn
apart by the mob.

On September 21, 1792, the National Convention met, separated between
the Girondins on the *Right* and the Jacobin-Montagnards (The Mountain)
on the *Left*. There were also those of the *Center,* sometimes referred to as the
*Plain.* Danton worked tirelessly to bridge both the left and the right.[91] In what
Gronlund referred to as the *"war of propaganda,"* the Convention committed
itself to spreading the principles of the Revolution to anyone—any nation,
any society—who opposed the old world of privilege, aristocracy, and monarchy. Since the "rights" articulated by Enlightenment thinkers and embodied
in the *Rights of Man and Citizen* were "absolute and universal, belonging to
all mankind," the arbitrary elevation of certain individuals over others was
considered unnatural and therefore illegitimate.[92] It was the responsibility
of free people everywhere to overthrow tyranny in their own country and
assist in doing the same in other countries. Danton feared the consequences
of such propaganda, one being that it would inspire further counterrevolutionary violence. Yet he found it difficult to swim against the current, so
he held his tongue.[93] The policy was nonetheless popular, especially during
France's success over Belgium. Indeed, the citizens of Belgium had become
increasingly persuaded by the ideals of the French Revolution, which encouraged the Convention to liberate Belgium from Austria. Eventually, the French
secured their own country and, at the same time, occupied Savoy "without
a blow."[94] Moved by such success, the Convention on November 19, 1792,

declared that it would offer support to any nation willing to *"recover their liberty,"* charging the executive to provide assistance in this endeavor.[95] Some of France's national legislators believed that such a policy would cost France a great deal. So, on December 15, 1792, the Convention decided to abolish "all feudal rights, duties, taxes, privileges, and corporations" of lands conquered. Likewise, as a "pledge for the costs of the war," all property "belonging to the treasury" was to be taken and held by the French government. As Gronlund noted, the object of this law, similar to the confiscation of the estates in France, was "to broaden the basis of the *assignats,* and thus extend their credit [and] to induce the protected nations to take and use this paper money as their currency."[96] By 1793, Danton succeeded in reversing the so-called "war for propaganda." He suggested that France turn to its own affairs and serve as an example to other nations of the benefits of liberty, fraternity, and equality. The Jacobin Constitution, proposed in early August 1793, affirmed that France would "never interfere with the government of other nations, nor suffer other nations to interfere with its own government."[97]

The execution of the king in 1793 dealt a heavy blow to the counterrevolutionary factions within France, but became, according to Gronlund, "a gage of battle to Europe."[98] On February 1, 1793, the Convention declared war on Britain. Britain had been an enemy of France since before the Revolution, but the annexation of Belgium, "on motion of Danton," threatened England's influence on the continent.[99] During his time in Belgium and monitoring the growing threat of England, Danton learned of the death of his wife, Antoinette Charpentier, and their young son. Despite his personal loss, he fulfilled his responsibilities as a patriot. He pushed the Convention to give aid to the forces in Belgium and called upon the citizens throughout France "to take up arms" and defend Belgium, invade Holland, and push back the English. While we wanted the Convention to act promptly, he did not want to see a revival of "the terrible days of last September [1792]."[100] He was eager, Gronlund said, "to deprive the populace of all excuse for perpetrating any more lawless murders, before they hurl themselves against the enemies." To wit, Danton persuaded the Convention to establish a "Revolution Tribunal" for the purpose of dissuading hysterical lawlessness, "so that the sword of the *law* shall be suspended over the heads of all who are guilty." It was important to Danton that French citizens hold back their emotions to prevent their "hatred from acting blindly."[101]

At the same time, Danton called out those who used (or manipulated) the Revolution for their own fiscal gain. He reprimanded greedy contractors for buying up vital resources like corn for the purpose of speculation, doing so at France's expense. In fact, the ministry of war, according to Gronlund, was staffed by profiteers, who engaged in numerous bribery schemes. The Girondins, for instance, not only turned a blind eye to the profiteers but also arrived at the Convention with their own "pockets full of petitions for placesfor their children, fathers, relatives, and friends, or friends of their mistresses." Danton hoped to correct this by strengthening the power of the executive.[102] He wanted to create a committee that would oversee the activities of key functionaries in the government, ensuring greater transparency and oversight. The goal was to create a nine-member committee with the "power to dismiss any executive or administrative agent." Danton argued that the Convention needed such a body to preserve the democratic progress of the Revolution. Democracy, in his mind, did not exclude an occasional "virtual dictatorship, provided the dictator was made responsible at stated times." The proposal was passed and called "The Committee of Public Welfare." Becoming its first president in the summer of 1793, Danton wished to execute his responsibilities with discretion. Unfortunately, the committee fell into such a momentum of overextending its authority that not even Danton could stop it.[103]

Earlier in 1793, the defection of General Charles-François du Périer Dumouriez dealt a "terrible blow to France and to Danton" by intensifying suspicions against nearly every "prominent man" in the Convention.[104] Danton was concerned about how this would increase the amount of discipline and violence, especially in the use of terror, that would tarnish the Revolution's legacy. Attempting to channel the enormous energy in this regard, Danton became the veritable head of the government by joining the Committee of Public Safety. The Committee would come to direct all the affairs of government, striking down "the rebels within and the enemies without." Danton worked to suspend the municipal laws and political machinery of the communes, republicanizing whole cities and villages. He likewise called for the arrest of "suspected persons," including royalists and members of the clergy.[105] Danton also helped to create the *levy en masse*. The day after the "Feast of Federation," celebrating the downfall of the monarchy, the Convention called for delegates throughout France to levy recruits for defense and take an inventory of corn. Danton successfully "conjured out of the ground fourteen grand armies and six hundred thousand soldiers"[106] A massive mobilization to route the enemy was embraced enthusiastically by the French citizenry.[107] This strengthened the republican army, making victory over the European coalition a real possibility. All these were necessary, Gronlund concluded, to save France. Danton's "great mistake," however, was his decision not to seek reelection to the Committee of Public Safety—a decision, according to Gronlund, that cleared the way for the Terror. The Convention attempted by way of a motion to persuade Danton to return to his place on the Committee, but he declined. He was not ignoring the work of the Revolutionary Government; he simply wanted to advance the revolution through other means—means outside the committee. Consequently, Gronlund argued, Danton lost "all influence with the multitude."[108] No other politician could take his place. No one could match his skills as a politician, and the government, according to Gronlund, drifted away from the path of such a sagacious leader.

In the early summer of 1793, thirty-two Girondin members were forcibly ejected from the Assembly. Members of this faction "were nothing but talkers," Gronlund wrote, who impeded the work of capable legislators. The "most damnable" charge leveled against the Girondins was that they cared little for the Revolution or the people of France. They were middle-class men who opposed the expansion of democracy; they had a particular aversion to the masses. As for policies, they had a "horror for centralization," preferring instead "unrestricted private enterprise." The immediate cause for the removal of the Girondins included their virulent attacks against certain members of the assembly, especially Danton, who "stood head and shoulders above them all in ability."[109] Danton, however, harbored no ill-will toward them, extolling the talented among them, though he did not consider them capable administrators. But why the hostility toward Danton, who worked to cool tensions between factions? Along with the blame cast upon him for the September Massacres, the Girondins charged Danton with misappropriating the funds used for Belgium and for conspiring with Charles-François du Périer Dumouriez; neither of which, in Gronlund's judgment, was true. Eventually, Danton and others had enough of the Girondin fanaticism. Consequently, on May 31, 1793, Danton presented a petition to the Convention calling for the "exclusion of thirty-two members."[110] On June 2, around 100,000 armed Parisians demanded the ejection of the Girondin members.

As these ex-members freely roamed Paris, a few began to foment rebellion against Convention. They were arrested and eventually executed, though no one fought as hard as Danton to save them from execution. The Montagnards now held power unopposed from June 2, 1793 to July 28, 1794.

Another reason for the resentment against Danton came in part because of his opposition to the Girondin plan of establishing independent communes throughout France. Danton believed that this federalism would necessarily weaken the bonds of unity—one of the "grand objects" of the Revolution of 1789. Such a plan was class-driven: "From demanding such liberty for their persons and their class, it was only a step to demanding liberty for their localities, where they, of course, could rule by virtue of the influence they possessed through their wealth." Despite the use of revolutionary language, the Girondins were motivated by a deep contempt for the popular masses. They wished only to protect their wealth and fetter the democratic impulses of France's citizenry. For Danton, all citizens were members of a united France, "an undivided whole with an undivided representation." His commitment to the unity of France reflected an understanding of the "doctrine of evolution," which rested on the premise that "progress lies in the development of larger and larger unities." It was through the unity of the nation that citizens would "enter into relation with humanity." The state manifested the highest development of humanity, the "law of our being"— a "sacred" law "worked out through us." It was the march of the Will of the Universe. Despite the fact that he was a middle-class man, Danton, Gronlund believed, was the "greatest statesmen of the Revolution." He was a proponent of industry, science, and philosophy and an advocate for the separation of church and state. Most importantly, for Gronlund, Danton had a "heart for the masses" and was a supporter of popular sovereignty over absolutism and of a social order that would quell passionate reactionaries.[111]

From June 2, 1793, when the Girondins were ejected from the Assembly, to the end of that year, the Jacobin Convention, "a most noble assembly," were in compliance with the "Will of the Universe." They labored to create a society that would benefit all citizens, including members of the laboring class, a class "to which not one of them belonged." This was the moment when Danton's influence reached its highest point. The first and most important order of business after the removal of the Girondin was to create a new constitution—the "Constitution of Ninety-Three."[112] Before the ascent of the

Jacobin Convention, the Girondins adopted one that had been authored by Condorcet.[113] Gronlund examined the difference between Condorcet's draft, which reflected the class interests of the Girondins, with that offered by the Jacobins of June 2. As to style, Condorcet's was "dry and diffuse," Gronlund noted; the Jacobin's was constructed of letters "hewn into granite and painted in warm colors." But the most important difference was the "spirit that pervaded the two documents." Condorcet's proposal was essentially, according to Gronlund, a *"charter of individualism"* with "no conception of *humanity."* This elevated middle-class plutocratic authority and ignored the sovereignty of the working classes. Gronlund looked at Concordet's push for universal suffrage with suspicion, since he argued that the Girondins, with their "narrowest of class interests," would use their wealth power to keep the poorer classes from voting.[114] Gronlund was not one to view the right to vote as the best means to secure the national democracy. At any rate, Condorcet's constitution did not appreciate the unity of humanity; it was silent on the "interdependence of men," the source of not only self-knowledge but also oneness with the Power behind Evolution.

The constitution drafted by the more radical Jacobins recognized society as an "organic whole." In supporting all citizens, especially the working classes, the Jacobins had a far better understanding, then, of the essence of society. Yet while not opposed to universal suffrage, the Jacobins had a keen understanding that the administration of the government would best be taken on by the most *"competent, skillful, and wise"* among them.[115] Such a governing arrangement, when done correctly, would maximize the reality of a democratic State. Yet a government even of the most competent did not guarantee that all the rights of citizens would be protected. Administrations could easily descend into dictatorships. The solution, derived from Jacobin radicalism, would be that while some citizens were "unfit" to choose competent representatives, all citizens would have the opportunity to vote on laws after they were made by administrators. This revolutionary proposal—the referendum—would allow citizens in France to approve or reject items of legislation proposed by legislators.

As to the public welfare, some among the Jacobins found that a "let alone" system vis-à-vis the economy would be far from beneficial to France.[116] The reason stemmed from the relationship between property and labor. The radicals believed that property meant the "fruits of a citizen's labors *which the law guarantees to him.*" They opposed modes of industrial organization that would be harmful to citizens—especially relations of competition. Members proposed measures that would counter the principles of competition, guarding against glut and scarcity and monitoring the distribution of wages by imposing a "maximum," "the *highest price* for wares." According to the first law of maximum, passed in early May 1793, corn and flour merchants were required to make a declaration as to the "quantity and nature" of their goods. These items had to be sold in the public markets. Although the price was set, it would gradually be reduced by the following proportions: "On the 1st of June by one-tenth, on the 1st of July by two-tenths, on the 1st of August by three-tenths, and on the 1st of September by four-tenths." Furthermore, fines would be imposed on anyone selling above the maximum; those who, through innovative financial schemes, destroyed or removed corn and floor for the purpose of driving up prices and selling privately in order to generate a profit would be punished by death. The maximum, according to Gronlund, "was in flagrant opposition to individualism and the doctrine of *laissez-faire*," contrary to middle class ideals. In order to defray "the difference" between the price of corn and wages, Danton convinced the Convention to levy a "contribution," presumably a tax, on the wealthy. This was made into law April 2, 1793. A maximum was also set for wages and prices on wheat, meat, pork, butter, cattle, salt-fish, wine, whiskey, vinegar, cider, beer, firewood, charcoal, coal, candles, salt, soap, honey, white paper, leather, iron, lead, steel, cloths, leather shoes, and tobacco. These anti-laissez-faire policies were enacted as "a kind of democratic protest against" how powerful plutocrats might try to control the economy.[117]

These laws, of course, did not go unchallenged. When supplies started to dry up after the declaration of the maximums, dealers and manufacturers threatened to close their shops and factories. Many did, in fact. Likewise, those with money quickly glutted the suppliers. The situation became so bad that law enforcement had to forbid "traders to deliver more of one merchandise to one than to another." The Convention determined that the price of items under the maximum would be "what is was in 1790, *at the place of its production, plus one-third* of said price, *plus five percent* for the wholesaler, *plus five percent* for the retailer, and, furthermore, a fixed price per mile of transport added." The Convention created, therefore, a table of maximum whereby the "cost of raw materials and the labor added to the products" would be better calculated, which would serve as a way to measure the health of the economy. The United States was the first country to create a Bureau of Statistics of Labor. As a result, the assignats rose and enough revenue was generated for France's fourteen armies. Such a rational calculation of the national economy (contra laissez-faire) added to France's stability. Moreover, as Gronlund was quick to note, the success of the maximum depended on the "intimate harmony between all interests"—i.e., social cooperation. Competition no doubt produced a greater amount of wealth. Yet the retention and augmentation of that wealth came not through equitable individualistic competition. It was through the cooperation of a few in competition with the many. Gronlund wanted his readers to see how an expansion of cooperation, encompassing all sectors of society, would be of greater benefit to the public. The strength of an economy would only come when all parties worked together. The fiscal management would circumvent the negative tendencies of competition, bringing order instead of anarchy. These policies gave knowledge to producers, how best to utilize their resources and organize industry. It would help in the transition to the commonwealth by mollifying the harm done by wage competition. Gronlund surmised that if the policies had been allowed to continue, Europe would have moved closer to the "New Social Order" in the commonwealth.[118]

Despite the opposition, the Jacobin Convention continued to formulate legislation for the benefit of the working masses. The members established new weights and measures, adopting the metric system, and a new calendar, though this last item unintentionally "wronged the working-people," Gronlund wrote, since they were largely unable to adjust to the abolition of Sunday. More importantly, they eliminated imprisonment for debt, provided for public assistance for children, the elderly, widows, and paupers as well as easier access to health care. Danton included provisions for injured soldiers, such as land in the Paris suburbs as a reward for those who fought for France. The Convention worked to end the warfare of the profiteers against the republic by suppressing every association "whose capital stock is based on shares to bearers, on negotiable instruments or titles, transferable at will" and, to strike a blow against speculation, by closing the Exchange. Because it owned up to half of the "soil of France," the state reappropriated the sales of the national estates by redistributing communal lands: "All inhabitants of the communes, farmers, agricultural laborers, servants, etc., are to have an equal share; the lands to be divided as much as possible into equal parts."[119] The Jacobins merged all debt in the Great Ledger for the purpose of shoring up the nation's credit. One of the most solemn moments came when the Convention abolished slavery, "the first great power in modern times to pass such a law," according to Timothy Tackett.[120] For Danton, abolishing slavery in the New World would "bear abundant fruit" throughout the globe. This made the French Republic "a part of the firmament of heaven."[121] Such efforts, revolutionary and future-looking, reflected a concern for national "fraternity," a commonwealth in the Jacobin mind.

The great love for fellow citizens shown by the members of the Jacobin Convention manifested itself in a public educational system created to foster French liberty. Children, Danton proposed, would be "fed, instructed, and lodged gratuitously" in "common education."[122] Sons and daughters belonged not to parents or an individual family, but to the organism of the republic. Private education kept children from learning how to become virtuous citizens and was, therefore, a threat to the republic. The public bore the responsibility of educating the nation's future members. Danton's public school system would be sectioned up in three parts: technical knowledge "indispensable to artisans and working-men"; technical knowledge related to professions; and, finally, advanced studies for "more gifted minds." Part of this general education, like weights and measures, included a shared language. The Jacobin Convention recognized its role as architect of a new nation. A strong nation demanded a shared sense of self. The way to accomplish this was through a shared language, which, Gronlund writes, "was the work of the Jacobins": "When they came to power, *nearly half of the twenty-five million Frenchmen did not speak or understand the French language,* but spoke innumerable dialects." Language become one important means for France to become "a homogenous nation." It was then decided that language teachers would be appointed in each district throughout France. Finally, the Convention created the following institutions for the educational benefit of the commonwealth: "The Normal School"; "The Conservatory of Arts"; "The Museum of Natural History"; and "The *Polytechnic School,*" of all the institutions "the most eminent." France's public educational system, Danton proposed, would be paid for by "the superfluities of men with scandalous fortunes."[123]

The Jacobin Convention intended for such measures to be permanent: the *maximum,* industrial statistics, a generous poor law, the closing of the exchange, land grants to the poor and soldiers, a system for primary and secondary education, the Polytechnic School, the universalization of the French language, the abolition of slavery, a decimal system of weights and measures, the Great Ledger. These all were to be part of France's historical transition—a transition made possible by the bourgeoisie. The men of property understood that increasing production and making "mental preparation" to reeducate the people were necessary to place France on the proper evolutionary path. France needed the men of property as leaders to push for "free competition and private enterprise" in order to increase production. But this needed to be limited; otherwise, it would have impeded the further developments of the Revolution. By preventing the "shameful excesses" of the plutocrats, the Jacobins, Gronlund believed, represented the "good genius of the French bourgeoisie."[124] The Jacobins would have "prevented gluts" by monitoring production. Overseeing the equitable distribution of wages, they would have satisfied the wants of the poorer classes, preventing, thereby, the poorer classes from unleashing their resentment toward the bourgeoisie through violence. In short, the Jacobins, Gronlund argues, would have provided a "smooth transition over into the permanent social order which approaches."[125]

Regrettably, Jacobin leadership soon came to an end when Jacques René Hébert and then Robespierre ignored "God's mysterious text," interrupting the progress of history.[126] This brought the Revolution into the phase of the Reign of Terror. It is important at this point to pause and take into account that which was central to Gronlund's philosophy of history—namely, that violence of whatever kind, including class violence, resulted from a failure to cooperate with the divine in evolution. And this could happen in at least three ways: (1) by an older establishment trying to return to earlier times, (2) by those who identified as supporters of the revolution using its language for their own profit, and (3) by true revolutionaries rushing the hand of providence. The Terror was the result of the third way. Members of the Convention were "misled" by Jacques Hebert and Maximilian Robespierre, both of whom cruelly and brutally destroyed the foundation laid by the Jacobin Convention. These individuals insisted on bringing the Revolution to its conclusion, not patiently waiting for the direction of history. Specifically, the Convention failed to assuage fears of counterrevolutionary forces that continued to threaten the Revolution. Danton believed that the "feverish excitement" regarding counterrevolutionaries both foreign and domestic would eventually cool and that the "severity of the government would then be more and more relaxed."[127] It was believed by Danton that the Revolutionary Tribunal would be abolished and that a liberal government would then commence its regular activities under the new constitution. Yet because he refused to continue his service on the Revolutionary Tribunal, Danton was unable to temper factions.

Gronlund pointed the finger at Hébert, not Robespierre, as "the true father of the terror." Driven by "malice and revengeful feelings" toward those of wealth and status, Hébert intensified class warfare and endangered the cooperation necessary for a healthy commonwealth.[128] He spoke of the people in the "coarsest and most vulgar language." Hébert, according to Gronlund, convinced the Convention on September 17, 1793, to approve of the "Law of Suspect." Accordingly, anyone who, in any way, demonstrated themselves as "partisans of tyranny," "enemies of liberty," and "who had not uninterruptedly manifested attachment to the Revolution," were identified as suspect. Lists were drawn up and arrests were made immediately. And what was Danton's response? Danton believed it was imprudent to oppose the law as it came, like a rush, "in the heat of passion." Instead, he waited for the right moment, and that sadly never came. Danton felt "grievously wounded" by the excesses of executions commenced under the instigation of Hébert.[129]

Gronlund believed that Hébert's "wrong-heartedness" came from his ardent atheism. Abandoning a belief in divine providence was to abandon all sense of morality necessary for social order. An opponent of atheism, Danton had once proposed festivals for the worship of the "Supreme Being," the "Lord of nature." This did not make him orthodox, however. He rejected traditional Christian dogma, which, to him, presented God as a *"lawless* despot, omnipotent, and consequently siding with the rich and powerful of this world."[130] He particularly repudiated the notion of immortality so popular among French citizens. The dead will not remember their past lives; such a belief rests on the continuation of the individual, though in spirit, "vouched for by consciousness." Death, for Gronlund, was a "sponge that wipes our *memory.*" Gronlund developed his understanding of the afterlife in *Our Destiny* (Chapter 4). However progressive his ideas regarding religion, Danton was "a faithful instrument to the Power behind Evolution," willing to lay down his own life to comply with the will of the people—that is, "to do the will of God." Accepting the Will of the Universe meant sharing in the "common well-being" of all citizens. The religion of the past separated citizens into individuals: "this is precisely what condemns it as essentially *vicious,* anti-social." The "religion of the future" would communicate to citizens that they were interdependent social beings: "It will inculcate that the same destiny, whatever it be, is awaiting us all." A step in that direction, for Danton, required a complete break with the church and its Pope, a *"separation of Church and State,* as practiced in the United States. Yet the situation became worse when the Convention closed churches, forcing the clergy to surrender their credentials and resign their positions. "A wave of insane fanaticism" passed over France; outrage against the clergy, in Danton's mind, could rarely be assuaged.[131]

Around the time Hébert unleashed his indignation against the enemies of France, Danton received a leave of absence from the Convention. He intended to spend time with his wife at Arcis-sur-Aube, his birthplace. While away, opposition to Danton grew. In her *Memoires,* Madame Roland, who was eventually imprisoned herself, charged Danton with sending the Girondins to be executed. Gronlund viewed this as egregiously slanderous, for, as he reasoned, Danton was at home "feeding his ducks," planting trees, and converting the meadow behind his house in a garden. Danton had been "walking in his garden" when he was interrupted by a courier relaying the news that the Girondins "lost their heads on the scaffold." Troubled by the news, Danton felt that such actions were ultimately unjust: all members of the Convention, including himself, had been factious. No one escaped such a charge. But unlike powerful figures like Robespierre, Danton exhibited greater patience with the mistakes made by fellow patriots: "It ought to be held a sacred principle that a patriot must do wrong three times" before using severe methods to punish him.[132] On his return to Paris, Danton and Camille Desmoulins, also member of the Cordeliers Club, walked "one evening along the Seine"; they both pursued clemency to stem the flow of blood.[133] Desmoulins used his pen: "*The Old Cordelier* was the result."[134] Desmoulins was highly critical of the Hébertists. When the third issue of the *Cordelier* appeared, the editor "lashed the system of the Terror."[135] For Gronlund, the *Cordelier* was largely welcomed, encouraging Camille in the fourth *Cordelier* to call for the opening of *"prisons to the two hundred thousand citizens [the Convention] calls suspects,* for in our Declaration of Rights there are not mentioned at all any prisons of suspicion" and to "exterminate all your enemies by the guillotine" represented a great folly. The Terror would make "ten enemies" of the victim's "family and friends."[136]

The Hébertist continued their relentless attacks on members, going so far as to accuse Danton and Robespierre of being traitorous moderates. Hébert and many of his supporters were eventually executed on March 24, 1794. Hébert apparently went kicking and screaming to the guillotine. The elimination of the Hébertists brought great satisfaction to both the government and the Dantonists. Hébert and his followers were too impatient to discern the Will of the Universe, according to Gronlund; they were unwilling to submit to that divine authority guiding history: "it is just the pity of every new movement that it is loaded with fanatics who often destroy it by carrying things to extremes."[137] It was during Hébert's arrest and execution that Danton's fate was determined.[138] Two of his closest friends were arrested when he gave his final speech to the Convention.[139] Marie-Jean Hérault de Séchelles, "who drafted the Jacobin Constitution," had been charged with giving shelter to an emigrant and revealing "secrets" to the Committee of Public Welfare. Philippe François Nazaire Fabre d'Églantine, who invented the new calendar, was accused of forging a decree of the Convention "in the interest of stock-jobbers and speculators."[140] The truth, according to Gronlund, was that d'Églantine was attempting to expose the forgers.

The elimination of the Hébertists not only encouraged the Dantonists, but it also gave "unbounded joy to the royalists and the counter-revolutionists," who, witnessing the demise of the radicals, believed that the end of the revolution was near. This provided the opportunity for Danton's enemies to strike out against him. His trial and execution came quickly after the arrests of Séchelles and d'Églantine. Many of the earliest historians of the Revolution, including Aulard, implicate Robespierre in Danton's demise, but Gronlund challenged this interpretation. Danton's greatest enemy was not Robespierre, who had been his friend up to that point, but Jacques-Nicolas Billaud-Varenne, an instigator of the September Massacre and one of the principal figures of the Montagnards.[141] Billaud-Varenne pursued Danton with "an implacable hostility." Gronlund concluded that although a man of "inflexible rectitude" and a patriot, Billaud was also an unwavering "terrorist." He hated the fact, according to Gronlund, that Danton was too soft, a "man of pity" and "chief of the party of clemency."[142] Danton was executed for his efforts to smooth out the divisions among revolutionary patriots—to compel them to cooperate with one another. After the fall of Robespierre, Billaud repented of his relentless pursuit of Danton: "If the death of Danton be a crime, I accuse myself of it, for I was the first to denounce [him]." Danton was also accused by Lafayette of accepting bribes and misappropriating large sums of state money—30,000 livres from the royal treasury—entrusted to him in 1792. This, according to Gronlund, was an unsubstantiated rumor. Nothing in the King's papers provided a shred of evidence to implicate Danton. The final accusation, a "still more untenable charge," was that Danton was "monstrously immoral."[143]

The mounting charges against this giant of the Revolution finally moved Robespierre to act. Warrants for Danton, Camille Desmoulins, and Jean-François de Lacroix were signed on March 30, 1794; they were soon arrested in their homes.[144] While in prison and awaiting his trial, Danton met Thomas Paine (also in prison); both had been placed in the same cell as the Girondins had been previously.[145] Danton confessed to Paine that he wished he had not created the Revolutionary Tribunal. The creation of such an executive council was done to prevent another event like the September massacres. Despite the "arrant nonsense" (Gronlund's words) against Danton during his trial before the Convention, he and his fellow defendants were convicted without evidence and without the opportunity to defend themselves. At the time of his conviction, Danton offered these memorable words: "I feel a consolation in believing that *the man who is to die as chief of the faction of the merciful, will find grace in the eyes of posterity.*" Citizens were completely silent as they watched these three men, patriots of the Revolution, carted to the guillotine. As he came to the executioner, according to one eyewitness, Danton, "this atlas of the Revolution," appeared "formidable" with a face that "defied the axe."[146] This "patriot *par excellence,* the disinterest hero" died, sending a great "chill," writes Tackett, "to the Convention and to the whole of Paris."[147] Gronlund laments the reality that France's greatest deliverer was to be laid hidden from mind for seventy years "under the heap of obloquy" before later thinkers revived his image and attempted to give him justice.[148] In his 1886 Edinburgh lecture mentioned above, Gronlund identified Danton as the "Socialist of that epoch." Had Danton lived, Gronlund continued, socialism would have come earlier to Europe.[149] Despite his faults, which included a possible bribe offered to the "mistress of the King of Prussia" and the use of gold to "conquer the Lyonnaise insurrection," Danton failed ultimately to curb the passions of the masses. He never intended for citizens to be ruled by their passions.[150]

Eventually, Robespierre, called to be arrested by Danton's former priest Louis Louchet, faced the guillotine, and with his death came the end of the "Revolutionary Government."[151] At one point, Gronlund complimented Robespierre in the way that he, like Danton, had the "masses at his back," advocating for economic policies "in the interest of the poor."[152] But his great error was his hubris in thinking himself "the very prophet of God." Robespierre became a kind of cult leader, assuming that no one else was competent or pious enough to govern and destroying anyone who opposed him. He lacked an understanding of historical developments and the Will of the Universe, believing that society was "independent of all its past development" and could only be refashioned via the guillotine "to suit himself."[153] With the fall of Robespierre, the plutocrats returned to power; their influence lasted up to the time of Gronlund.[154] Many of the Girondins returned to their seats in the Convention. After taking their revenge against the remaining Jacobins, the returning Girondins implemented policies, including abolishing the *maximum,* in order to make way for free competition, land speculation, and the reopening of the exchange. Such actions were protected in the Constitution of 1795, a constitution that reflected the interests of plutocrats to protect their property.

Soon thereafter, the National Convention was replaced by the Directory. One last effort was made by François-Noël Babeuf to establish a "communist" republic.[155] Babeuf envisioned the equal enjoyment through the common possession of everything.[156] Tragically, Babeuf had been motivated, Gronlund argued, by a false interpretation of God's historical text, but one different from the counterrevolutionaries. Babeuf's mistake came in the belief that the collective state could be achieved solely through human efforts. What is more, news of Napoleon Bonaparte's victories diverted attention away from the domestic concerns in France. Bonaparte's military leadership made him immensely popular among the citizens of France, allowing him to launch his successful coup on November 9, 1799, bringing an end to the Directory in the same year. Bonaparte's *coup d'etat* was the "death blow to the Revolution."[157] Bonaparte protected the interests of the plutocrats who had taken back the government of France. For instance, in 1803, Bonaparte gave to the capitalists—not the public—control of the Bank of France.[158] He also reversed the policy of the previous assembly in nationalizing the mines, privatizing them in 1810. After "granting the wishes of the propertied classes, Bonaparte sought to create a dynasty of his own. Tensions arose when Bonaparte, "who," Gronlund wrote, "preferred himself to all humanity" and to whom patriotism was an "unknown sentiment," worked against the middle class in his intent to extract funds for the military. The plutocrats responded by "throwing him overboard," delaying provisions during his campaign against Russia. Eventually, the plutocrats removed Bonaparte. Gronlund reminds his readers, if Danton had been alive, the situation in France would have been quite different.[159] Napoleon would not have had the opportunity to create a new empire, the revolutions of 1830 and 1848 would have been avoided, church and state would not have been humiliated as they had been, Paris would not be transformed by Louis-Napoleon "into a city of mere pleasure," and the class hostilities in France would have been avoided.

Victorious and unassailable, the bourgeoisie returned to power and abandoned the Revolution. The church and nobility of the Old Regime were able to avoid paying taxes; members of the middle class attempted the same, placing much of the country's financial burdens on the working class. Referencing Édouard Adolphe Drumont's anti-Semitic *La France Juive,* Gronlund intimated that the financial manipulations of the propertied classes of the immediate post-Napoleonic period came ultimately from French Jews. France's plutocrats employed, as he said, "[Jewish] trickery of *indirect* taxation to escape their just share of the public burdens."[160] A tax, called the "*octroi,*" was imposed on "nearly all articles of consumption and prime necessity on entering the cities and towns." This cost the working class about 20 percent of their annual income, as opposed to the 4.5 percent among bourgeoisie households. When it came to the alleviation of poverty or the reduction of the public debt, the plutocrats would loan money to the state at high rates of interest, further grinding down their poorer citizens. The mission of the bourgeoisie, in the end, was to protect capitalist accumulation. This was at first a boon to society. Production and productivity through the wage system and competition provided for immediate social needs. But, as is the nature of capitalism, such practices would inevitably come to a crisis point. And instead of wealthy elites becoming "sufficiently *moralized*" in the sense of not only preventing future crises but also caring for the needs of the poor, to "extirpate all misery and pauperism," they would hold on to their hegemony.[161] France's revolutionary Left demonstrated the possibility of a real fraternity between the middle class and the laboring classes. But it was not to be. Once the men of property regained power, all thoughts of fraternity evaporated. Competitive individualism and the pursuit of profit calcified the hearts of the bourgeoisie, betraying the legacy of the Revolution and defying the Will of the Universe.[162]

Yet despite those who would impede the progress of the divine for their own greed, history would continue along its path. And here is where Gronlund turned his attention to the United States. Modern history began with competition, but it would end with cooperation—true liberty, equality, and fraternity. No other country besides Britain was as developed as the United States to reach such a goal. The great revolutionary innovation of the capitalists in the late nineteenth century, Gronlund reminded his readers, was the trust, "a monopoly in its most concentrated form."[163] The trust—with Gronlund using Standard Oil as the prime example—was symptomatic of the great reversal (i.e., contradictions) within capitalism. Just as the language of revolution was liberating in the abstract but then perverted in the particular by the bourgeoisie, the effectiveness of the trust would move beyond the control of elites to the wider public. The idea of the trust could not be contained; its very function had to spread throughout society. Evolution-to-revolution could not be stopped. Evolution led the nation to the trust; revolution would come when leading individuals harnessed its power for the benefit of society at large. Cooperative ventures were established in agriculture in states and territories across the country. Wage earning laborers were also recognizing the importance of cooperation, as they created insurance companies and trade unions for workers. The unintended, though inevitable, consequence of anarchistic individualism, gathering together huge armies of laborers, taught workers the importance of interdependence, which, after further growth, would counter the efforts to perpetuate isolated individuals. Individualism would eventually contradict itself. Those who chose cooperation via the example of the trust—whether among the working class or the capitalist class—veritably rejected competition; that is, companies knew that cooperation was better than competition. Commenting on what Marx and Engels argued in the *Communist Manifesto*, Gronlund noted that the true and "greatest revolutionists in the world," were among the capitalists, though unconscious of their revolutionary activity. Thus, it was not only foolish to deny the progress of the Power behind Evolution—to crush the trusts and thereby capitalism and the capitalist class—it was impossible.[164]

The "Power behind Evolution" selected individuals to guide society, but much of its work was done through the state, the most practical body to organize the collective laborers of citizens. This did not mean that the government would be absolute, running everything in an economy. Its main job would be that of a "statistician," "general manager," and "general arbitrator."[165] Indeed, Gronlund conceived of a small government composed of administrative agencies with specific responsibilities—agencies overseen and populated by competent individuals democratically chosen and monitored by the citizenry.[166] The democratization of governing agencies was necessary for the development toward the commonwealth. Collectivizing banking, the postal system, the telegraph service, public education, factory legislation, the establishment of a bureau of labor, the railway system, interstate commerce, and land use would move society closer to the realization of social consciousness and the social organism manifested in the State. It would put an end to fractious individualism and provide greater freedom. Every individual "wittingly or unwittingly," he said, necessarily contributed to the collective will. And, again, regardless of their own self-interest, legislators would not be able to resist the imminency of this "new social order."[167]

These governing administrations, essential to the advancement toward the commonwealth, required gifted humans. Evolutionary providence was "at work on certain *minds*": "As the French Revolution was made in the minds of Danton and his contemporaries before 1789, so the Coming Revolution is now being prepared among [Americans]." Individuals like Danton stood as "*conscious actors*" advancing the Will of the Universe. No doubt there were "stupid men in the world" who contribute nothing to society. And then, of course, there were the selfish ones, those who sought to advance their own power in wealth. This latter class was "especially numerous in the United States," Gronlund believed.[168] Whether ignorant or arrogant, the majority of citizens of a country did not understand the flow of history. The Will of the Universe "irresistibly pushes us all—the stupid, the selfish, the indolent multitude" onward and upwards. Yet this divine "Will" did not need all to actively do so; it needed only a few "discontented" individuals. Discontent is to evolution, Gronlund compared, "what steam is to the engineer." Only those with "both discontent *and* right convictions" were fit to be "co-workers of the Power behind Evolution," for only they had "truly deciphered 'God's mysterious text.'"[169]

Where, Gronlund asked, would these figures come from? First, they would come from among the educated who drew inspiration from Henri de Saint-Simon and Karl Marx.[170] French collectivism, especially among the Saint-Simonians, insisted that the commonwealth would develop "into an association exclusively of workers," wresting ownership of capital from private hands. Second, such leaders would be those who recognized the "Supreme Will" behind evolution. The Saint-Simonians erred in believing that they could force the new social order into existence, Gronlund believed, on their own terms, essentially ignoring the "Will behind evolution." German collectivists fell into a similar line of thinking. Prescient individuals from Britain and America, on the other hand, who, from Gronlund's perspective, faced less opposition than their counterparts on the European continent, would complete the "mental preparation for the Coming Revolution." What gave "Anglo-Saxon Collectivism" its "peculiar force" was the belief in a providential agent directing events. The closer these individuals brought the majority of citizens to the brink of collectivism the more the individual nation would *bring itself into harmony with* the Supreme Will. Citizens would "see the hand of Providence in human affairs"—"a Will, an Intelligence, a helpful Presence."[171]

# CHAPTER THREE

# STONE-BLIND IN ONE EYE

## Henry George's Historical Myopia

All "progressive societies," Gronlund wrote in *Commonwealth*, tend "toward socialist democracy."[1] It is difficult for the contemporary mind to imagine a society that can avoid the arduous phase of industrial capitalism on its way to becoming a more progressive state. And if it is a necessary step, it certainly is not an easy one. First, changes in the means of production and the creation of new social relations on the way to capitalism generate serious social anxiety. Radical changes wrought by capitalism (or emerging capitalism) can be quite unsettling to traditional ways of life. Second, once the habits of capitalism settle into a given society, the need to protect such an economic system becomes paramount. One way to safeguard the accumulation of wealth is for governments to implement strategies to make sure an economy remains open (i.e., to liberalize it)—open, that is, for wealth. It is truly a vicious circle. This, however, while benefiting a few, creates hardship for the majority of a nation's population and its environment. In the era of globalization, unfettered neoliberal capitalism has augmented the negative impact on the world's geography, resources, climate, and populations. It is hard (and foolish) to deny that under capitalism profits take precedence over people and place. The movement toward a more democratic society, in contrast, does not depend on liberalizing capitalism but directly confronting the negative consequences of such an economy by mindful human beings. When historic capitalism goes through its cyclical downturn—and it always does—problems inherent to capitalism come into sharp relief. One such problem relates to how great wealth can grow along with great poverty, an enduring theme in boom-and-bust economies.

Those concerned with the recuring highs and lows in America's economy have offered plenty of reformist programs to ameliorate the gap between the "haves" (the less than 1 percent) and the "have nots" (the remaining 99 percent)—with an equal concern for the natural environment. But such strategies, Gronlund boldly proclaimed, would ultimately fail not only because they ignored the root problem of capitalism itself, but also because they exhibited a woefully deficient philosophical outlook. One of the most popular reformers during the Gilded Age was journalist and political economist Henry George, a largely self-educated individual who experienced firsthand the challenging social realities of industrial capitalism in the late nineteenth century, whose ideas had a profound influence not just on America but countries around the globe.[2] After a few years in the newspaper business, George published *Progress and Poverty* in 1879, the most-widely read economics text at the time. The central issue addressed in the book was how a country like the United States could become so prosperous, so extremely wealthy, and yet at the same time create such widespread poverty. George's son Henry Jr. articulated his father's observation of this point: "On every hand [Henry Sr.] beheld evidences of advancing civilization, but of a civilization that was one-sided; that piled up riches for the few and huddled the many in filth and poverty"[3] What was behind such disparity? In George's mind, land was both the problem and the solution to America's great dilemma.

Land, for George, took on (if I may) biblical imagery in that it was the origin of life (creation) and the source of its demise (the fall). Land "is the home of humans," he wrote in *Progress and Poverty,* "the storehouse we must draw upon for all our needs. Land is the material to which we must apply our labor to supply all our desires."[4] It is the well-spring of life: "On land we are born, from it we live, to it we return again—children of the soil as truly as is the blade of grass or flower of the field. Take away from man all that belongs to land, and he is but a disembodied spirit. Material progress cannot rid us of our dependence upon land; it can but add to the power of producing wealth."[5] Yet this well-spring of life could be used to cut life short. From its founding, the United States had its eye on reappropriating land across the continent. This intensified after the Civil War, when land was turned over to the appetites of big capital. By the late nineteenth century, land was increasingly set aside for railroad companies, bonanza farmers, and land-grant educational institutions for the continuing expansion of private wealth. Congress consistently and egregiously violated (and continues to do so) the agreements made with Native American communities, granting railroad companies large swaths of land in order to build lines—some of which were not even used. And the growth in scale of America's postbellum communication and transportation infrastructure necessitated the creation of large agribusiness commercial farms. The land acquisition needed to fuel capitalist expansion had a direct impact on labor, which was itself rapidly increasing given the influx of immigrants from eastern Europe and Asia, particularly China. For idealists, the supposed "free-land" out west—the frontier—would act as a means to escape the nation's troubled urban centers; it was also a place in which white Americans created themselves, dominating the landscape and sowing the seeds of American empire. But the myth of the frontier did not square with many of the challenges of real life. Native Americans, their people and culture, were removed from ever-shrinking colonies within America's emerging empire—their presence largely forgotten in the nation's historical memory.[6] As new laborers moved onto these not-so-open lands, tenants would face increasing rent from landlords and speculators. When "land is monopolized," George said, "progress might go on to infinity without increasing wages or improving the condition of those who have only their labor. It can only add to the value of land and the power its possession gives . . . the speculative advance in land values tends to press the margins of cultivation, or production, beyond its normal limits, thus compelling labor and capital to accept a smaller return, or . . . to cease production."[7] Large landowners prevented workers from benefiting from social and economic improvements. This was the reason behind the growing gap between wealth and poverty: "The great cause of inequality in the distribution of wealth is inequality in the ownership of land."[8]

Yet it was also through land that society would be restored (redemption). The monopolization of land motivated George's single tax proposal. The value of land would rise because of the production and community in and around it. But that value, for the most part, benefited the landowner, not the ones who produced that value. The property owner (landowner) could then receive double (or more) of what he originally paid. Placing a land tax on the "unearned increments," taken as profit, would compel corporations to use the land more efficiently, but it would also ease the burden of workers by alleviating the pressures of rent and curbing the loss of wages caused by privatized land ownership: "wages depend upon the margin of production, or upon the produce which labor can obtain at the highest point of natural productiveness open to it without the payment of rent."[9] Recasting decades-old assumptions about that which was common to all—namely, land—George's single-tax policy was actually quite conservative, since land, the source of wealth, predated capitalism. Land, as well as air and water, was a key resource given to all humans equally. There were no *a priori* laws, whether from nature or God, that dictated that such resources, prior to the human labor applied to making things from nature (e.g., property), could be the exclusive right of certain individuals—most certainly not those who refused to apply their labor to nature. A tax on land was an indirect way of returning value to those who created it and alleviating the tension between labor and capital.

An instant success, *Progress and Poverty* sold millions and was eventually translated into eleven different languages. Writers, intellectuals, and influential political figures as far away as Australia, New Zealand, Russia, and China sought to implement George's remedy.[10] Yet despite his wide-spread popularity in his day and beyond, George was not without his critics. There were, of course, the obvious greedy robber-barons of the Gilded Age who advocated for the "free" acquisition of land to maintain a "planless" economy. Likewise, radical and reformist critics of the capitalist establishment, including Thomas Huxley, Alfred Marshall, J. B. Clark, F. A. Walker, and Edward Bellamy, to name a few, expressed concern over the efficacy of the single tax. William Dean Howells rejected George because his doctrine was tantamount to land confiscation, though he admitted that George's plan turned many reformers toward socialism.[11] Karl Marx viewed George's single tax as "utterly backwards," since it failed to understand "the nature of surplus value."[12] In the end, Marx bluntly stated that George was the worst among the "panacea-mongers without exception" and that his *Progress and Poverty* stood as "a last attempt to save the capitalist regime."[13] In his *Conditions of the Working Classes in England,* Frederick Engels articulated the fundamental difference between socialists and Georgists: "What the socialists demand implies a total revolution of the whole system of social production; what Henry George demands leaves the present mode of social production untouched."[14]

Notwithstanding his comment that *Progress and Poverty* was "the best forerunner a Socialist could wish to have" in the movement toward the collective state (as plenty of British Fabians turned to socialism because of George), Gronlund echoed the sentiments of Marx and Engels. "[S]tone-blind in one eye" and "near-sighted as the Jacobins of 93"—the architect of the single tax was ultimately "in love with the wage-system."[15] The fiery debate between these two great minds, Henry George and Laurence Gronlund, after George's failed bid for mayor of New York in 1886, caused a "profound sensation in the labor world," argued Gemorah.[16] The socialists' position against George, according to author George Raymond Geiger, was "perhaps most effectively presented" by Gronlund.[17] From a wider lens, the irreconcilable tension between George and Gronlund over strategies for reform, which weakened what might have been a stronger leftist front, supports the conclusions made by twentieth-century scholars as to why socialism failed to take a greater hold on America's political culture.

While writing *Ça Ira* in Europe, Gronlund spent a good deal of time reflecting on George's single tax policy.[18] Around the time of George's first mayoral campaign, Gronlund, despite his and other socialist's initial support for George's United Labor Party (ULP), wrote two pamphlets, the contents of which "represent the most considerable effort ever made," according to Fred Harrison, "to refute George on Marxist grounds."[19] In the first, *Insufficiency of Henry George's Theory* (1887), Gronlund argued that George's reformist policy did not go far enough.[20] *Insufficiency* began by restating what was written in *Commonwealth*—namely, that Henry George was a "forerunner of Socialism in the United States."[21] In his 1904 tribute to George, George Bernard Shaw admitted that he been swept up into socialism via the works of George.[22] Richard Ely recognized George's "distinct services" in advancing the cause of socialism. Sidney Webb too recognized George's unintended role in consolidating "a popular Socialist Movement" in England.[23] Despite his influence in converting a number of reformers to socialism, George, according to Gronlund, provided only a partial remedy to the socioeconomic problems of the mid-1880s. Gronlund was certainly willing to accept incremental changes like a single tax. But to limit social amelioration to this reform measure, ignoring "who should control the instruments of production and transportation," was not enough.[24] Although a step in the right direction, that "one step," Gronlund says, "must involve and be followed by another"—like the popular ownership of the country's infrastructure.[25] The remedy George offered reached "only a part of the evils of the present condition of society."[26]

Here again, Gronlund is careful to maintain historical development. Central to both pamphlets was Gronlund's concern that George's "land question" was pushed "so much into the foreground" that it lost sight of "who should control the instruments of production and transportation."[27] In true Marxist form, Gronlund was concerned with the fleecings that would always appear within capitalism, the value created by labor, and who rightly owned and therefore could properly distribute that value. It seemed that George carved out an indirect path to allay the human consequence of capitalism while Gronlund focused on its very root.

The second, *Socialism vs. Tax Reform,* written and published in the late summer of 1887, was a passionate response to George's misguided frustrations with the socialists, who, according to George, were dividing the ULP.[28] Gronlund's language had become increasingly bitter. George finished second to Tammany Hall's Abram Hewitt, with Theodore Roosevelt trailing George by a little less than 8,000 votes. He ran again in 1898 but tragically died of a stroke during the campaign. George assigned much of the blame on the socialists. He published his very harsh opinions about them in the *Standard.* Historians have argued that George, who, early on, sought to gain wide support from among reformers and radicals, took direct aim at socialists in general but Gronlund in particular.[29] Along with the ULP chairman John McMackin, George sought to reorganize the ULP by purging all radical factions, "notably the socialists," from its roll. [30] Socialists responded by forming the Progressive Labor Party, running a candidate against George in the 1887 election. Authorized by the socialists, George responded by not only reiterating his critique of George's policy but also answering George's charge that his mayoral loss was due to the weakening of the United Labor Party by factional socialists. George's comments regarding socialism, especially after the election, and Gronlund's riposte undoubtedly deepened the division between socialists and Georgeists. Unlike the first pamphlet, "Gronlund forcefully attacked George" in *Socialism vs. Tax Reform.*[31]

Both essays were united by a shared argument. George's central failure was his historical myopia, the inability to see the "historical development which the means of production had undergone in the course of civilization."[32] At the end of *Ça Ira,* Gronlund wrote that both European and American reformers, including America's "own Henry George," had "a wrong interpretation, a false translation, of 'God's mysterious text.'"[33] This "wrong interpretation" reflected, to be clear, a failure to view major moments in history, especially that of the French Revolution, as part of a greater divine scheme to advance societies closer to the commonwealth. America in the late nineteenth century was at a transition stage: the stage in which capitalism was reaching its crisis point, preparing the way thereby for the collective commonwealth. George could not see this; he seemed to feel comfortable with preserving capitalism. Nonetheless, he offered a partial plan to alleviate the struggles of the working classes. Unfortunately, Gronlund believed, it did not go far enough. George needed to look beyond the immediate, according to Gronlund, to consider the internal contradictions within history as that which fueled the development of civilization. In short, by assuming that the single-tax policy would provide ultimate and final relief, George ignored the "Power behind evolution," and thereby halted the developments toward socialism. Thankfully, however, the Will of the Universe would eventually eradicate competitive individualism, wage slavery, exploitation, and, hence, capitalism all together, taking along with it any plan that would simply reform capitalism. Evolution was on a course—a course orchestrated by the "Power" and "Will" behind it— that would end in the collective commonwealth.[34] George's failure to address the root conditions of capitalism meant that he did not fully grasp the march of history, slowing, thereby, the movement toward the commonwealth. Although more narrowly technical, Gronlund's argument against George and the ULP was undergirded by his nascent theo-historical perspective—a perspective that would mature in Gronlund's mind a few years later (see Chapter 4).

Before the election of 1886, George "had displayed a consistent toleration of socialists and an open admiration of their goals," writes Henry O'Donnell.[35] He honestly believed that his single tax would help to "realize the dream of socialism." What is more, he admitted in his 1883 *Social Problems* that the American economy was moving toward cooperation "or, if the word is preferred, socialism."[36] And he singled out Gronlund as the one who offered the "best exposition" of the German socialist school of Marx. He accepted Gronlund's definition of capitalism as that "part of wealth employed productively, with a view to profit by the sale of the produce" and favored Gronlund's term *fleecing* over the more abstruse "surplus value."[37] But this was not the source of their disagreement. At first, George accused the socialists of confusing their terminology, but such a criticism did not stand, especially with Gronlund. In contradistinction to the socialists, Gronlund believed that "oppression did not come from the nature of capital, but from the wrong that robs labor of capital by divorcing it from land."[38] The source of confusion, according to George, related to how socialists did away with "private ownership of land," and failed to accept the true source behind workers' "helplessness": land monopoly.[39] Yet Gronlund never wavered from the "theories" of the socialists "in their entirety," which included "the nationalization not only of land but of all the products of land."[40] The socialists incorrectly argued that the real problem faced by the laboring masses centered on the wage system.

The disagreement between George and Gronlund, which opened the discussion in *Insufficiency,* related to their opposing view of human nature in relation to the capitalist system. For George, humanity's natural condition was one of competition. George recognized "no evil in competition." Competition became perverted, he admitted, when it turned into "restricted competition"—"one-sided competition to which men are forced when deprived of land." Unrestricted competition, George believed, was indeed "necessary to the health of the industrial and social organism as the free circulation of the blood is to the health of the bodily organism. . . . We would simply take for the community what belongs to the community, the value that attaches to land by the growth of the community; leave sacredly to the individual all that belongs to the individual; and, treating necessary monopolies as functions of the state, abolish all restrictions and prohibitions save those required for public health, safety, morals, and convenience."[41] Solving the land question would then make competition morally acceptable. From George's perspective, there did not seem to be a way to overcome competition. To a degree, it was part of human nature. What is more, competitive "individualism" was so deeply entrenched in America, as compared to what it was in Europe. "This is the reason why," George stated, socialism "can never make the headway that it has on the continent of Europe." The people of Europe had become familiar with looking to the government "as a sort of special providence," supervising and directing much of life. Recall that Gronlund made a distinction between "individualism" and "individuality." He brought up the same distinction in his interaction with George. George, according to Gronlund, simply wanted to "cure the bad effects" of the country's competitive social structure. Agreeing that workers should retain the fruits of their labor, Gronlund took the opposite view when it came to human nature. Humans were morally drawn toward cooperation, to work with and for one another for the purposes of maintaining a well-working social contract. They were made, he argued, to be dependent on one another. There was no isolated individual; consequently, there was certainly no individual that could survive by eliminating other "individuals": "Society is an organism, whose members are interdependent even now to a much greater degree than it seems."[42]

George never denied that there existed "a domain of individual action and a domain of social action," affirming both individualism *and* communalism.[43] He accepted this truth of socialism that individualists forgot; yet he also charged socialists with ignoring the inevitability of individualism. For Gronlund, the two terms, individualism and communalism, "mutually *exclude* each other."[44] There was no such isolated entity as an individual. Furthermore, the ideology of "individualism" stood as the powerful propaganda necessary to fuel competition, pursuing one's own aim against others "by elbowing them aside." Each person was not his or her own but belonged to and depended on others. Individual identity did not arise from an internal self, but rather from external "selves." Likewise, every ostensibly free action made by an individual could be traced back to the influences of a particular social context. This is why socialists, then, favored *"co-operation and emulation"* with their fellows.[45] Gronlund would agree that individualism had been favored at certain times in American history, but, "like the pendulum of a clock," individualism was giving way to communalism, only because capitalism was nearing its collapse. Late-nineteenth-century citizens in North America and Europe were witnessing the decline of individualism and "nurturing that new sentiment" of socialism. The growth in trade unions signaled this shift. And through the trade unions, the individual learned to subordinate "his interest to the interest of the organization." Each person would merge "himself in the whole body."[46]

Gronlund's main criticism in *Insufficiency* revolved around George's refusal to centralize the reality of surplus value as the defining feature of capitalism and the source of labor exploitation. This is not to suggest that George was ignorant of this fundamental element of capitalism. As mentioned above, George approved of Gronlund's "fleecing" concept vis-à-vis surplus value. While he saw this as a problem, it was not his central concern. Exploitation could be eased. George believed that the social problem created by capitalism require getting "rid of those bad landowners" through taxation, which would lead to the sharing of "their advantages with the laborers." But the idea of ridding the capitalists of "all taxation" was a farce. Surplus value generated through labor would continue as the true source of wealth for the plutocrats. Gronlund believed that the income of the capitalist grew *"much faster than the income of the landlord* from increasing rent."[47] A tax on these unearned increments of land would certainly shake the foundations of land monopoly. But even with such a tax, the capitalist would continue to accumulate his own profits by fleecing workers. There might be a modicum of relief through a land tax, the revenue of which would go back to the people, but this will not deal with the continued alienation workers face within the wage system. Others shared Gronlund's criticism on this point, adding that a land tax would allow the continuation of fleecing and would do nothing to reduce worker hours. Editors of the *Cigar Makers' Official Journal* stated, "Henry George's theory that the taxation of land values will relieve the work-people employed in factories, mines and mills of their present misery and poverty is a snare and a delusion . . . No financial scheme or novel plan of taxation will shorten hours of labor."[48]

Given his underrating of surplus value, George was also wrong, according to Gronlund, when it came to the creation of value (and, of course, how it was distributed). For George, land was neither wealth nor capital, though the latter two were drawn from the former. George assumed that "landlords grow richer and richer by material progress, while capitalists do not get their proper share and are, in fact, in the same boat as the wage workers"; but landlords, Gronlund says, "constitute but a small portion of our monied class."[49] Land was, however, "that original factor of production from which labor produces wealth and capital"—the "original" means of production. Without land (i.e., land that is monopolized in private hands) there is no means of production and hence no labor. Land is the resource given to all equally. But it was not the ultimate source of value. What people produced *from* the land was what they rightfully may call their property. George admitted that an individual worker had "a right to the fruits of his own exertions."[50] He retained a place for private property as it came from the fruits of one's labor: "There is nothing in [Gronlund's commonwealth] that destroys the opportunity for individual effort or property. If one man works harder than another he will get more of the product of labor, be it represented in money or goods."[51] The rising value of land, and hence the rise in rent, was the result of labor. Value "is created by the labor of other people," Gronlund wrote.[52] Hence, "valuable land stands exactly on the same footing as capital." Whatever is taken from the added value of land in the form of profits is to fleece the labor that went into creating that value. The value of land corresponds to the labor put into it, which then constitutes "means of labor, means of production," which then should be under the ownership and administration of those who create the value. Progress demanded, according to Gronlund, "that both land and capital be placed under collective control."[53]

Gronlund did not deny that land was a necessary feature in the process of production: "there is not a Socialist who will not admit that, that land is primary as to time."[54] But land alone was not enough, and it certainly could not be separated from the elements that went into capitalist production. The landless worker "would be just as sure of dying by starvation, as if he was suspended in mid-air." Humans had always been able to live off the land—hunting, gathering, planting, harvesting, etc. But the use of land in this sense did not equal capital. Capitalism required the instruments of capital: tools, mass labor, commodities, and land. Such instruments were "indispensable to production," which George designated as secondary factors. Yet they were "as much a part of Nature as land."[55] Tools themselves derived from nature. They were made by the laborer. And as means of production, tools had to be owned and operated by those who used them in the process of making marketable commodities. In this way, Gronlund saw a negligible difference between primary and secondary factors in value creation: all the elements of capitalist production were inextricably tied to nature. Humanity took from the natural world (land), turning raw nature into items of property. Land was given to all, of course, but once it was used for capitalist production, it quickly became a foreign and alienated object—transferred from public to private hands. To return land to its original state, a resource for everyone, reformers needed to dismantle capitalism itself.

George was the one who confused "nature and land with value together." Gronlund agreed that capital "derived from Nature": "When labor is applied to Nature, wealth is the result and Capital is a certain part of wealth." But labor, not an inert natural resource, "gives wealth or Capital its value." The product *from* nature—though still connected to the original material—would become something different: property. The value of land was derived from labor, since labor was *the* source of value itself: "[I]t is the Labor that has brought the land nearer to market, has made it accessible; it is the Labor that has made the surrounding improvements, that has built railroads, that has paved and graded the streets, laid sewers, built the side-walks, planted the trees, created the city." This is what placed land "on the same footing as Capital."[56] The value of land fluctuated with labor. If land could be sold, Gronlund argued, then there would be no exchange value and thus no capital. Land was sold because of its value—value created by labor. A factory required land, and a factory could only run because of labor. Land was, therefore, a "necessary means of production, a 'primary' means of production."[57] A crisis caused by overproduction would impact negatively the value of land only because it would negatively impact labor. Workers would be laid off, and the land would plummet in value. The continuation of a tax on valueless land would then be a waste.

Placing a tax on the value of land would certainly break the monopoly of the landlord and ease the burdens of labor. But it would not eliminate the wage system. Consequently, it would not eliminate exploitation. The capitalist would still be able to get rich through surplus capital. Likewise, it would not eliminate what Gronlund identified as the central crisis of overproduction. There was no doubt that speculation in land certainly contributed to economic stress in an industrial economy. For George, an economic downturn could ultimately be traced back to land speculation, which necessarily impacted production, wages, and consumption. Gronlund disagreed, tracing the origins back to labor. Capitalist crises came primarily from overproduction: "It is to the rule of these selfish plutocrats, and to their wage-system, competition and 'private enterprise' that the so-called 'over-production' and our crises are due, and *not at all* to the speculative rise in the value of land, as George declares."[58] Again, for George, this was not *the* problem. For George, the wage system, where, in his mind, the value of a product in relation to supply and demand connected to the dynamics of wages, did not need to be eradicated. In fact, doing away with wages without addressing the primary factor in production, originating in land and its common resources, would be even more of a detriment to labor. The law of supply and demand would be much more efficient in determining the value of products than a collectivist government. And if the unchecked "laws" of supply and demand resulted in the crisis of overproduction, which inevitably it would, society would have a fiscal reserve drawn from the land tax that would quell the crisis. George's remedy did not require revolution, certainly not violent revolution, to which Gronlund would have agreed. It would, however, quell the social unrest caused by capitalism's cyclical crises. The single tax would also help to shrink the unequal distribution of wealth. In one sense, the single tax would be kind of indirect redistribution. Maher points out that George never offered "a budget on this single tax," which led Gronlund to dismiss the benefits of George's scheme as merely assumed.[59]

The "grand question" proposed by Gronlund was whether George's land tax would indeed help the workers? Taxing the land, its natural and therefore common resources, would allow workers to retain their labor. It would also relieve the burden of rent, which George included under the category of "fleecing," collected by private ownership. His proposal was an indirect recovery of what the capitalists stole via surplus value; it would have gone a long way in alleviating the consequences of advanced capitalism. The revenue generated from the tax would eventually go back to the community—the community that generated the value in the first place. This "simple yet radical reform," George argued, "would do away with all injustice" related to America's economic situation.[60] The tax on land would go back to workers, those responsible for augmenting land value—thereby levelling out the distribution of wealth. George's plan fixed not just an economic problem, but a social one as well. It would have eased the plight of struggling workers without upsetting contemporary socioeconomic arrangements.

For Gronlund, however, George's solution would not ease the burden of workers. If anything, it would make their situation much worse. First, even with a land tax, capitalists could implement any number of strategies to protect their wealth. Immediately, they could force laborers to work longer hours, thus increasing the surplus and the profits that they gained through fleecing. And while the tax would eventually adjust to meet changes in labor, it would be a little too late since the capitalist had already received his profit. What is more, the value generated through land use had the appearance of that which was natural, but capitalists could arbitrarily force a surplus without an increase in the value of land. Second, the revenue collected from the tax, all things being equal, would not be sufficient to run federal and state government programs. Third, George's land tax would do away with protective tariffs, which Gronlund believed would give aid to workers.[61] Eliminating protective tariffs would insure, Gronlund wrote, "big profits" for owners and employers, protecting "the private interests of the plutocrats" but not necessarily the jobs of those selling their labor.[62] Finally, Gronlund challenged the notion that "immunity from taxes" would increase wages and allow workers to purchase homes or procure capital. How did he arrive at such a conclusion, Gronlund inquired? George failed to lay out the logic of such a claim. The single tax would allow workers to build their own homes, but, as Gronlund suggests, with little money and certainly no capital, they would be free to build themselves "some sort of shanties": "the poor can go down to the river and fish out old, rotten boards with which they build most miserable 'shanties.'"[63] Beyond building shanties, where would the poor be able to get the materials necessary to live in better circumstances? The poor could not save their measly wages to be able to build their own homes. Laborers could earn money (however much), but this was not the same as earning capital. It bears repeating for our own age: earning money is not the same as accumulating capital. Money without capital was archaic, and there was no sense, Gronlund believed, in turning back "the wheel of progress." The poor might escape land monopoly, but they would never be able to escape exploitation. Labor had become dependent on the "concentration of industry." Even with reforms to make small improvements in the lives of workers, labor would remain subject to the trajectory of capitalism.

George accused the socialists of attempting to hijack the ULP, to brook no compromise with their socialist agenda. But it was George, not the socialists, in Gronlund's estimation, who was acting as the single-minded partisan. The United Labor Party had been created by a coalition of labor organizations, which included socialists. Many of these organizations took central aim at abolishing the wage system. George, according Gronlund, knew this. The only way, in their minds, to do that was to "abolish private property in capital."[64] According to socialists, land was "a most important bastion in the fortress [of] Capital"; even the Georgists understood this, hence the reason why they were often equated with socialists. Gronlund challenged the claim that the socialists wanted to take the "rudder" of the new party, as George charged. Rather, Gronlund argued, the socialists had "left the machinery entirely in the hand of Henry George and his friends." But Gronlund and the socialists came to regret such a concession, since the Georgists eventually "emasculated the constitution" of the ULP. The new constitution would ignore the goal of eliminating the wage system and narrowly impose George's land doctrine, "undermining," according to Gronlund, "the principles of the party with a vengeance."[65] George continued his opposition to socialism in his 1890 *Science of Political Economy*. In it, he highlighted "four major faults" of socialism. First, it was unscientific in that it denied natural laws. Second, it was anti-religious and thus "destitute of any central and guiding principle." Third, it was unable to protect individual rights. Finally, there was the problem of cooperation—directed and unconscious. The "fatal defect" of socialism was its managerial overreach: "any attempt to carry conscious regulation and direction beyond the narrow sphere of social life in which it is necessary, inevitably works injury, hindering even what it is intended to help."[66] Gronlund lamented that he and fellow socialists "were kicked out" of the ULP. George created a split that "may be more serious than George seems to suppose."[67] Such a move would have alienated, Gronlund added, the "conservative Powderly" and the Knights of Labor as well as the Central Labor Union. Gronlund was not the only one concerned over George's efforts to focus the ULP along the strict lines of the single tax. Socialist and editor of *Leader*, Serge Schevitsch not only expressed his criticism of George's attempts but also showed his preference for Gronlund's socialism. The removal of socialists played an important role in the demise of the ULP as well as George's involvement in politics. Emma Goldman intimated that the fall of the ULP and the strength of labor politics in general came not at the hands of socialists but, ironically, from those of Henry George himself.[68] George, Gronlund charged, "opposes himself to the efforts and aspirations of the working-classes everywhere."[69] For Morris Hillquit, "[t]he expulsion of the socialists from the United Labor Party had the effect of weakening the organization to a great extent."[70]

It was George, Gronlund suggested, who had "done all he could to switch the party off the track, changing it from a *party of the workers*, that is a party of the fleeced against the parties of the fleecers, of the monopolists of the means of production, into a *Free Trade Party*."[71] The socialists, Gronlund asserts, "care for the cause, not for persons"; that is, they were interested in preserving principles not in the political aspirations of single individuals. The question as to whether the ULP should have been altered to conform to German Socialism was a "question no man living," Gronlund concluded, could "now determine." It was the Power behind Evolution at work among the various labor organizations. Gronlund thus encouraged socialists to continue supporting the candidates of the ULP. Yet the socialists would need to rethink their alliance if core principles were abandoned, which had been instigated by George. For instance, if the demands of doing away with the wage system were indeed ignored, then the socialists would be unable to continue supporting the ULP. George's restricted focus on land and his unwillingness to compromise with other labor organizations, including those among farmers, would be political suicide. What did George mean when he said that the socialists "lack[ed] radicalism." Gronlund interpreted this to mean that the socialists failed to distinguish between "land as primary and capital as derivative."[72]

A tax on the unearned increments of land, George earnestly believed, would shake the foundations of land monopoly, and not just land monopoly, but all other monopolies. But even with such a tax on land, the capitalist would continue to accumulate his own profits by fleecing workers. Gronlund assumed that the working classes would consider George's policy a "most unpopular doctrine."[73] He appealed to the example of the workingmen of England and France to support his claim that the move toward the elimination of the wage system was a viable plan. In England, considerable gains were made for the rights of labor, but then there came those "not imbued with the co-operative spirit, men who simply wanted to amass a little capital." The English working class detracted from their main goal of dismantling the wage system. A similar situation inflicted France when in 1886, Charles Gide, professor of political economy at the University of Montpellier, charged an assembly of "French co-operators," that the wage system was "an inferior condition of Labor and should be abolished."[74] Though not a socialist himself, as he informed Gronlund in a letter, Giles nonetheless favored replacing the wage system with "voluntary co-operation." But would the single tax be permitted in the American context? Gronlund questioned whether it could be accomplished constitutionally. Even if George convinced every state legislature to pass a land tax, the courts would eventually overturn such decisions since it would become clear to the judges of the land that such taxing is nothing more than confiscation. For the single tax plan is to "hide confiscation with a thin veil."[75] George's plan would require a revolution of mind, a completely new way of understanding land, value, capitalism, and taxation.

While disagreeing on root causes as well as a secure remedy to deal with America's economic and social troubles, George, wanting to preserve capitalism, and Gronlund, intent on dismantling it, did not need to be enemies. Despite his strong skepticism that cooperation would lead to an overall increase in wages for laborers or "relieve poverty," George believed in the benefit of cooperation for civilization over the long term.[76] Humans, he believed, were "*made for co-operation—like feet, like hands, like eyelids, like the rows of the upper and lower teeth.*"[77] Association, he said, was the "first essential of progress."[78] While purging competition and individuality of their "destructive tendencies," the single tax would have been a step toward cooperation.[79] And over time, the "government would change its character and would become the administration of a great co-operative society. It would become merely the agency by which the common property was administered for the common benefit."[80] George's fatal error was not opposing cooperation as a practical scheme but his dogged pursuit to rid the ULP of socialists. In light of George's position on cooperation, Gronlund too may have been overly zealous in opposing the single tax. Perhaps Gronlund took George's attacks personally. Such was—and continues to be—a common dilemma among reformers and radicals: to what degree would they be willing to compromise. Should one be ideologically pure in every way, or was their room to appropriate reformist platforms? I cannot help but imagine the powerful political coalition that could have been had George and Gronlund continued to work together. Perhaps Gronlund did not quite understand George's scheme. Was Gronlund so committed to his brand of socialism that he could not be as politically dexterous? Was George himself too narrowly committed to his agenda? Was the source of disagreement really one of strategy and timing or hubris?

As to the growing factionalism within the ULP, George believed that the socialists were resolutely focused on turning the party "to their own peculiar views and plans."[81] George was not completely wrong on this point. Friedrich Sorge, like George, recognized the factionalism of the socialists after the 1886 election as a political liability, reprimanding them for supporting the Progressive Labor Party, for "failing to come to the defense of the Haymarket Square martyrs," writes Daniel Gaido, "on the grounds that they were anarchists, and for belittling the trade-union movement on the basis that it was not socialist."[82] Monitoring the movements of American socialists arguably through Sorge's eyes and other correspondents of *Die Neue Zeit,* Karl Kautsky, the "pope of Marxism," would come to a similar conclusion:

> Just now Social Democracy had nowhere to struggle against such difficulties as in America. The disunion and petty jealousies among the different

socialist organizations are, if possible, even greater than in England. While in the latter these drawbacks have to a certain extent been balanced by great advances in the socialist consciousness of the proletariat, the mental effervescence lately to be seen in America has not yet led to a considerable furtherance of the socialist movement . . . Whether the fault lies in the American workers or in the socialists, whether the former are too limited and egotistical or the latter do not sufficiently understand the workers, or finally whether both are to be blamed for that situation—that is difficult to determine from here. But it is clear that just as such a situation demands criticism, it must lead to particularly irritable reactions to it.[83]

Gronlund admitted that the socialists sought the "advance toward [the] perfection" of the ULP, "not the breaking up" of it.[84] His criticism of the single tax did not take away from an interest in maintaining an alliance. "Have socialists been hypocrites," he asked George directly, "in working for your election last fall? . . . Of course not."[85] Gronlund never wavered from remaining on George's "ship," though the scheme of his and his followers was off course. Evolution would inevitably right the Georgist vessel, though it would take a bit longer to reach the destination then if the socialists were at the helm. "So, we stay on board," Gronlund concluded.[86] Gronlund rejected the charge that the socialists were trying to break up the ULP. Regardless of George's success, the socialists, Gronlund argued, would have refused to quit the party, or if they did leave the ULP they would continue to "give it our best support." Gronlund and fellow socialists recognized "much good for the world" the United Labor Party had done in advancing "toward the realization of our ideal nation, where all competition will be destroyed and the means of labor shall be in the hands of the State."[87] But it must be emphasized that Gronlund's interest to maintain a political coalition stemmed from his view of history—namely, that the ideas among radicals and reformers, especially on the areas in which they agreed, was necessary to move closer to a cooperative society. Gronlund admitted that George's run for mayor, while ultimately a loss, was a successful step toward socialism, whether or not George himself and his followers realized it.

Gronlund ends both pamphlets, as he did many of his other works, by assuring his readers that his commonwealth would not only protect but cultivate American liberty. In this regard, Gronlund responded to George's description of socialism as "an exotic born of European conditions," which would not be able to "take root and flourish in American soil."[88] George could not see that capitalism and freedom were at odds with one another. Preserving capitalism would necessarily threaten American democracy. But returning to a familiar anti-socialist argument, George and other critics feared that socialism would create too large of a state, crushing thereby individual freedom. By freedom, George meant "absence of restraints," especially from the government, to which Gronlund would have agreed in part. Freedom meant more than this; it included "living the life worthy of a human being"—not only a freedom "to" but a freedom "from." Gronlund did not want a large state either; rather, he and fellow socialists sought "to institute *the most perfect self-government.*"[89] Gronlund preferred the use of bottom-up administrations to address the everyday functions of society. He envisioned a Commonwealth made up of representatives from every industry in society, public and private. Each board or bureau would be composed of individuals elected from each industry—historic-minded individuals who would carefully and nonviolently lead people closer to the final age. The obvious challenge was to find the most "competent, wise, and skillful persons to direct affairs."[90] This would not lend itself to an overbearing state in Gronlund's mind. The nation would undergo a social transformation when trades unions took responsibility for their own members, the hours they worked, and the distribution of their earnings, displacing thereby the tyranny of the plutocrats. As a governing body, the collective state would have only three functions: general manager, general statistician, and general arbitrator.[91] The work of the statistician would be to determine how much is to be produced. The manager would distribute work and assess the performance of labor. The arbitrator would make sure that justice was done between the different associations and between each association and its members. George, however, thought that such a move would become an undue burden on liberty, for it will tend toward the elimination of individuality and by extension all personal property. But nothing in Gronlund's arrangement would preclude the ability to acquire property, other than the elimination of the conditions that would enable greed and exploitation.

At first glance, readers may draw the conclusion that *Insufficiency of Henry George's Theory* and *Socialism vs. Tax Reform* are—in relation to the thesis of the present work—the most secular of Gronlund's works. The disagreement between George and Gronlund revolved around competing reform policies as well as perspectives on history. George supported cooperation in all levels of the economy, yet he was unwilling to disturb an economic system, historic in nature, that created isolated individuals, fractured communities, and practiced cooperation in a very restricted sense. George was caught in an irreconcilable dilemma. There would be no cooperative commonwealth so long as capitalism continued. Another of George's problems, and perhaps the most serious one according to Gronlund, was that he understood America's social dilemma abstractly; he needed to see it as a necessary contradiction in the outworking of history. Recognizing cooperation in a historical way would have allowed Gronlund to accept much of George's position. Though George's plan was incomplete, it nonetheless was, for Gronlund, a step in the right direction. In the end, however, Gronlund was the one willing to compromise. The goal of both the Georgists and socialists, he said, ran parallel to one another: "While we are travelling those paths there is no use for our quarrelling."[92] If the commonwealth, as Gronlund believed, was inevitable, then both reformers would have ended up in the same place. It is true that both pamphlets were largely focused on the details of George's policy, but it is not entirely accurate to say that they ignored Gronlund's historical perspective, including his view of the divine in evolution. Both pamphlets assumed the "Will of the Universe"—the force that would fulfill its teleological purpose regardless of the various efforts to slow it down or stop it altogether. In *Insufficiency,* Gronlund positioned the socialists as "the true co-operators of the Power behind Evolution," offering the only plan that could "forestall the catastrophe and crash that is surely approaching."[93] But this was not a belief stubbornly enforced. Gronlund was open to the leading of the Power behind Evolution. When engaging George's complex question as to whether the ULP should fall in line with German Socialism (and George never clarified what he meant by German Socialism), Gronlund responded that this was "a question no man living can now determine; that is a question for what I call 'the Power behind Evolution' to determine."[94] George was much too dogmatic and stubborn to open himself up to the Will of the Universe.

# CHAPTER FOUR

# RESTORATION OF A BROKEN BOND

## Toward a Sacred Socialism

In 1890, Russian novelist Leo Tolstoy read, "with more than great interest," Gronlund's *Our Destiny: The Influence of Socialism on Morals and Religion.* "I quite conscientiously say that I highly appreciate your book," Tolstoy wrote in a letter to Gronlund, "the ideas espoused in it, and the expression of them."[1] Although a Christian anarchist favorable to Henry George's single tax policy, two positions for which Gronlund was particularly critical (as discussed in previous chapters), the acclaimed author of *War and Peace* and *Anna Karenina* expressed his agreement with one of the central arguments in the book: "That morality must be the basis of progress; and that morality is true only when it is an effort to promote [the] organic unity of society."[2] Unrestrained industrial capitalism created competitive and tragically forlorn individuals, which in turn stalled the evolution of humanity toward a collective state of being—what Tolstoy considered "the Kingdom of God on earth." This collectivist kingdom—where humans would exhibit, Gronlund added, a "developed intelligence," an "irresistible belief in God," and a true love for humanity— rested on a cooperative morality.[3] *Our Destiny* confirmed the author's subtle move away from Spencer's organicism and toward an older philosophical idealism wherein cooperation revealed humanity's identity with the Power behind evolution. Specifically, it was Hegel, according to Joseph Blau, who "struck the keynote" for Gronlund's moral collectivism.[4] Gronlund could not accept evolution without postulating a divine architect to direct it, nor was he able to conceive of a coherent moral theory without that same divine force. Morality was the tie that held the metaphysical and the material together in the process of evolution. In other words, it was not a matter of elevating one over the other—for instance, the force of ideas over productive forces in constituting existence or vice versa. Ethical directives did not descend as pre-arranged rules for humans to follow as traditionalists held. Rather, morality arose out of human cooperation. In this way, cooperation manifested not only the oneness of humanity but also a unifying alliance with the divine.

Gronlund's religious and moral beliefs had always remained the most consistent feature of his philosophy. Recall his reception of socialism after reading the meditations of the very religious Pascal. Whatever may have changed in Gronlund's understanding of the role of intellectuals, strategies regarding labor activism, effectiveness of reformist policies, or political associations he was involved in, his religious perspective seemed only to mature. References to the divine were muted, as one would notice, in the first edition of his *Co-operative Commonwealth* (1884). The only words remotely related to this cosmic director appeared toward the end of the book, when Gronlund wrote of a "great mystery" navigating history. The phrase seemed to be pragmatic: *"some* theory of life is needed to give harmony, purpose and vigor to active life."[5] Irish playwright George Bernard Shaw, who edited the 1884 version of *Commonwealth* for a London publisher, added "will of the universe" (not capitalized) and changed "Great Mystery" to "supreme will" (again, not capitalized) and, elsewhere, "Providence."[6] Gronlund approved and used the terms "God," "Power behind Evolution," and "Will of the Universe" in subsequent editions of *Commonwealth.* This made his "Supreme Will" less of a justifying theory and more a concrete existing being. Soon after the release of *Commonwealth* and during his time in Europe, Gronlund, in a more formal manner, introduced his views regarding the divine—and thus the religious implications of his socialism—at a reform society lecture in Edinburgh.[7] In *Ça Ira,* he made reference to Thomas Carlyle's vague concept of a supreme power (an "Eternal Silence") guiding human history. Carlyle's "Eternal Silence," for Gronlund, had little connection to a distinct willful entity and was far from a direct aid to humanity.[8] By the time he wrote *Our Destiny,* however, Gronlund was committed to the divine as an integral agent cooperating with humanity in the unfolding of history.

Gronlund's initial motivation for writing *Our Destiny,* however, was to respond to the criticism that socialism was inherently opposed to religion. Such a conclusion is understandable after a cursory reading of Karl Marx's reference to religion as an opiate. First, religion was a "protest against real suffering," Marx claimed, "the sigh of the oppressed class, the heart of a heartless world, and the soul of soulless conditions."[9] Second, it was a panacea that numbed the pain of modern life, the only salve workers had against the brutality of industrial capitalism. As that which provided a psychological escape into a metaphysical realm where toil and exploitation would be imagined away, religion allowed members of society, especially those among the working classes, to endure hardships caused by capitalism. Marx, an atheist, did not concern himself with the doctrinal content of religion. From the earliest days of his intellectual career, he rejected the whole "pack of gods," but doing so not from any deep philosophical reflection.[10] Technically, however, his comment was not a disparagement of religion, for indeed religion can provide solace in difficult times. If we were to press the analogy, however, we should say that while an opiate provides temporary relief, it also takes a good portion of our life away. Understood solely as a means of comfort and not of action, this kind of religion fails to confront the realities of capitalist power (or any power for that matter).[11] But what if the central tenet of faith—namely, God—worked with laborers to break their chains, to reclaim their humanity and dignity, to restore an intimate fellowship (unity) between humanity and the divine? This, of course, was Gronlund's objective.

But more to Marx's intent, such a soporific faith was something created and used as a means of oppression by those in power. Bourgeois businessmen and their sycophantic disciples, including religious leaders, have been able to manipulate the minds of citizens to serve the interests of capital. "The theology of evangelical laissez-faire," according to historian Eugene McCarraher, "remained vibrant among businesspeople and their apologists" in postbellum America.[12] "The abolition of religion," Marx argued, "as the *illusory* happiness of the people is the demand for their *real* happiness."[13] The "robber barons" of the Gilded Age used such a position to their advantage. Capitalist leaders and those loyal to them incessantly decried the anti-religious sentiments and the penchant for horrific violence among socialists, strengthening thereby capitalism's association with doctrinal orthodoxy. Anti-capitalists, whether reformers or radicals, threatened God's providential (in truth, "bourgeois") order.[14] But it should be made clear that the immersion of the "let alone system" into the baptismal waters of evangelicalism has never been natural nor inevitable. Nothing *a priori* in the essence of capitalism requires or suggests an amicable relationship with religion, though one could say that greed can be pursued "religiously." That is, one could be a "good" capitalist without religion. The real question, however, is whether the so-called "good" capitalist, the one consistently motivated by profit and engaged in the labor exploitation endemic to the system itself, can be a "good" (i.e., faithful) religious adherent, especially if that religion prioritizes a love of God and neighbor. At any rate, plenty of capitalists since the late nineteenth century have availed themselves of a variety of disciplinary tools—rhetorical propaganda and the power of the state—to canonize their economic ideology.

From the Gilded Age to today, there has been an underlying assumption among the champions of capitalism, especially the religiously devout, that speaking against capitalism is indicative of godless heresy. But this belies cogent reasoning. *Our Destiny* challenged the idea that atheism was *"an integral part of Socialism."*[15] Turning Marx's hackneyed phrase on its head, Gronlund suggested that a rejection of religion among atheistic socialists—and there were, of course, plenty—was the "cry of an outraged conscience" dismayed by how religion became the slave of capital.[16] Such frustration, although understandable, was no reason to abandon religion altogether. Not all socialists were hostile to religion—a truth that the supporters of capitalism, especially among evangelicals, have been loath to admit. Many found common ground with religion, especially Christianity. Fourierist "Associationists," according to Carl Guarneri, rejected the idea that Christianity and socialism were "inevitable antagonists"; they were, in fact, "indispensable allies."[17] Methodist minister, socialist, and settlement house advocate John Spargo, author of a handful of works dealing with religion and socialism, including *Marxian Socialism and Religion* (1915), believed that there was "no reason to consider socialism hostile to religion in general or Christianity in particular."[18] Charles Fanani was much bolder: "Socialism *is* Christianity; and Christianity *is* Socialism."[19] Socialism for J. Stitt Wilson represented "applied Christianity."[20] Gronlund's colleague W. D. P. Bliss proposed that "the aim of Socialism is embraced in the aim of Christianity."[21] Throughout the pages of the Old and New Testament, God himself confronted the greed and arrogance of the wealthy—time and again warning of imminent judgment against those who neglected or directly antagonized the poor. New Testament Christianity offered a message of selflessness, a love for God and neighbor over neighbor-hating competitive individualism; it was a religion that revolved around the sacrifice of self, taking the life of Jesus as the example, for the purpose of ministering to the marginalized, the forgotten, and the economically exploited. Christian socialists took seriously the reality of ushering in God's kingdom on earth as it existed in heaven through acts of love and mercy to the marginalized. A pure religion was one that addressed the spiritual and physical needs of widows and orphans, the lowliest of the lowly, and by implication, supported by numerous other passages in the Old and New Testaments, all those cheated and exploited by their plutocratic overlords.[22]

Gronlund's theology, far from traditional Protestantism, had more of a philosophical quality to it—a quality undoubtedly shaped by different strands of idealism in America. Despite the growing popularity and intellectual formidability of Spencer and Darwin in the late nineteenth-century, idealism continued to cling to the American mind. In 1895, Berkeley philosopher George Holmes Howison articulated the limits of evolution by stressing the country's pre-eminent commitment to reality as essentially mind. Howison defined idealism as an "explanation of the world which maintains that the only thing absolutely real is mind; that all material and all temporal existences take their being from mind."[23] Although there was hardly a consensus regarding idealism, it could not be ignored—appealed to often, says Bruce Kuklick, "only to be disparaged."[24] Among the variations of idealism, none seemed more formidable in Europe or America than Hegel's.[25] And the great German thinker had plenty of followers in the United States. He was, in Walt Whitman's estimation, "fit for America"—particularly the nation's ongoing democratic development.[26] Hegel himself viewed the United States as the "land of the future, where, in the ages that lie before us, the burden of the World's History shall reveal itself."[27] Intellectuals in New England, Pennsylvania, Ohio, California, and, of course, St. Louis mined the major works of Europe's greatest systems-builder, stretching him along the political spectrum so as to justify competing visions of the nation's destiny.[28] A few among the Ohio Hegelians swung closer to a progressive left than their more right-leaning colleagues in St. Louis, who begrudgingly and condescendingly agreed to incorporate workers into their ranks upon condition of their becoming "properly philosophic."[29] Hegel was often used by progressive reformers to fight against slavery and justify advocacy for the rights of labor. Prussian-born military professional, communist, and "forty-eighter" August Willich, who migrated to the U.S. in 1851 and later became a general in the Union Army during the

Civil War, abandoned neither his socialist concern for workers, including the rights of slaves, nor the Hegelianism that underwrote it, though he did break with Marx in a rather acrimonious manner.[30] Hegelians like Willich, Peter Kauffman, and Burnette Haskell were attracted to the cooperative efforts of utopian communities in the spirit of the Fourierists, the Saint Simonians, and the Owenites, each inspired to build communities in the northwest and far west.[31]

Caught up in this intellectual current, Gronlund's evolutionary idealism was tipping increasingly toward Hegel as he entered the 1890s.[32] For one, he believed that a "new wave of thought" turning against Spencer was on the rise in America. Spencer's popularity was, he continued, "evidently declining" at the close of the century.[33] This may have been Gronlund's own opinion, for he provided no evidence to support such a turn. If it was solely his opinion, it was an odd one, since he praised the evolution that "English scientists have installed on the throne of the human mind," identifying it as "the greatest intellectual revolutionary achievement since Copernicus."[34] Furthermore, he had early on affirmed Spencer's organicism as laying the foundation for socialism.[35] Yet it was hardly a decade after the publication of *Commonwealth* that Gronlund came to recognize the "curious contradiction" inherent to Spencer's organicism—again, an organicism that had initially informed his socialism. This became clear to him after a critical reexamination of Spencer's concept of the individual and the state[36] The ultimate truth, that which was "real," for Spencer, was the disconnected individual, who stood above the artificiality of the state. The state was nothing more than an accumulated "crowd of monads"—a phrase Gronlund used often. This would have made organicism unnecessary; that is, both society and state seemed to terminate in the collected (not collective) crowd, so to speak, since, from a dialectical method, no clue to an opening toward cooperation could be induced. Spencer's social philosophy would "evidently end in Anarchism," not organicism.[37]

For this reason, Gronlund would not have been cast among the handful of British and American idealists who attempted to reconcile Hegel with the "evolutionary doctrine" of Darwin and Spencer.[38] British Emergentist Samuel Alexander noted "how great the likeness" was between evolution and Hegel's idealism: "Hegel's philosophy is in fact an evolution, called by the name of dialectic, which is the counterpart in philosophy of what evolution is in science."[39] Scottish philosopher David George Ritchie, once president of the

Aristotelian Society in London, focused his intellectual energy on "Hegelian-izing natural selection."[40] Postbellum American thinkers, Kuklick has argued, linked "evolutionary ideas—Darwinism—into an idealistic, quasi-Hegelian religious framework."[41] It seems as though variations on Hegel were favorable to those straddling modern evolutionary science and traditional religious belief. America's Charles Saunders Peirce admitted that his own formulation of pragmatism—what he designated as "pragmaticism"—was "closely allied to Hegelian absolute idealism." Another influential American thinker John Dewey affirmed his "special attraction" to Hegel in his early career.[42] And both thinkers were likewise proponents of evolution.

Incorporating Hegel's philosophical understanding of history into discussions regarding both biological and economic developments was not a matter of turning the old man on his head, but rather of placing his feet firmly on the ground. On the biological plane, both the human subject and the external environment mutually constituted one another in the process of becoming. British physiologist John Scott Haldane would later write in the early twentieth century that an "organism is determined by its own influencing acting through its surroundings. The surroundings in acting on the organism are therefore at the same acted on by it. The organism is thus no more determined by the surroundings that it at the same time determines them. The two stand to one another, not in the relation of cause and effect, but in that of reciprocity."[43] In *Moral Order and Progress,* Alexander made a similar claim when he wrote that "adaptation can only be understood as a joint action of the individual and his environment." Both the individual and the environment were interdependent: "the act of adaptation is thus not a mere one-sided modification, but a process of selection from both sides."[44] And this was more than just a Mind-Spirit dialectic. Such dynamism included cooperation in the material world. A few American socialists followed Hegel in positing the existence of an "Absolute Idea" as the agent behind historical development, yet they challenged the notion that the "Absolute" worked independently from the "forces of production."[45] The Absolute manifested itself within socioeconomic cooperative relations. For Gronlund, humanity would evolve toward full consciousness and, consequently, absorption into the divine through productive cooperation.[46] The interdependence of the human community would end in the "restoration of a broken bond," the bond between humans and the divine, which the morality of competitive individualism—that "satanic element of our nature"—had shattered. The divine did not live above humanity, but within it—particularly within cooperative production. Divorcing humanity from the Will of the Universe, a form of competition, was both anti-human and anti-divine. The kind of socialistic religion proposed by Gronlund would "make holiness consist of identifying ourselves with Humanity—the redeemed form of man—as the lover merges himself in the beloved."[47]

The contingent and, thus, mutually constituting nature of all life tied all things together. Scottish Hegelian Edward Caird argued for a fundamental unity between subject and environment, between being and nothing. It was "not a struggle," he argued, "between two independent and unrelated forces, but the evolution by antagonism of one spiritual principle. It is, on this view, the same life which within us is striving for development, and which without us conditions that development."[48] Combining philosophical idealism with evolutionary naturalism, however, left open the question not only of meaning and purpose in evolution but also whether there existed an animating agent behind it. Suspending judgment about a personal architect of evolution had the potential of leading one toward agnosticism, historicism, or, even worse, atheism, which Hegelians could not digest. Hegelians posited the end of history as the full realization (and liberation) of the Absolute—of God. And if this was the case, then God (the Absolute) was the first and continual cause of becoming. This may have satisfied some, but it presented a serious difficulty for those coming from a naturalistic or materialistic perspective. The "Power which the Universe manifests to us," Spencer wrote in *First Principles*, "is utterly inscrutable."[49] Though he may have granted the reality of a metaphysical force directing the course of events, Spencer was skeptical as to whether this force could be known. This ontological challenge—if one takes it as such—had been intensified by Immanuel Kant's distinction between what could be known by way of appearances (*phenomena*) and what could be known of things in themselves (*noumena*). American philosopher and Unitarian minister Francis Ellingwood Abbot identified this Kantian problem as *the* fundamental dilemma "at the bottom of all other issues of modern thought."[50] The wall separating *noumena* and *phenomena* seemed to grow even higher with the coming of Darwin and Spencer, whose work, according to David Watson, led to a denial of "transcendental properties of mind" and the reduction of "human relations, both interpersonal and between the species and the environment, to mechanical relativity."[51] Some, like Spencer, never crossed the *noumenal* Rubicon: knowledge remained on the phenomenal side of the Kantian divide. The one thing that the scientist could know for certain, Spencer argued in *First Principles,* was that knowledge of the "Actuality lying behind Appearances" was, in fact, unknowable.[52] While admitting the insurmountable difficulty of completely abandoning a belief in the absolute, "a positive and indestructible element of thought," Spencer argued that it was not possible "to give this consciousness any qualitative or quantitative expression whatever."[53] The different names that thinkers gave to this force was symptomatic of its unknowability. As Gronlund observed, Spencer called it the "Unknowable," atheists, the "Laws of Life," and theists, "God." Not even Gronlund provided a precise definition of this absolute being, though he was open to interchanging "Power behind evolution" with "God." Yet whatever its name, it was an unavoidable reality.[54]

Because Spencer's "whole philosophy," according to Walter Muelder and Laurence Sears, was "sense-bound," it seemed easy for critics to attack him for threatening metaphysics.[55] But to be fair, the notion of a self-existing Being as the force behind evolution was not, for Spencer, a matter of "probability" or "credibility," but rather of "conceivability."[56] Spencer's "Unknowable" did not require, in a strictly logical sense, a complete break with God, challenging thereby the argument offered by Princeton Theological Seminary's Charles Hodge that the theory of evolution—and Hodge included Spencer in his critique—was "tantamount to Atheism."[57] Elaboration on this point required a kind of Kantian negative theology. Kant sought to liberate God from the suffocating restrictions of empiricism á la David Hume: one could not dismiss that which was non-sensory (e.g., causation, time, space, morality, and God) because of its failure to comply with the methods of sensory perception. Hume's error rested on confusing categories. Empiricism restricted itself to that which could be perceived by the senses (i.e., phenomena). God was not something that could be sensorially perceived as other objects in human experience could be. He was, in what one might consider a normal experiential sense, "non-sensory," but this did not make him epistemologically nonsensical. What is more, God could not be confined to the limits of the human mind. For someone to say that they "knew" God would be to deny his radical freedom. Likewise, if God was infinite and infinitely free of his own volition, then it would be foolish for finite humans, however intellectually astute, to subject God to the narrow boundaries of the individual's mental faculties or the tighter restrictions of language. The human mind, in a sense, had to let go of God. God had to remain open; in a negative sense, this meant that he could not be fully known. One could certainly know that a supreme being existed, like claiming to have a concept of infinity, but they could not—again, like infinity—measure it out completely. This was not a problem for some. There were American thinkers who reconciled Spencer with religious belief by directly embracing the unknowability of whatever was behind evolution, going so far as to suggest that this was the proper attitude one needed in accepting the reality of the divine. In his effort to harmonize religion and science in *Outlines of Cosmic Philosophy,* John Fiske, for instance, who voraciously devoured Spencer's early writings, was one such thinker. For Fiske, Spencer had greater integrity in accepting the limitations of human thought than traditional creedal dogmatists. Not even conservative Christian leaders, at the end of their long theological meditations, could deny that the identity of God—his essence and persons—could be known absolutely. The idea that the "Deity *per se,*" according to Fiske, could not be epistemologically exhausted was not a "truth which originated with [Spencer]: "all the Christian theologians that have lived . . . also regarded [the] Deity *per se* as unknowable, being revealed to mankind only through [the] incarnation in Christ."[58]

The solidarity of humanity with the divine in the process of cooperative self-realization required overcoming the *noumenal-phenomenal* divide. Solving this dilemma, in a way, gave birth to Hegel's dialectical logic. The "divorce between thought and thing," according to Hegel, ran counter to the "conviction of all previous ages, that their agreement was a matter of course."[59] What cannot be known (*noumenon*) cannot be separated from the "be" in the sentence "What can or cannot *be* known"—hence being/knowing. Thus, that which we might consider *noumenal is* being. In asking the question, "Who am I," from a Hegelian perspective, humans are confronted with the "nothing" or the "negation" of their own existence—what they *are not.* And for the idealist, these are connected to being. Indeed, the essence of the phenomenal "I" is noumenal; thus, there is a knowing and not knowing concurrently when considering the "I." Both of which are united in being. The same occurs when asking, "Who is God?" God himself is confronted with his own negation. This "nothing," as Hegel argues in his *Science of Logic,* is not that which simply accompanies "being": it *is* being itself. "*Pure being* and *pure nothing*," he wrote, "are the same": "Nothing, taken in its immediacy, shows itself as affirmative, as *being;* for according to its nature it is the same as being. Nothing is thought of, imagined, spoken of, and therefore it *is;* in the thinking, imagining, speaking and so on, nothing has its being."[60] Being and nothing are identical, and this initiates the process of coming to know: the emergence of a new being/nothing. Not only does the same apply to that which is beyond individual things (i.e., anything collective), but also that which is finite and infinite. The inquiry into humanity is similar to the inquiry concerning God. That is, the question, "What is humanity," is, like the problem of God, an immediate awareness of humanity's negation. So, for instance, in traditional Christian orthodoxy, humanity is distinct from God. Humans are *not* God, which is to recognize the prime negation of humanity. Using Hegel's logic, however, if humanity is the negation of God (i.e., *not* God), then they are, at the same time, God—the positive being of God. In truth, therefore, humans are, to use the words of Ralph Waldo Emerson, "part and particle" of God. By the same logic, if God is *not* humanity, remembering that *being* and *nothing* are one and the same, then God is also humanity. The existence of finite things is, Hegel said elsewhere, "founded not in themselves but in the universal divine idea."[61] The identity of being and nothing of both God and humanity, indeed of all existence, is tied together in dialectical becoming—that is, in evolution—overcoming the negations that they encounter in coming to full consciousness.[62]

Taking this into account, it is difficult to deny what appears strikingly Hegelian in Gronlund's *Our Destiny.*[63] Humanity would grow into the realization of the self and the divine by engaging the conditions of existence, which began with knowing the other. When addressing the issue of an individual's *telos* or ultimate purpose, therefore, the attraction to a collectivist philosophy seemed quite strong. The maturing "self" demanded the cultivation of the well-being of "others." An individual could not "aim at one's own true well-being," Gronlund wrote, "without aiming at that of others."[64] "These others," he continued, "are not mere means to myself, but are involved in my essence."[65] That which is *not* is the essence of self. Man's natural relationship to himself compels him toward others: "only in unity with one's fellows does the individual ego realize its being."[66] The self grew into its negation by working with the other. The individual likewise gained a meaningful sense of self by cultivating his natural environment—yet another negation that went into a positive and higher state of being. What he accomplished vis-à-vis producing his material world was what he incorporated into to his own identity. In this way, self-meaning was fundamentally social and tied to labor. And the accumulation of humans into this fuller consciousness represented the evolutionary process of humanity participating in the Power behind evolution. Humanity cooperated with the divine; such cooperation represented humanity's advancement through history into the fullness of the divine. Eventually, Gronlund believed, American cooperative socialism would give a "profound conviction of the presence of God in Humanity."[67] Hegel argued that self-consciousness "achieves its satisfaction only in another self-consciousness," which is concurrently the process of coming to know the Absolute. God's "self-knowledge of himself," Hegel wrote, is "his self-consciousness in men, it is man's knowledge *of* God that goes on to become the self-knowledge of man *in* God."[68]

The social nature of being and the cooperation between the human and the divine, as stated above, were foundational to Gronlund's morality. If the divine appeared through social cooperation, then how individuals treated one another, morality on a practical level, would become the primary concern in the development of humanity. "Morality," as he defined it in *Our Destiny*, "is the conscious and voluntary co-operation of men towards the *brotherhood and fellowship of man*": "To be 'moral' can thus be said to be synonymous with being' in its profound sense."[69] This made "being" a matter of moral action toward others. Sadly, however, plutocratic elites and their supporters, including religious leaders, imposed a morality contrary to the Will of the Universe. Some late-nineteenth-century Americans exhibited a moral ethos shaped by Protestant individualism that identified competition as an immutable law of nature. For Gronlund, this was nothing more than a hellish reality of "penal servitude." The end of competition, "an ultimate, instead of a mediate end," meant the sacrificing of "human beings to capital." The pursuit of profit was the highest virtue, "the chief and only incentive" in American society. Under capitalism, workers were compelled to abandon their empathy for others and adopt an ethic that centered on the cash value of an individual's work. But humans by nature were drawn together by an "innate social sentiment." The ethics of individualism severed the bonds of humanity and thus shattered the source of human flourishing. Even America's "conventional morality"—"purity, temperance, and honor"—seemed much too focused on the self, though Gronlund did not completely reject such virtues (more on this below). The problem was that such bourgeois virtue ignored the importance of the other. True self-reform, for Gronlund, required cultivating the well-being of one's neighbor. Repudiating laissez-faire "planlessness," what society currently suffered from, and organizing "a system," which included associations of "complementary trades," was needed for the moral health of American society.[70]

Gronlund's moral idealism in *Our Destiny*, however, raises a problem in relation to his earlier work. He made the case in *Commonwealth* that "morals and religion" are "gradually built up" from the economic base, "the foundation of every social system."[71] Yet he consistently rejected a purely "materialistic morality," a morality derived *solely* as a response to the social difficulties arising from industrialization. In his history of the French Revolution, *Ça Ira*, written a few years before *Our Destiny*, Gronlund wrote that historical movements were "always under the empire of ideas, consciously or unconsciously." Strong ideas cultivated "a ferment in the minds of the people" and compelled action.[72] In this sense, ideas seemed to be supreme. How does one account for this apparent dilemma? Did Gronlund change his mind in the short time from *Commonwealth* and *Ça Ira* to *Our Destiny*? This does not seem likely. One might deny that this is a serious problem for Gronlund. Material conditions and the relationships that they created would eventually break down, laborers would become conscious of such decline, and act quickly to formulate strategies for a new material existence. This would, of course, necessitate new ideas—innovative ideas derived from a pre-theoretical faith in what could be. Ideas, then, would become concrete as individuals tested and worked out that which they imagined in faith.[73] Another approach would be to consider the supremacy of the divine in directing material and ideological relations, which then would resolve the issue by reducing it to chronology (i.e., the order of development). It is important to remember the place of the divine in Gronlund's historical perspective. It might be easy to assume that human evolution began with the actions of the divine—a kind of prime mover, an uncaused causal agent. But Gronlund avoided any discussion of a theogony; he simply assumed the cooperation of the divine and human in evolution. The Will of the Universe used human relations at the economic level to cultivate ideas that would help build up cooperative consciousness—material to ideas, ideas back to material. The "germ of morality," Gronlund wrote, came somewhere "from on high," yet it was never divorced from the material conditions of humanity.[74] Morality was *immanent,* horizontal rather than vertical, expressing itself within the dialectic of labor production and mutual aid. It was not a premade morality that simply dropped down from heaven nor was it a delusional ideology created out of thin air to cope with the challenges of material existence. Morality evolved from within, Gronlund argued, "man's social, and especially, industrial relations, each stage developing morality up to a certain point."[75] Moreover, the ideas that advanced the commonwealth were also God's thoughts. Ideas were not merely corresponding descriptions of existence. Cooperative labor was humanity thinking as the divine: the evolving consciousness of humanity as the evolving conscious of the Power behind evolution.

In the later portions of *Our Destiny,* Gronlund addressed a few of the false assumptions about the morality of socialism. The first had to do with the loss of the individual in a collectivist society. A socialist commonwealth, his critics charged, would create an authoritarian state and "crush out all individuality."[76] This so-called "loss," for Gronlund, was misleading, since no such thing existed to be lost in the first place. The growth in human consciousness and, thus, the knowledge of God came through social institutions—institutions formed through social cooperation. The first social "force that binds us together," Gronlund wrote, began with the family. This was, for Hegel, an undifferentiated unity; that is, the members of the family were drawn together by mutual love and support for each member. Through the family, an individual would enter society, which itself was made up of multiple families. Yet society, given its "differentiated disunity," was where individualism emerged, especially in its economic relations. Of course, society, a conglomerate of individuals, also contributed to the individual's identity, though in a contradictory manner. Finally, there was the "differentiated unity" of the State, where both the pure homogeneity of the family and the heteronomy of society were subsumed, preserving thereby the many (individuality) with the one (the organism of the State). The State represented the highest form of individual and social development. The material form of the State came in the country or nation. "One's country," Gronlund continued, was "the practical force, where primary authority resides."[77]

Thus, it was impossible to speak of single individuals; every individual originated from and subsequently developed within a tripartite social order. Sadly, however, capitalism, by its own nature, eviscerated these social bonds—bonds necessary for human moral and religious evolution. This was experienced most acutely in the lives of workers. Working class men and women, especially husbands and wives, toiled away as isolated individuals in the factories or on commercial farms, spending the majority of their lives away from each other. The system forced young people into loveless marriages, where two people established a conjugal relationship not because of affection for one another but for the purposes of combining wages to survive. Neither husband nor wife could "make both ends meet without the wages of their children."[78] Neither children nor their parents had any freedom to live life as they chose. Indeed, parents were forced to defy state laws (for example, a law in Massachusetts that Gronlund references) that required a minimal education for children—an education that complied with the dictates of the market. Children were "robbed of the years during which character is formed."[79] Unable to maintain the cohesive meaningfulness of social bonds, society would break down—from the State, to society, the family, and finally, the individual. Civilization would be ultimately destroyed as a result, as would the identity of God within human consciousness.[80]

It was capitalism that alienated individuals and set them against one another. Gronlund blamed this on Spencer. Despite the claim that Americans were turning their backs on Spencer, many continued to hold tenaciously to his competitive individualism.[81] In this way, Gronlund was swimming against a portion of American culture that made Spencer so attractive—the appeal of "self-reliance and self-improvement."[82] The survival of the dominant species may have reflected the biological world, the savagery of the animal kingdom, Gronlund admitted, but it had no place in the civilizing efforts of humans. Such a "satanic" scheme, to use Gronlund's signifier, was "anti-social and in the highest degree wasteful."[83] Associating competitive individualism with the survival of the fittest was damaging to the moral health of the country. Society had lost that which was dear to past civilizations—namely, the "conviction of our belonging together, the sense of man's organic unity, of the solidarity of man . . . devotion to the commonwealth . . . the vital principle of [classical] polity."[84] Spencer was, he concluded, "wholly incapable" of understanding such a loss. The fullness of being came through the cultivation of "collective well-being." All "personal morality," he said, would become "a servant of social morality."[85]

Most tragic of all—not to mention ironic given their opposition to Spencerianism—was the fact that conservative religious leaders were the main propagators of this competitive social struggle. The only function of these "unfaithful ministers," as Gronlund labeled them, was to "drug the world's conscience."[86] The dominant morality espoused by church leaders served to disrupt social harmony, constituting America's "greatest misfortune" when it came to true morality. If Jesus himself had come to visit America's plutocratic elites, Gronlund imagined, he "would flog every one of them out of the temple."[87] Anticipating the language of the Social Gospel, Gronlund portrayed Christ as a radical who "would not content himself with denouncing sin as merely spiritual evil; he would go into its economic causes, and destroy the flower by cutting at the roots—poverty and ignorance."[88] The very core of Christianity had become rotten and required fundamental change. Religious leaders mirrored a "survival of the fittest" ethic and fused it with the Christian doctrine of providence, extolling the sacredness of individual struggle. The Bible could be used to argue that competitive selfishness was a natural reality after Adam and Eve's fall in the garden, regardless of what this same Bible said about exploitation, the oppression of the poor, the evils of mammon, and the mandate to protect the image of God in all humanity. Individualism mixed with the doctrine of providence reflected, Gronlund wrote, the "trait of the present narrow-minded ruling classes, the 'bourgeoisie.'"[89] The attempt to idolize the bourgeoisie and compel all members of society to conform to this cultural class, punishing them in various ways if they failed to do so, was contrary to the nature of reality and only intensified the divisions among citizens. Confusing the dominance of wealth with how the world should be was a great detriment to morality and, thus, humanity. Indeed, if individuals were, by nature, forced to compete endlessly against others for the end goal of accumulating wealth, there would be no need for morality. Eliminating the lives of others would also destroy human life.

This did not mean that Gronlund rejected the many (individuals) for the one (the collective). He returned to an earlier distinction he had made between "individuality" and "individualism." Individuality referred to the ways in which each citizen, as part of a distinct laboring body, employed his or her talents to become a contributing member of society. This reflected Gronlund's commitment to America's republican tradition, contradicted by the dominant economic ethos of the late nineteenth century. "While I detest individualism," Gronlund admitted, "I hold Individuality—that is, the sum of all the qualities which differentiate me from others—most sacred. It is not what entitles us to the divine regard, but it is that *which enables us to serve our country and humanity,* and to wipe it out would, indeed, be a calamity, greater even to society than to ourselves."[90] Far from losing their unique self, individuals would preserve their identity by cooperating to benefit the whole. Individuality would appear when citizens worked to preserve the life of others. Empathy and love were the primary motivators in this regard. If citizens battled to destroy the life of their neighbors, they would threaten their own, since humans needed others for self-realization. Apart from society, the individual was an illusion: "The 'social self' accounts for our personality; it accounts for conscience as being the object mind, self-conscious in the individual, the voice of the whole in the breast of each citizen, the utterance of the public spirit of the race in each social self." Instead of seeking the removal of others, which would logically lead to the nullification of the self, citizens needed to rely on their natural tendency toward sympathy and love, Gronlund advised, "the very reverse of the struggle for existence." Love was the kernel of morality, displaying itself in an attitude of sympathy: "without sympathy there is absolutely no morality, and by itself sympathy may almost be said to constitute morality." As the "alpha and omega of morality—its commencement and its end," sympathy would come only as humans conjured "vivid mental representations" of the "suffering of others." Caring for the plight of others would not only draw out an individual's essential humanity, but it would also draw humanity together. Sympathy, which revolved around appreciating the "purposes of others," contradicted struggle.[91]

Critics also feared that a socialist collective would expand the size of the government. Gronlund intimated that the size of government was not an *a priori* detriment to society. This was coupled with the claim that the commonwealth would not be able "to exist without government." But the size of the government was nothing in comparison to those who held the real power in America: wealthy elites. Was America committed to a government dedicated to the "public authority," governance derived from the will of the governed, or to private interest (i.e., corporate capitalism)? This is where "more" or "less" vis-à-vis the government came into the equation. Capitalists favored private authority to preserve their own self-interest, doing so at the expense of communities. The government existed *by* and *for* all the people; it was not something that could be owned by corporate elites. The public, Gronlund argued, recognized the state not as a force of restraint but of efficient admin- istration, for citizens understood the need for "a guide, a director, a regulator." This "reversed conception," differing from self-interest of private authority, represented, Gronlund said, "true democracy." Capitalists who pushed for a less intrusive state did so based on the belief that the best way for the "average businessmen" to make a profit was to be left alone—hence, once again, the need for small government. Gronlund questioned whether wealth could be generated apart *from* the public. The corporate individualist, the chief de- fender of privatization, failed to see that he could not extirpate himself from society; using the rhetoric of privacy would not hide his widespread influence on and responsibilities toward society, especially in the way that he employed citizens and tugged at the levers of government. "Have I not the right to do what I please with my own?" the capitalist gambler asked. "My own what?" Gronlund responded. That is, what was it that the capitalist owned to freely use? That which he owned was a creation of labor. Thus, workers, those who produced "things owned," were the true proprietors. Such plutocratic thieves wanted the public to believe that they were the ones who created.[92]

Although supportive of a larger, more efficient social administration, Gronlund was mindful of the dangers of an overextended government. What he meant by an expansion of governing authority was essentially greater de- mocracy. One way for citizens to reduce the size of government—to make it more local and hence democratic—was through democratic trade unionism. Gronlund anticipated that the "future Social Order" would be established by such "corporate bodies," whereby every citizen would play an integrally "collective bearing" on the whole. This, too, echoed, writes political philos- opher Charles Taylor, "Hegel's insistence that men [should] not enter the political arena directly, but through their associations, corporations, etc., in a more organic fashion."[93] Such unions stood as the best means to effectively move the country toward democracy. Leaders were chosen by workers and accountable to them. Trade union members would elect their own admin- istrators, in Gronlund's words, "from below,"—those competent enough to choose their "immediate foremen."[94] These institutions would direct their own affairs, "each group to decide with authority on all matters, especially concerning their own interests." In a sense, Gronlund seemed to favor a kind of institutional pluralism, whereby businesses, schools, educational institutions, and religious organizations would be responsible to contribute to the betterment of society as each saw fit. Democratic accountability was the key to greater cooperation and thus "a true *Civitas Dei.*"[95]

Another concern was that socialism would unfairly distribute goods to everyone regardless of individual effort. But this confused socialism with communism. The cooperative nature of human production—production that moved toward absolute freedom by the Will of the cosmos—would not require the equal distribution of material goods. Communism allocated goods to members of society with no concern for those who created the goods or who should be compensated for their work. For Gronlund, laborers should have the sovereignty over the products of their making. Non-producing capitalists were the ones who stole products from labor and distributed them as they pleased. Communism was, he went on to say, as alienating as capitalism, for it removed the human laborer from his or her own product. Contrary to communism, Gronlund's collectivism rested on the equality of conditions. Equitable social and economic circumstances meant something different, he argued, "from the suggestion that all citizens should receive equal remuneration." Equality in this sense would be "social rather than economic": "*all citizens will be independent of each other,* but all equality dependent on the commonwealth." The economic conditions of the commonwealth were created by the individuals who made up the social order; the moral wrong, then, rested on not having proprietary rights over the apparatuses of production. This economic equality would be preserved by a new kind of political equality: "the co-ordination of equal corporate bodies," which would be "secured by having all useful citizens gathered intro trade-unions . . . all, however, distinctly unlike, ranking as equals, on account of the equally essential services which each renders." The kind of equality in which each person participated in the governance of their union will have no need for "standing parties, or rather factions, hence no 'bosses.'"[96]

In the end, however, critics never tired of pushing the argument that socialism was immoral by design. Once again, Gronlund turned this on capitalism itself. Moral anarchism (that is to say, anti-morality) was more the result of capitalism than socialism. For one, capitalism did not derive from a benevolent concern for the wellbeing of humanity; it was motivated by the laws of the jungle and focused solely on profit, which set humans against one another with no affiliations, allegiances, obedience, or higher morality outside the individual person. Gronlund believed that this was the epitome of "amorality." The selfish individual was driven by his or her own interests. There was no need for capitalists to abide by a higher law (or any law)? The only appeal to morality—an empty morality—came when their profits sunk for whatever reason. And the idea that socialism would dismantle all forms of authority was to conflate it with anarchism: "Anarchism wants to abolish and discredit authority. Socialism, on the contrary, exalts it." The "germ of morals," which unfolded naturally, was obedience, a fundamental attribute of human nature: "Man is truly made to obey, and to feel remorse if he does not obey."[97] If humans were by nature interdependent, there had to be a higher authority to which humans would submit. Morality came from the collective; the collective, in turn, submitted to an even higher authority: "the order of the world, the Universal Order." The cosmic Will was the source of morality and "the natural foundation for Socialism." This "Supreme will," he wrote, represented "providence for humanity" and entered "into vital relations with the individual only through humanity as mediator," commanding interdependence and obedience "for there is no other thing we can do." Gronlund was confident that his theory would overturn "a barbarous and crude conception" of God and his world. A spark of divinity, located in the moments of creative genius that made humans human, was, at the same time, a taste of the divine itself. The accumulation of these divine flashes, as more and more humans forged a greater humanity through collective activity, would eventually provide a "bird's-eye view" of the "superior power" guiding history, which would then lead to a collective comprehension of the divine.[98]

The idea that a divine agent guided the course of events might have suggested a determinism whereby humans would take a passive role in evolution. But if both the divine and humanity were part of the same process of becoming, then both, by nature, actively cooperated with one another. Cooperation was the law of reality—physical and metaphysical; materially and ideally; earthly and heavenly. Humanity would not simply sit back while events unfolded: "We cannot, as Spencer seems to want to have it, fold our hands and await events." God, Gronlund continued, "needs our co-operation." We are compelled to cooperate with the divine. On this point, Gronlund made a distinction between unconscious evolution (what he called natural evolution) and conscious evolution. The former moved humans along the course of evolution's *longue durée*. Humans would eventually reach a point of waking up;

they would see the hand of the divine in history. But such a decisive historical moment would not come until hunger ceased and leisure was attained. If individuals attempted to counter the inevitable, life would be one of consistent toil and degradation, but only for a time. Evolution would eventually defeat the immorality of the capitalist ethos; it would move society toward higher stages of human consciousness and thus toward a fuller realization of the divine. All that "religious people" needed to do was help build "the universal human instinct" and become aware of how God revealed himself in the evolution of humanity. Cooperating in the unfolding of history was a matter of *"acting God's thoughts"*: "It is self-expanding morality, love and sympathy, that will make man 'in action like an angel, in comprehension like God.'" The moral achievement, ushered in by socialism, "as a tree bears blossoms of fruit," was the "necessarily evolving belief in God and immortality." It was *"through human history,"* and especially the period of the late nineteenth century, the transition from capitalism to socialism, that the "revelation from God," according to Gronlund, would come. To deny the existence of God would be to deny the destiny of humanity: "the history of man will appear like a whole divine drama unrolling before the very eyes of humanity."[99]

A crucial element in humanity's cooperation with the divine came from the work of a few prescient intellectuals, historical figures chosen by the Will of the Universe to lead the masses toward collective freedom. This, too, sounded quite like Hegel's idea of a world-historical individual. More than any other figure, Jesus Christ provided the model for a universal socialist morality. Christ forfeited his own life so that the world might have life, to reunite humanity with God. This was precisely what socialism set out to do: "its doctrine of the organic unity of man, will surely put a supreme value on self-sacrifice." The moral strength of the commonwealth depended on voluntary Christ-like selflessness, "deliberately sacrificing all that we hold dear in this life, our liberty and personal existence, for a great object." The reason why God took on a human form and became a mediator between God and man was to begin the process by which humanity would regain its God consciousness. The power of Christ, which included his identity with the "personality of God," rested on his union "with the personality of humanity." No other human in history provided such a pure model of empathy. Ministering to the poor, the outcast, the downtrodden—these were divine acts of cooperative love. A pure morality was one which the individual gave himself for the other. This was what it meant to be human. And to be properly human, it was necessary to act as God acted. Jesus represented, he says, the "symbol of humanity"; humanity, in turn, stood as "the medium through which we enter into communion with God . . . the keystone of any coherent system of morality and the crown of all preceding speculations." Humans were unable to access God without imitating Christ—that is to say, without giving up the self. Caring for others was how humanity accessed God. Pure and undefiled religion, according to James 1:27, including serving the poorest members of society. Those who addressed the needs of the poor, the hungry, and the marginalized were also those who came into contact with Christ himself, as Matthew 25:40 says: "whatever you did for one of the least of these brothers and sisters of mind, you did for me." These "little ones" had their identity in the divine. And since all humans had their identity in and through each other, how they interacted (morally) with one another was concurrently a unifying activity in God. Only by working with humanity, could individuals know one another and God. God would be "intimately known" in history and "later, still better, through institutions, and our organic unity"—that is, through cooperation.[100] What Vaneesa Cook has written about mid-twentieth-century "spiritual socialists" would certainly apply to Gronlund and others like him in the late nineteenth century. Spiritual socialists, Cook argues, "emphasized the social message of Jesus, who repeatedly told his disciplines to love and care for each other and the members of their community through simple acts of compassion and cooperation."[101]

As shown above, Gronlund argued that individual identity and the maturation of religion/morality were inextricably connected to the lives of others. In the final sections of *Our Destiny*, Gronlund applied this notion of a collective identity to the afterlife. Socialism would not only reconnect the development of humanity with emerging consciousness of the divine, but it would also alter the "belief in Immortality." Recognizing the increasing social, philosophical, and cultural changes at the end of America's long nineteenth century, Gronlund showed an interest in the teachings of eastern religions—particularly "the modern tendency [toward] Buddhism"—and the many burgeoning "Psychic Societies" that helped open the "hidden forces of the soul."[102] He had expressed interest in studies of "cataleptic patients" that demonstrated "extraordinary capacities" of the mind, an organ "independent of the orderly agency of its bodily machinery."[103] He offered a favorable nod to non-western religions to offer a brief reflection on the challenge of under-standing the nature of an immortal soul. Central to this was his belief that death was not the "annihilation of consciousness." After death, a person's soul would be transported into a collective consciousness—"the second religious achievement of American Socialism."[104] But how did one identify the soul, he asked? Where was it located? Gronlund did not dismiss the existence of the soul simply because it could not be seen. "Electricians do not perceive by sense the thing called magnetism or electricity. They cannot see, feel, nor hear their immaterial forces, but are, nevertheless, assured of their existence." The soul, wherever it might have been located, had some relationship to the seat of consciousness in the brain. The soul and the brain were so mingled together that it was basically impossible "to show their mutual relation." He did, however, assume a distinction between the body and the soul. Why else would he use the example of somnambulism (sleepwalking), which proved that the "soul can exist distinct from the body"? In the case of trances and psychism, which he drew from the practice of mesmerism, consciousness could be suspended; the soul had the ability to cease to "communicate through the body with the external world." The reality of the trance, more directly, had raised, Gronlund suggested, "a strong probability of immortality by proving that even in this life Soul and Body can be partially severed and preserve distinct existences."[105]

Not even memory played a role in "our inmost being," since cases like amnesia, self-induced drunkenness, and dreaming contributed to a loss of memory (connected to the soul) but not the cessation of bodily activity. De-spite the loss of memory, individuals retained their "identity from childhood to old age." What did this have to do with *a future life*," asked Gronlund? Life after death, in Gronlund's day, was understood as a "second volume" of our current lives, just in a different form. That is to say, the next life began with the memory of our former lives: "If we pass away as a beggar, we enter the other life with the memory of a beggar; if as an emperor, *with the memory of an emperor.*" But socialism would teach something different—namely, that humans would "enter upon the other life with our personality alone," not our memories. Remember what Gronlund said about "the self." There was no existence apart from others. An individual's personality was the "innermost being," but an inner being that was essentially a "social self," what we "have in common with other men—this we may call Self-hood, and this it is which entitles me to the divine regard." Our individuality came by way of the "exterior circumstances that distinguish one man from another." Gronlund referenced here George Talbot's *The New Ideal* (1890), in which Talbot stated that whatever "exists in the condition of *individuality* is necessarily transient." The soul continued as part of a universal collective soul after death. Socialism aligned with such a divine truth: "that each person is an eternal, integral part of Humanity, that the fibers of each 'self' are, and will eternally remain, intertwined with those of posterity and our ancestor." The social self would continue after death, but the incidentals of our specific identity (e.g., memory) would not. "Immortality," for the socialists, would "mean *continuity*"—continuity of our "social self exclusively." Borrowing from Paul Janet's *La Morale*, Gronlund noted, "*Eternal Life is the consummation* (not annihilation) *of personality*."[106] The absorption of the self into the wider consciousness of humanity was like an artist who "loses himself in the masterpieces he has created." While there is a loss of the self in each case, the subjects are still conscious of their "absorption." The soul, according to Janet, was the "highest and best part of his nature—his personality, that is, his reasonable will": "[T]he excellency of his personality does not consist merely in itself: it consists also in its union with the personality of other men."[107] After death, the individual would be consumed by a universal social self, like a drop of rain in the ocean. If in earthly existence, identity was inextricably linked to the existence of other individuals, so the continuation of the soul after death, then the metaphysical self would be brought into a universal social self.

Gronlund concluded *Our Destiny* by discussing the methods of those prescient leaders (like Danton and Christ) who would guide humanity boldly and courageously toward its true destiny.[108] The means employed to move toward the commonwealth would not include violence. Intellectuals would guide the moral passions driving "the social train for weal or woe," directing humans toward who they "ought to be." Discerning the metaphysical "benevolent power" outlining the "road for [humanity]" required moral reflection. Although critical of the individualistic bourgeois morality of the Gilded Age, Gronlund affirmed the need to "cherish our own life," for if we failed to take care of ourselves how then would we be able to "live for others": "we must make ourselves pure, since my own life must be precious to me before I can attach much preciousness to the life of others." Thus, he encouraged those willing to prepare for the coming of the commonwealth to embrace temperance and sexual purity, both of which address temptations (drunkenness and illicit sexual relations) created by the ethics of capitalist competition. Yet such moral reform should not terminate with the individual; self-reform must be initiated for the sake of the commonwealth. This was, for Gronlund, evolution.[109]

The adoption of socialism would strengthen more affectionate bonds among humans. Only when a shift in mindset away from production for profit would humanity be able to cultivate a healthy morality. "This is what Nationalism or Socialism means," he wrote.[110] Incremental steps toward socialism, even within a functioning capitalist society, would give the laboring masses the time ("blessed Leisure") necessary to cultivate their morality. Capitalist defenders among the middle class argued that ameliorating the toil of the working class would lead to idleness: an argument utilized by the defenders of capitalism for decades. Gronlund believed otherwise. The leisure of the cooperate state would be that of a reward for a "decent existence." Furthermore, it is leisure that leads necessarily to the cultivation of the mind, which, in turn, would lead to reflections on morality. The defenders of capitalism believed that competition contributed to the development of the mind. Gronlund disagreed: "genius is not strengthened by struggling."[111] It is quite the opposite. Competition—especially competition under conditions that rarely if ever allow the vast majority of competitors to advance—actually dampens the intellect.[112] Capitalism also "dampens" the intellect when it forces individuals to become functioning cogs in a mindless laboring machine.

Gronlund appealed to the nation's most "profoundly religious minds" to take the responsibility in ushering in this sacred socialism. This may seem to be contradictory, given his frustrations with the religious establishment in America. But recall that Gronlund was willing to work with like-minded reformers and radicals, despite disagreements over strategies for change. In his essay "Why I am a Socialist," written the same year as the publication of *Our Destiny,* Gronlund expressed optimism that a "quickening of the moral sense" was awakening many American citizens to the righteous cause of democratic socialism. He himself witnessed many "Christian ministers step forth and testify that the fulness of truth," the fullness of humanity and the divine, was on the horizon. The rich and those who supported them, including religious leaders, were the "real thieves and murderers"—possessed by Satan himself. "But all signs and portents," he concluded, "bear witness that Satan will be dethroned."[113] This, of course, was the inevitable course of evolution. Ranked highest among the nation's intellectuals, according to Gronlund, religious leaders had to convince members of society to "carry out God's thoughts" in their immediate lives. Next, they needed to connect with one another, "form a brotherhood," a common friendship, to "grasp the hands of similar broth-erhoods in surrounding towns." It would then take only a couple decades to establish the "Socialist Commonwealth."[114] When American citizens realize the benefits of working with one another and commit to the future common-wealth, the last thing they will need to do is organize, to band together the myriad trade-unions throughout the country. But such social bonding should never congeal into "a clique of unpractical doctrinaires—a mutual admiration society." Anticipating the commonwealth should compel citizens to push for "socialistic measures" like the nationalization of the nation's communication infrastructure and a civil service.[115]

While he privileged religious intellectuals as those who would help the intelligence behind evolution, Gronlund did not neglect workers. Workers too demonstrated their commitment to religious thinking, and Gronlund encouraged them to use their faith to achieve liberation. Labor's religious commitments were not tied to dogma so much as to "a firm faith in Prov-idence," a belief that provided "the only solid foundation for a hope in the future of human societies."[116] This trust in the evolutionary work of divine providence made workers the champions of morality as well as the agents of revolutionary change. They would not use religion as an opiate; they would demolish the bourgeois morality that kept them down. Consciously labor-ing with the Will of the Universe, workers held the responsibility to raise America, Gronlund wrote, "from the low moral plan to which our plutocrats have dragged it down": "Workmen, be conscious of your high mission! It is this high morality that places your course on the same high plane that the abolitionists occupied."[117]

In his *Social Darwinism in American Thought*, Richard Hofstadter wrote that the "social-gospel prophets drew many of their ideas" from Gronlund's writings.[118] According to contemporary theologian, philosopher, historian, and activist Gary Dorrien, Gronlund's *Cooperative Commonwealth* antici-pated "the signature phrase of the social gospel."[119] An important tenet of the Social Gospel theology was the idea that the kingdom of heaven would be established on earth through human cooperation. Such a belief was drawn from George Herron's "Kingdom Movement," which Gronlund was swept up in.[120] Indeed, the Kingdom Movement echoed much of Gronlund's religious and moral commitments presented in *Our Destiny*, particularly the moral imperative to prepare society for the second coming of Christ and the establishment of his kingdom, which had galvanized evangelicals, conservative and liberal, throughout the long nineteenth century. Of course, the precise timing of the arrival of the cooperative kingdom was unknown. With very few exceptions (the Millerites being one), most evangelicals heeded the teaching of Christ in Matthew 24:36 that no one—not even the son of God—would know the day or hour when the kingdom would arrive. Nonetheless, Christians were called, first, to identify the signs of Christ's impending return and, second, to morally prepare themselves and society for it. George Herron, working closely with Gronlund for a time, spoke of the coming of the kingdom in terminology that pictured the agency of a power within a collective consciousness: "the consciousness of a power to act together as one man, in the development of one common life and destiny." Gronlund shared Herron's conclusion that such a realization was "slowly awakening" in society.[121] Furthermore, God's preparation for a new world required the cooperation of humanity itself: "The idea of brotherhood, co-operation, unity, is both destroying and recreating the world . . . The belief that sacrifice and not self-interest is the social foundation, that the Golden Rule is natural law, is everywhere gaining disciples and power."[122]

The architects of the Social Gospel, especially Walter Rauschenbusch and Washington Gladden, confronted the moral destructiveness endemic to late-nineteenth-century competitive capitalism by embracing key aspects of Gronlund's commonwealth.[123] Notwithstanding his favoring of George's single tax, Rauschenbusch believed that "new forms of association" had to be established. The only thing that will save America's "disorganized competitive" society is to create "an organic cooperative life": "Individualism means tyranny."[124] While applauding Gronlund's emphasis on changing material conditions, which would "successfully tempt [citizens] to do right," Gladden expressed skepticism as to whether Gronlund's "great governmental machine will be able to carry on its work successfully."[125] Americans needed to see themselves as "parts of a whole": "To live is not to separate ourselves from our fellows, but to unite with them in multiform ministries of giving and receiving."[126] For Christian socialist Richard Ely "true welfare is not an individual matter purely, but likewise a social affair." Citizens would thrive "only in a commonwealth," he continued: "[O]ur exaltation is the exaltation of all our fellow men; their elevation is our enlargement."[127] Socialism was not simply religious, according to Herron; indeed, it was a religion: "it stands for the harmonious relating of the whole life of man; it stands for a vast and collective fulfilling of the law of love. As the socialist movement grows, its religious force will come for from the furnace of experience."[128] Universalist clergyman and author of *Modern Socialism* Charles H. Vail suggested that substituting "combination for competition" was the most sacred aspect of socialism. He found it "useless to hope that the ideal of the ages—peace, justice, and plenty—would be realized under the antagonisms of our competitive system."[129] The ethical goals of Social Gospelers and Socialists, in other words, aligned with the idea that the ultimate redemptive act was to give one's life for others. African American ministerial leaders likewise understood this relationship between social solidarity and full—body and soul, individual and social—liberation. Many knew that socialism was the practical means toward such a reality. African Methodist Episcopal minister Reverdy Ransom believed that African Americans would "enthusiastically espouse the cause of socialism." When Black people attained the "freedom of opportunity to cooperate with all men upon terms of equality in every avenue of life," they would be quick to accept "social emancipation."[130] Such sentiments continued well into the next century.

The consequence of human cooperation was the establishment of the kingdom of heaven on earth.[131] Social Gospel leaders heeded Gronlund's call for "Americans to bring heaven down to earth, end the reign of Mammon, and live in beloved, sacramental community."[132] In 1907, editors in the *Christian Socialist* boldly wrote that "brotherhood and comradeship which Jesus loved and labored to bring about" would arrive when "the Cooperative Commonwealth of Humanity, is established in the world."[133] As Stow Persons wrote in the 1965 preface to Gronlund's *Co-operative Commonwealth*, "revolutionary leadership would be assumed by devoutly religious minds. After the fashion of George Herron and the Christian Socialists, he [Gronlund] identified the cooperative commonwealth with the Kingdom of Heaven on earth."[134] The final passages of the revised edition, Stow continued, "contained an eloquent invocation of the religious spirit of solidarity."[135] Dan McKanan defines religion as "all practices, ideas, and institutions that connect people to what Paul Tillich called 'ultimate concern,' providing a frame of reference that reaches beyond pragmatic adjustment to the here and now."[136] And it is difficult to separate religion from radicalism. Religiously motivated "ideas, institutions, and practices have always been intertwined with radical activism," McKanan correctly notes.[137] Radicals, McKanan adds, "are drawn to religious communities and radical organizations in order to connect their daily routines to a more transcendent vision of heaven, salvation, or a new society."[138]

Religious faith commitments could be found in antislavery, women's rights, the various utopian movements, early labor activism, dietary reformism, and even the Free Love movements. Many, in fact, were impacted by the revivals of the Second Great Awakening, especially in the area most effected by the emerging Market Revolution, the burned-over district in New York. Charles Finney himself "set countless evangelicals on the path to radicalisms."[139] Revivalism has often been restricted to individual reform, but many who were ignited by the flames of revival engaged issues of labor, property, and the negative consequences of the market well into the next century. Plenty of backcountry revivalists were not only anti-authoritarian, a central tenet of American evangelicalism, but also egalitarian in the sense that a fair distribution of property, according to one Baptist minister, was "the basis of free and equal government." The Lowell factory girls' "dedication to scripture," Milton Cantor observed, "did not appear inconsistent with labor militancy."[140] Quakers and Methodists were major supporters of the Working Man's Party in the early nineteenth-century, along with Freethinkers and Universalists. The use of religion in this way continued into the postbellum world. Leilah Danielson, Marian Mollin, and Doug Rossinow have lamented the fact that the "historiography on social movements in modern industrial twentieth-century America has little to say on religion."[141] There is an assumption that after the Civil War, religion had a diminished role in shaping some of the most pressing issues of the day, especially in the realm of labor, immigration, racial, and gender injustices. But this is not completely accurate. The radical movements during the Gilded Age and Progressive Era, Henry George's single tax, Muckraking journalism, Christian socialism, urban reform, and antilynching activists, "integrated questions of poverty and class into religion." The faith that drove many (though, of course, not all) of these movements continued well into the twentieth century, providing "a home for pacifism, the Civil Rights movement, antiracism and left-wing interna-tionalism as well as anti-capitalism."[142] Historians have largely forgotten the place of religion in radicalism in the last century, but it is definitely there. The teachings of Jesus were incorporated into "the theology of labor."[143] Labor unions provided the "most important base of support" for those on the Left, especially socialists, argues McKanan, and "congregations were a significant second."[144] Miners in West Virginia and Kentucky sang traditional Christian hymns while on strike. Plenty of socialists in Gilded Age utilized the rhet-oric of Protestantism in their battle against industrial capitalism. Christian socialist George McNeill, for instance, used the Westminster Shorter Cat-echism to denounce industrial slavery; many abolitionists had done much the same. It also may be surprising to contemporary conservatives to read fundamentalist evangelical William Jennings Bryan's 1896 criticism of what later became known as "trickle-down" economics, a sacred doctrine among fiscal conservatives. The antiwar and anti-capitalist activism of A. J. Muste was fueled in large ways by his Dutch Calvinist roots, including his knowl-edge of the Heidelberg Catechism. David Burgess, leader of the Fellowship of Southern Churchmen's labor commission, said it best when campaigning for Christian support of labor unions in the postwar South that he "did not want to cheapen religion by using it as a secondary instrument."[145] "Jesus," Vander-bilt Professor and Disciples of Christ minister Alva Taylor proclaimed in the late 1930s, "was the 'real progenitor of a democracy that would sweep away class and racial distinctions and pursue social justice." Although identifying himself as a progressive, not a radical, Taylor believed, Ken and Elizabeth Fones-Wolf have shown, "that if Jesus were alive . . . he would be 'at the head of these vast, marching columns of labor."[146] In his 1946 essay "The Root is Man," Dwight MacDonald observed what had been lost in the Old Left: "We feel that the firmest ground from which to struggle for that human liberation which was the goal of the Old Left is the ground not [of a rigid teleological materialism] but of those non-historical"—or transhistorical—"values (truth, justice, love, etc.) which Marx has made unfashionable among socialists."[147]

Nationally recognized labor activist and former presidential candidate Eugene V. Debs spoke of Jesus as the "master proletarian revolutionist," who offered a model of pure self-sacrifice. Debs became a socialist because he was an advocate of humanity. And in answering the question "What is socialism," he wrote that it was, at root, "Christianity in action."[148] Socialism was humanitarianism and Christianity marbled together. Debs spoke of Gronlund as someone inspired by the "vision of a prophet." His "ripest thought and unrelaxing energy" was akin to "the old Hebrew prophet[s]," announcing the coming millennium when nations would "beat their swords into pruning-hoods and their spears into plow-shares." With "unbowed head" yet always in the "shadow of death," Gronlund never wavered from the goal of making the "deaf hear, the dumb speak, the lame walk." His religion was a "new dispensation of liberty" for the workers of the world, those who would soon be "redeemed from the enthrallments of wage slavery."[149] Gronlund indeed took on the role of a prophet. His objective was to introduce, as he had in *Ça Ira,* a "religion of the future"—a religion that would "teach us that we are, above all, *social* beings," striving cooperatively to realize the Absolute.[150] This was the destiny of humanity.

# CHAPTER FIVE

# SOMETHING, INDEED, MUST BE DONE

## From National to Global Cooperation

Henry George's mayoral campaign and the purging of the socialists from the ULP dealt a heavy blow to a much-needed unified front among reformers and radicals. But socialists were divided amongst themselves, weakening thereby, as thinkers throughout the twentieth century have concluded, socialism's efforts to take a deeper hold on American society and politics. In 1898, a year after his official turn to socialism, Eugene Debs and other prominent socialists organized the Social Democracy of America. The SDA had been divided almost from the beginning between "colonizationists," those who supported the creation of a socialist colony in "one of the states of the Union," and those who favored political actions plans to implement elements toward a socialist commonwealth. The latter group, under the leadership of Victor Berger, abandoned the SDA when a meeting of the delegates adopted a colonization program—a program supported by Gronlund. A portion of this faction created the Social Democratic Party, which focused on revolutionary class consciousness and a variety of practical political and economic policies (e.g., the initiative and referendum, a national insurance plan, and the end of America's expansive capitalistic wars). Gronlund believed that Berger and his followers acted rashly, describing the secession as a "childish procedure."[1] Berger, in Gronlund's estimation, should have submitted to the decision of the SDA and worked to persuade those who opposed them. In 1901, two years after Gronlund's death, the faction of the Socialist Labor Party merged with the Social Democrats to form the Socialist Party of America.

Gronlund's desire for unity among socialists was indicative of his commitment to cooperation. Cooperation was the necessary course of history. While the divine power behind evolution could not be stopped in any ultimate or final sense, it could be slowed by factions—especially those that centered on the implementation of practical programs for reform. Failing to "connect with reality," Gronlund observed, Berger and his supporters, were taken by the "entirely un-American" theory of class warfare. As we have seen, the *telos* of Gronlund's collectivist philosophy was the organic unity of society.[2] A carefully planned and unified strategy, despite internal differences, would peacefully transition society toward the collective. Violence, the result of irreconcilable factions, was not the course of history, Gronlund believed. Besides, the emphasis on class antagonism was misguided since Providence was already turning society's evils (e.g., the trust) into blessings. The plutocrats stood as both enemies and benefactors of society. As mentioned earlier in this study, the trust, albeit created for the selfish consolidation of wealth, unwittingly fashioned "the most tremendous instrument in the hands of Democracy for [the plutocrats] own destruction."[3] Such a method would play *the* decisive role in advancing humanity. These were not simply the inevitable contradictions of capitalism; they were the divine hand of Providence—contradictions as the plan of the divine. Violence ignored the evolution of history and rendered inert the incremental steps within capitalism as directed by the Will of the Universe, hence the reason Gronlund spent his later years laying out a practical plan for the establishment of a socialist commonwealth. Radicals and reformers worked to persuade citizens to become a "solid phalanx" against the "absolutism of capital," but divisions, Gronlund lamented, strengthened capitalism and slowed the progress of history.[4]

In the last decade of the nineteenth century, those associated with the Left demanded a wise and practical plan to prepare for the commonwealth. The way to do this was to recognize, "the whole trend of history," the partnership of the divine with humanity where national democracy would be secured through combination.[5] But plenty of socialists fell far short of a workable plan, according to Gronlund. Karl Marx, for instance, portrayed the end of capitalism, Gronlund concluded in *Ça Ira*, through "catastrophe and a crash." His philosophy of history was one of *"evolution toward destruction"* with little to offer in terms of "positive formulas" in preparing for capitalism's demise.[6] The end of capitalism could not be stopped, but Gronlund believed that socialists had a responsibility to work toward that end. For Seymour Stedman, Secretary of the Social Democratic Party and later vice-presidential running mate with Eugene V. Debs in the 1920 presidential election, Gronlund had always been someone who "treated the subject of Socialism plainly," stripping it of its "utopianism."[7]

A year before his death, Gronlund published *The New Economy: A Peaceable Solution of the Social Problem* (1898).[8] Written at a time when its author lived in poverty and suffered from what the contemporary observer might consider as a serious case of depression, *New Economy* provided a more scientific approach in "production and distribution" that would mitigate the evils of competition and remove the obstacles that would impede the advent of cooperative collectivism. While he argued for the expansion of the powers of the government, Gronlund believed that the actual work of building the commonwealth began not at the level of the central government but on the ground, so to speak, hence the reason he supported colonization. These smaller communities would act as a model for the nation.[9]

*New Economy* was also written at a time, when America, stretching beyond its own geopolitical borders because of its own industrial capitalism, was ascending as a global power.[10] "The feverish activity of our competitive system, far from cooling down, becomes more and more intense," Gronlund wrote in Bellamy's *Nationalist*, "[and it] must go on enlarging and concentrating."[11] This echoed what Marx and Engels wrote in the *Communist Manifesto*—namely, that capitalism "must nestle everywhere, settle everywhere, establish connections everywhere."[12] Christian Socialist George Herron likewise observed that the growth of American capitalism was "merely the carrying out of the program of greed by which the holders of stocks and bonds propose to industrially subject the world—the bond-holders and stockholders who are today the emperors of the emperors and their empires."[13] Capitalism reached its highest stage of development in imperialism, an insight articulated by Vladimir Ilyich Lenin nearly two decades after Gronlund's death: "If it were necessary to give the briefest possible definition of imperialism we should have to say that imperialism is the monopoly stage of capitalism."[14] And, of course, one should be able to see the colonizing tendencies in the primitive accumulation efforts within the enclosure movement that helped give rise to capitalism. Colonial conquest is the origin as well as lifeblood of capitalism. As he had written in the *Commonwealth*, Gronlund noted the imperialistic consequences of generating new markets: "[they would] immolate men, ruin cities, annex or conquer half-civilized countries, shake up by the roar of cannon the sleeping Chinese, encourage the building of railways in Mexico and incursions into the heart of Africa; in brief, penetrate into and ransack with feverish and frantic energy every nook and corner of the globe where human beings are found that can be coaxed or driven to—trade."[15] In 1898, the United States went to war against the dying imperial power of Spain, doing so not for democracy or the benefit of humanity, but for profit.[16] It was the nature of capitalism to expand, conquering new lands by forcing open new markets, "a matter of life or death to the system," Gronlund argued.[17] American business leaders recognized the immense commercial opportunities in Cuba, the Philippines, and among the islands across the Pacific (Hawaii in particular), coercing foreign governments to protect their expansionist interests. The war "greatly increased the resources of [America's] plutocracy."[18] If wars were lucrative for the plutocracy, human civilization would see more of them. War would exist so long as competitive capitalism did: "Competition is war, and as long as the war-spirit is the rule within every civilized nation, it naturally governs the conduct of nations with each other."[19] "Imperialism," Herron wrote in *Why I am a Socialist*, "has always been the immediate result of the centralization of wealth in the hands of a few and can be dealt with only by changing the order of things from which it naturally springs."[20] It was the expansion of the U.S. nation via its economy that demanded, Gronlund wrote in the opening pages of *New Economy*, an immediate practical plan for the commonwealth: "Something, indeed, must be done!" Something needed to be done "before [America's] war with Spain— it is still more true after it."[21]

The expansion of empire was one of the reasons why many socialists rightly viewed their cause as international. Battling capitalism at that level was the best way to keep capitalism from spreading everywhere. Gronlund disagreed, however. He understood the capitalist logic of imperialism, but he stopped short when the focus on empire abroad distracted from the building of socialist states at home. In this way, *New Economy* was not only Gronlund's most practical work, it was also his most nationalistic. His practical plan for the nation was, he wrote, "an anti-imperialistic program in itself" and "more persuasive than a mere abstract declaration against imperialism." American citizens needed to turn their focus away from the Philippines and Cuba to establish a national collective.[22] This form of anti-imperialist nationalism was undeniably Fabian, distinct from Marxian internationalism. Fabians socialists had, according to Sidney Webb, "little sympathy with the idea of a universal cosmopolitanism," advocating instead that each nation should prioritize the pursuit of their own socialist commonwealth.[23] This was, however, a matter of course; that is, the Fabians were not calling nations to completely seal themselves off from the international community. Nations had to develop their own socialism first, securing their place in the march of history to serve as a model for other nations. "The Fabians," Gemorah noted, forged a "synthesis between patriotism and internationalism."[24] Loyalty to country was essentially a collectivist virtue, "the natural intermediate step in the evolution of organic humanity, and further, a precious organ of social progress." A well-functioning commonwealth would be "a model to other peoples and an effective organ of humanity and of progress," Gronlund argued. Along with their internationalism, Marxian socialists, because they "deliberately preach a war of classes," move "away from all love of country."[25] Socialists of Gronlund's kind were, in Gronlund's terms, "proud of Uncle Sam."[26] But we must make clear that "nations," not to mention an "international" (however conceived), were not ends in themselves. The nation was the developing organism of the State, a moral and divine unfolding of the Power behind evolution. What this meant was that the establishment of the State via the cooperative progress of the nation was concurrently the revelation of the will of God. This makes sense when considered in the light of Hegel's understanding of both God and the state: "The state is the march of God in the world, its ground or cause is the power of reason realizing itself as will. When thinking of the idea of the state, we must not have in our mind any particular state, or particular institution, but must rather contemplate the idea, this actual God, by itself."[27]

The contradictions that would ultimately consume capitalism would at the same time expand democracy. Evolution, the cooperation between Providence and humanity, aimed at total democracy, what Gronlund referred to as "rational Socialism." The stages of history brought citizens to higher states of democratic consciousness. The end of history was absolute liberation, the overcoming of obstacles in the way of full cooperation. As a kind of barometer to measure the advancement of history, labor would occasionally receive glimpses of that liberation as it prevailed over impediments blocking self-realization. The growth in self-realization centered on changes in modes of production that included increased interaction (mutual cooperation) with others. Of course, such changes, marking what Gronlund understood as the battle for civilization, were never smooth for the laborer.[28] Civilization began, "in its most brutal form," with the workingman as a slave, a mere laboring brute, unconscious of the relationship between his identity and what he produced. As the master took away the product of the laborer, he also took away the identity of the laborer and the relationship the laborer has with his fellows. After the "lapse of centuries, the laborer became a serf," and it was Christianity via the "monastic orders" of the medieval west "that first conferred dignity on the manual workers."[29] The laborer became aware of the power he had over that which he produced and sought to harness that power through cooperation, moving slowly away from slavery to serfdom. As a serf, the laborer would retain a little of his identity by holding on to what he produced. This was determined, as mentioned above, by custom and created through community, though the full value of his production was still in the hands of another (the lord). Yet production was done by all; thus, the identity of one was constituted by the identity of all. Each stage of cooperation was preceded by the trials labor had to face—a kind of crucible necessary for liberation.

Gronlund noted four historical periods that were at the same time giant leaps in the forging of cooperative ideology. The Italian Renaissance and the Protestant Reformation helped cultivate a new sense of worth for the individual. The Renaissance came at a time and place when the old medieval world was in sharp decline and citizens, especially in northern Italy, were compelled to implement innovative ways to reconstitute both self and society. The Renaissance "man," the idea goes, was not only well-rounded but self-made; he was not a figure born into a condition—a condition created by the labor of others (i.e., the relationship between peasants and the aristocracy). Likewise, the Reformation freed individuals from the overbearing supremacy of the Catholic Church. They no longer needed to appease a hierarchical class of domineering priests. They were free to commune with God directly. This provided a modicum of liberation and a new sense of the value of the individual, which, in turn, cultivated a renewed attitude toward labor, sanctifying even mundane and moiling work. Individuals could demonstrate their devotion to God even through the most tedious of tasks, to help them live as God intended. The irony—or perhaps its dialectical antithesis—was that the

Renaissance and Reformation planted the seeds of competitive individualism, slowly eclipsing the individual's responsibility to the community, since in part the Renaissance and Reformation individual was made through a rebellion against community. Inevitably, however, a new form (synthesis) of author-itarianism emerged. Protestant clergymen and proto-capitalist merchants and bankers, derived from competitive individualism, slowed the growth in cooperation necessary for the flourishing of the human community, counter-ing the efforts to return to a purer humanism and more authentic Christian faith. Jesus Christ, Gronlund believed, preached a message of solidarity, that all humans are endowed with a "common dignity" and "identical glory." Yet Protestantism, despite the way in which the period reconnected all humans directly with God, "paved the way" for "unbridled individualism."[30]

The next major period, the critical breakthrough in labor consciousness, where combination enabled a more radical democracy, came in the French Revolution. The ideas of liberty, equality, and fraternity touched every mem-ber of French society; they could not be restricted to one class. This was a boon to the working classes, who, because of the Revolution, were able to rec-ognize the "potential power" of their labor. Never before had they engaged in "asserting their importance." The Revolution was the catalyst to move workers to recognize their value to the advancement of civilization. Labor started on a course of greater self-consciousness. And like the Renaissance and the Reformation there were those who sought to thwart the expansion of this liberating self-consciousness. Eventually, France's bourgeoisie, those who employed liberty, fraternity, and equality to liberalize the nation's economy, withheld from the working class the ideals forged in the democratic crucible of the revolution, creating a new form of absolutism. The French Revolution dismantled the divine right of kings and exchanged it with the "divine right of plutocrats."[31] Modern society returned to a new form of dependency. The same had occurred in America, where "moneyed men" used the language of revolution to gain control over the country's citizens. Indeed, this was the governing ethics in Gronlund's day—not just competition between businesses but also competition between isolated humans.

The final contradiction for history to overcome, both in terms of modes of production and the dialectics of ideas, came in the latter half of the nine-teenth century. The individualism and ascendancy of an authoritarian plu-tocracy, planted by the Renaissance and Reformation and maturing in the

French Revolution, came to full bloom in the Industrial Revolution, which directed civilization, Gronlund argued, "toward concentration [and] centralization in all human affairs." This was the end of history where cooperation and democracy had other antitheses to overcome. And there was no better place to see this reality than in the United States, Gronlund assumed, a country that modeled these "two great tendencies." Combination, exemplified in the trust, began in opposition to democracy. The trust was an example of the power (and inevitability) of cooperation; business leaders would combine "to stop competition between themselves" in order to augment production and their wealth. Eventually all sectors of society would recognize the democratic effectiveness of the Trust—of cooperation. In the 1890s, the trust and democracy were irreconcilable. Gronlund hoped that by the turn of the century, the trust and democracy would come closer together: the former used by citizens of all classes for the well-being of society as a whole. "[A]ll industrial activities," Gronlund believed, would adopt the practical model of the trust, raising "business one rung higher up on the ladder of evolution."[32] The end of the nineteenth century was a period which democracy edged closer to the final act of evolution: the abolition of the wage system. This required allowing history to run its course—that is, to let the trust mature. Gronlund admitted that while it was currently an obstacle in the way of progress, the trust was nonetheless admirable for its basic function, for it proved an undeniable truth: "Effective labor organizations will enable [all citizens] to meet even the haughtiest trusts on an equal footing.[33]

Gronlund's collective democracy, modeled after the trust, would allow citizens the freedom to choose their work: "if a citizen has aptitude for, say, teaching or wood-carving, and especially if he has been trained up to this occupation as such a man is sure to be in the Cooperative Commonwealth— then teaching or wood-carving is his function in the state, and it would be an injustice to society, even greater than to him personally, to require him at any time to do another kind of work."[34] Collective democracy of this kind would also allow workers to determine their own compensation.[35] But how would that be decided? First, compensation would be determined by the complexity of the labor itself—time multiplied by the amount of labor that went into production. A watchmaker would be paid more for a day's work than a "hod-carrier" (someone who carries materials for bricklayers and stonemasons). On a commonsense level, the latter knew that his work was not as complicated as that of the former. Rather than determined by what a consumer was willing to pay, compensation would be apportioned according to the "sum of socially necessary labor embodied in a given product."[36] Second, Gronlund did not restrict his discussion on compensation to manual labor alone. Teachers and doctors, for instance, spent years of training for the greater good of the community, and their compensation would have taken those years into account. But what about the mental labors of those who managed the greater army of labor? The able leader (essentially a manager), who found "his interest in the Collectivist Republic," would be paid slightly more than the average laborer, since his mental labor would be a matter of coordinating the labor of the collective. It was crucial for the collective to carefully search out such capable men, those focused on the well-being of the people instead of those focused on profits. The workers would identify such individuals and give to them such authority. Yet because they were chosen by workers, these leaders would be accountable to the people directly. Thus, in a very real sense, the workers were ultimately the ones who made decisions regarding management. The process of choosing leaders would begin in the schools established by the commonwealth (more on this below). Commonwealth schools would raise up a generation of educated people who placed the well-being of society above "profit-mongering."[37] Finally, compensation would be determined by social necessity. A teacher, doctor, and manager held a necessary place in society—those who would give instruction for good citizenship, provide health and healing for the citizenry, and coordinate the production of citizens. The greater concern, for Gronlund, was to eliminate the "fleecers," the non-producers who enriched themselves on the labor of others—whatever the type of labor. Even the "hod-carrier" served the wider community, in one sense, by helping to build the places for doctors, teachers, managers, and laborers to work.

What needed to change were the various attitudes toward different types of work and the corresponding value related to the consequences of that work. Capitalist society came to despise the disagreeable work of the one whose boot was daily blackened. Why, Gronlund wondered, "turn away in disgust from the scavenger?"[38] The reason centered on the relationship between what was produced and what it cost, ignoring, of course, the labor that went into the object. What fixed *a priori* law of nature demonstrated an undeniable correspondence between the price of something with its intrinsic worth? There is a tendency created within the capitalist nexus that the cost of an item corresponds to that item's inherent worth, when in fact the cost, represented in a strictly phenomenological sense through money, hides the true value of a product. While identifying this as artificial (i.e., intrinsic value confused with monetary value), Gronlund nonetheless followed its logic. He even suggested that raising wages for moiling work, like hod-carrying, would add value to that work (though not its true source), especially if those seeking work were driven by wages. An individual's wage impacted not only how society valued the labor but also how it valued the laborers.

Likewise, Gronlund believed that the laborer and labor, though tied to one another, should not be a fixed relation. The choice of work, whatever it may be and however long someone wished to remain in it, was to be decided by workers themselves. Because he held a necessary position in society and in the absence of competition, the hod-carrier and scavenger (the equivalent of a garbage collector) would be well compensated. He may not be paid the same as one engaged in "higher" forms of labor (with higher not meaning more valuable), but he would certainly be paid well above subsistence wages, a symptom of competition. Regardless of the type of work, remuneration, Gronlund stressed, would be democratically determined. The relationship between the complexity of labor and socially necessary labor would be strengthened in the absence of competition, when the watchmaker, hod-carrier, and manager recognized their interdependence. The complexity of labor and the differences between mental and manual labor were contributing factors that would guide in the decision making of the entire laboring community—by all workers. This all rested on mutual dependence, democratic decision making, and the abolition of competition. Sadly, however, America's late-nineteenth-century culture inhibit the "potential energy" within society that could only be harnessed by the collective will.

Gronlund continued to address the "perfectly groundless" accusation that his collective would lead to the degradation of all morality. On the contrary, Gronlund argued, turn-of-the century capitalism was the source of moral decline. The collective would create a new moral order, one grounded in the community. Individualism referred to the individual acting selfishly and in a way that neutralized or eliminated the threat of another individual; this represented what he called "gross egoism," characteristic of the competitive ethos of late-nineteenth-century America. Individuality, on the other hand, produced by collectivism, constituted what he called "rational morality" or a "moralized ego."[39] "Rational morality" referred to the individual who worked for the benefit of others, a calculated selflessness. Gronlund defined morality as conduct "conforming to right convictions as to the meaning of life."[40] Competition produced a savage, dog-eat-dog world—a world destructive of nature and morality. Such individualism was contrary to the laws of nature. Humans were "indissolubly and organically bound together."[41] This was the foundation of morality. Any effort to disrupt this law of nature corrupted morality. Working against nature, for Gronlund, was the epitome of irrationality. Citizens would do well to care for one another, for the destiny of the individual (moralized ego) was concurrently humanity's destiny. Gronlund was advocating an extreme self-abnegation; he did not mean that individuals should abandon the care of their own lives. Referencing French philosopher and economist Pierre Leroux, Gronlund reinforced the point that an individual's solemn duty in pursuing his or her own welfare could only be accomplished through securing of the well-being of the collective. Moralized egoism meant self-cultivation that upheld the well-being of the collective, a deep-rooted and lasting altruism that Gronlund referred to as "fellow feeling."[42] On this point, Gronlund repeated much of what he said in *Our Destiny:* "[I] mean the conviction of our belonging together, the sense of man's organic unity, of the solidarity of men." Working together would not only reveal the oneness of humanity, but also its divinity. The cooperative commonwealth manifested "Providence on earth to man."[43] Spencer, Gronlund now believed, was misguided in his views of the "Unknowable" moving evolution. As Hegel said in his *Philosophy of Right:* "[God] is no more on the other side—an unknown—for he has made known to man what he is, and not merely in an external history, but in consciousness."[44] Gronlund would have connected labor to Hegel's consciousness.

The end of an individual's becoming in and through the social context was freedom. In fact, freedom would grow as the self in society progressed toward consciousness. Such a process was not only natural, but also voluntaristic. Many Americans, Gronlund and others pointed out, held the belief that freedom meant the right of citizens to do as they pleased: "our competitive system has given some Americans, a very few, such a right, and it is looked upon by altogether too many as our 'ideal of manhood.'"[45] Such a view of liberty, however, was mere license. Gronlund preferred a positive freedom, the "inclination to do right" in relation to others—a "rational morality."[46] Unfortunately, citizens in Gronlund's day were not free in this positive sense, only because a small elite had far too much liberty. Not even the American farmer, "looked upon as par excellence a free and independent class," had the kind of positive freedom envisioned by agrarian republicans, since he had little to no access to the material conditions that would allow him to pursue the good. As a "means to his master's private ends," the morally de-graded wage-earner was closer to that of a slave.[47] Wage slaves, given their meager compensation, did not have the freedom to escape such "fixed rules" of dependency. While abiding by the dictates of the master was no better, complete resistance, breaking with the capitalist master, was a huge gamble for workers but only because of the fortuitous possibilities that would come if successful.

In part III of *New Economy*, essentially the meat of the book, Gronlund began the tedious work of laying out his practical plan. Before doing so, however, he surveyed a few of the political efforts offered by reformers (early progressives), like William Jennings Bryan and the Populists, who proposed ways of restoring worker autonomy and democratic participation. These in-cluded profit-sharing, the initiative and referendum, and the expansion of the vote for women.[48] The first, profit-sharing, came from moderate social critic Nicolas Paine Gilman, a fierce critic of Gronlund's collectivism, Bellamy's "Nationalism," and the "anarchistic individualism" of Herbert Spencer.[49] In *Socialism and the American Spirit*, Gilman argued that socialism was not only detriment to moral and intellectual development but that the American char-acter itself was incompatible with it. Gilman's profit-sharing plan could be summed up in this way: when a company made a profit, especially one higher than the previous year, the employer would then give workers, apart from wages, "half of these profits to divide among themselves," while the employer would keep the remaining profits.[50] Such a practice presented the employer as benevolent, graciously gifting his employees. But as Gronlund wrote years earlier, it was the worker who created the value and hence the profit; thus, a keener mind would hold that whatever profit the employer received would be a "donation to the employer from the workmen."[51] But this was not how American society in Gronlund's day framed the picture.

The second proposal was the initiative and referendum. Gronlund favored the latter but advised against the former. The initiative allowed voters to frame legislation for their fellow citizens. The mistake of the initiative was that it presupposed "no particular wisdom and training in the citizen" to shape legislative proposals. Adopting or rejecting proposed legislation demanded an understanding of the law. The referendum, on the other hand, provided that all laws passed by a legislature be submitted to public scrutiny and approval; no law would be enforced until it received "such sanction of a majority of the voters."[52]

Third, some reformers believed that extending the right to vote to women would be a constructive means of moving society closer to collective democracy. Gronlund was skeptical. "Women have always exercised great political power," he admitted, especially in "teaching and persuading the less progressive male voters." But they were by nature, he said in the same breath, unfit to participate in electoral politics, because they lacked a "due sense of the proportion of things." Women were "less amenable to reason" and "more subject to fanaticism"—"illiberal, unprogressive, [and] reactionary to a greater extent than the men."[53] Yet Gronlund went beyond basic suffrage. First, most citizens approached voting as an individual right, exercised for selfish ends. Gronlund held a counterview nearer to that of Hegel. For Hegel, the call for suffrage rested on an "atomistic and abstract point of view," especially as it related to the organism of the State. "To hold," he continued, " that every single person should share in deliberating and deciding on political matters of general concern on the ground that all individuals are members of the state . . . is tantamount to a proposal to put the democratic element without any rational form into the organism of the state."[54] The right to vote was not a right but a trust, according to Gronlund, "granted by the state" for the purposes of contributing to the welfare of the whole. Second, offering the trust to just anyone or any group, in this case women, would not necessarily curb the abuses of industrial capitalism. Enlarging the vote could strengthen capitalism and the power of the plutocracy, necessarily hindering the progress of the Commonwealth. Male voters had shown their true interest in preserving an economic system fueled by competitive individualism. There was no evidence to suggest that women would confront capitalist exploitation. He did, however, believe that with the arrival of the "Collectivist Republic," once the obstacles of capitalism were removed, women would gain the opportunity to vote.[55]

No reforms, in any final sense, would be of much help until the power of America's wealthy elites was broken down. The way to do this was by eliminating the wage system, which would "cut away the very function from under the feet of our plutocrats."[56] There were, however, a few suggestions toward which Gronlund showed a modicum of favor. One included the passage of a protective tariff, since it would protect American industry.[57] Opponents argued that it would lead to higher consumer prices, creating a burden on workers. Gronlund rejected such disingenuous reasoning from among free-trade capitalists since the tariff would be for the "foreign manufacturer to pay." And besides, the revenue generated by the protective tariffs would go straight into the "pockets of the employers and of the well-to-do classes," not the workers.'[58] Gronlund reminded his critics that the true source of wealth came from fleecing the value created by the worker: "That which causes the advantages which flow from protection to fill the pockets of the rich instead of the pockets of the poor is not the tariff at all, but it is the wage-system, and the wage-system exclusively." But Gronlund's position seems to be a contradiction. Since the tariff protected an industry, it would in turn protect the employer's exploitation of the worker. This is true. But it would also protect industry and provide jobs, creating work for "the greater part of the army of unemployed, running into the millions." While the tariff would not relieve exploitation, it would protect the jobs necessary for labor to continue on its necessary historical trajectory—granted, through exploitation—toward greater consciousness. Under late-1890s capitalism, Gronlund admitted that there was no way to provide an immediate benefit to the poor without also benefiting the rich. The protective tariff was a minor and short-term remedy.

Another reform favorable to Gronlund was the establishment of an eight-hour day. This too would ease the burdens of labor by protecting both workers' rest (eight hours) and leisure (eight hours), leaving the other eight hours for work. And although providing some relief, the eight-hour day did nothing to remedy capitalist "fleecing." Workers would continue to produce a surplus in that time. What is more, not every job, Gronlund suggested, required eight hours. In more dangerous economic sectors, laborers should work less than eight hours: "if any worker's time ought to be reduced below eight hours a day, that of the miners surely is!" This was, in his mind, the most dangerous form of labor, "where one must constantly breath unhealthy gasses or poisonous particles; where one is now exposed to extreme heat, now to extreme cold."[59] It would be up to the trade unions, after taking charge of the means of production, to decide the appropriate amount of labor.

Finally, to ease the burden of domestic labor, Gronlund supported strict though temporary immigration restrictions. By the late 1880s, immigrants from eastern Europe and Asia, particularly China, constituting what has been labeled as the "New Immigration," were changing the face of American society and culture. As an important source of cheap and exploitable labor, these new immigrants were certainly a boon to capitalists.[60] Gronlund favored a policy of immigration restriction to protect American workers. To soften his anti-immigration position, however, he added that such restrictions would only be a couple years until the country established a more secure footing for the socialist state: "let those who take the lead in this movement be themselves conscious, and impress it on all others, that the object of such limitation on the immigration of foreigners must not be a selfish one, but that it is for the ultimate benefit of all our fellowmen."[61] Remember, Gronlund, in Fabian fashion, sought first to establish socialism in America so that it would be a model for other nations and thus secure for foreigners the blessings of a democratic commonwealth. Unfortunately, Gronlund's hostility to foreigners did more to intensify the racial and ethnic hostilities dividing and thus weakening American labor.

Following his examination of these reform proposals, Gronlund laid out his own ideas for a practical working commonwealth. Around the time that *New Economy* appeared, Gronlund wrote an essay for *Social Democracy* entitled "Socializing the State." In it, he presented "seven grand measures" that would bring the country to the threshold of socialism: (1) State productive work for the unemployed; (2) effective trade unions and obligatory industrial arbitration; (3) State management of the liquor traffic; (4) State control of the mines; (5) municipalization of lighting, electric power, street cars, and the telephone; (6) State saving banks and loan offices; (7) compulsory education of children from four to fourteen years. Gronlund expanded on such measures, turning each—with minor adjustments—into separate chapters for *New Economy*.[62] Given that such proposals make up the heart of Gronlund's final work, I will explore each in turn. Before I do, however, it is important to reiterate that these proposals were penultimate. They were preparatory elements in the coming revolution. Gronlund wanted to follow the incremental steps of evolution as the proper way to inaugurate the revolution. Once such practices were established, it would not take too much time for society to tip over into a full revolutionary inauguration of the collective commonwealth.

*State productive work for the unemployed.* This plan considered the role of government in welfare programs. For the defenders of capitalism, it was not the job of government to guarantee work for citizens. Doing so would place citizens into the habit of relying on government welfare, robbing citizens of not only their individuality but also their responsibility to take care of themselves. Furthermore, as is the constant refrain among opponents today, government welfare programs would produce lazy and unproductive workers. Gronlund disagreed. The government should be involved in creating jobs—jobs for public benefit, not private profit. From the perspective of exploited workers, government aid was the only legitimate and nonviolent means for poorer Americans to protect themselves against an oppressively dehumanizing economic system. This was not a matter of paternalism, but of fraternity. And the goal was self-sufficiency. Gronlund was not thinking of "tramps, loafers, and criminals," those who would take advantage of the system; capitalism would always "go on breeding" such groups.[63] Rather, his concern revolved around those who had the ability to work but lacked the opportunities to do so. What aid, then, might the state provide for wage earners to become self-reliant? While strikes would play a beneficial role for the working masses, Gronlund admitted, state aid for the unemployed would be even better. The state would provide employment for public works and offer aid to cooperative associations.[64] The need was urgent. Gronlund feared that unemployment was reaching levels similar to that of Europe. As unemployment rose, he thought, so would resentment toward a system that took jobs away. To reverse the loss of jobs, and to cool the frustrations of workers against capitalists, legislators would have to interfere in the economy. Gronlund appealed to the founders of the republic, many of whom believed that "state productive work for the unemployed was right and practical." He even cited an early Pennsylvania statute still in effect in his day: "Whenever a citizen of this state is out of work the overseers of the poor shall furnish him with the necessary raw-materials, with tools and a work-shop."[65] He intimated that a substantial reduction in unemployment could be achieved if other states followed a similar law.

A federal income tax administered by a savings and loan bank (more on this below) would also benefit the unemployed. This would have required,

Gronlund suggested, either an amendment to the Constitution, which eventually came in the Sixteenth Amendment nearly a decade and a half after Gronlund's death, or until reformed-minded policy makers restructured the judicial system.[66] In the absence of an income tax, how would the government be able to generate revenue? Tariffs were not enough. Could the states jump in and impose a tax on capitalist profits? Critics responded by saying that if the states provided for workers in this way, then unemployed hundreds would "swamp our own people" with tramps and loafers looking not just for work but for state aid.[67] The solution was that state aid would be given upon condition that those who received aid would be required to work. At the same time, the guarantee for a job would bring a host of able-bodied and willing laborers to augment the productivity of sectors of the countries. The more populated and productive a state became, the greater influence it would have in national governance. Another option related to workers' assistance would be the establishment of voluntary cooperative societies specifically set up to address the needs of those needing work. Gronlund excitedly offered as an example the recent cooperative colony proposal of Eugene V. Debs. In fact, a year before the publication of *New Economy*, Gronlund had been chosen as one of three commissioners to "find a site for Debs' co-operative colony."[68] What was particularly encouraging to Gronlund was that a cooperative colony of this kind would be an example for a national collective.

*Trade Unions and Obligatory Industrial Arbitration.* In Gronlund's mind, there needed to be a fundamental change in how labor and capital practiced arbitration. Arbitration did not work "from the standpoint of one who believes in the supremacy of the individual." This is to say that it would not work in a context that prioritized the power of wealthy individuals. This was illustrated quite saliently, Gronlund highlighted, during the Great Strike of 1877 and the Homestead Strike of 1892—conflicts in which employers refused to arbitrate. The assumption was that employers had no obligation to negotiate with workers since they held absolute authority over workers. But according to Gronlund's scheme, capitalist owners and employers would be forced to parley with workers. He proposed legislation to establish settlement boards, summoning representatives of both capital and labor to the table. The board would then adjudicate between labor and management, "just as courts adjudicate contracts."[69] Revising the rules of arbitration would compel workers to create stronger unions. But this would have been the biggest challenge. A rooted idea in the minds of capitalists was that the employer was superior and the employee inferior. The most powerful means to uproot this stubborn ideological consistency, Gronlund believed, came through the trust. Negotiations combined with a unified (combined) labor union would be a most powerful force to break this hegemonic ideology of the plutocracy: "The most important element in the successful working of such arbitration laws is, naturally, that the arbitrators be men who have the confidence of the working-class; and it is very likely that to secure such arbitrators these effective unions are needed."[70]

*State management of the liquor traffic.* Gronlund, like other socialists, showed his middle-class moral sentiment in the way he understood the impact of alcohol in relation to the market. Competitive capitalism drove workers to drink; it became a way to escape the daily grind of industrial labor. But in dealing with the morality of consumption, reformers needed to address the ways in which morality was impacted by the economy. Socializing the production and distribution of liquor would curb "the most pernicious influence" of public institutions like saloons, he argued, "while not depriving anyone of the indulgence in moderate drinking."[71] Drinking would be done in the home, "in the presence of wife and children," not with fellow laborers at the saloon. It would also do away with the "American custom of treating" and the "pecuniary interest" of an individual seller to provide as many drinks as possible in order to make a profit.[72]

*State control of the mines.* Gronlund saw mining as not only one of the most exploitative but also the most dangerous of labor activities. Agreeing with what William Graham wrote in *Socialism: New and Old,* Gronlund argued that municipalizing mining would give the state the responsibility for the "safety and the health of the miners." Privatizing the mines shifted production away from the safety and well-being of workers to profits. Said differently, a restricted focus on profit, under the unwavering commitment to the sanctity of private property, would disastrously sanction the ignoring of workers' welfare. Gronlund believed that the silver controversy, a major campaign issue in the 1896 election, would have been easily dealt with had the mines transferred from a private enterprise to a public interest. He believed strongly that the nationalization of the mining industry was "bound to come sometime."[73]

*Municipalization of lighting, electric power, street cars, and the telephone.*

The state should take charge of municipal enterprises like electricity and gas. On this point, Gronlund cited examples in Europe, particularly Germany, a country with "a higher capacity for organized social action than the Anglo-Saxon" people of Britain or the US. Two-thirds of the cities in Germany owned gas utilities, electric lighting, and water utilities. Publicly owned slaughterhouses and cattle markets were quite productive. Each municipality, including sewage works, would be managed not by a city council but by "capable commissions, consisting of eminent experts" with the mayor as the chief executive. Germany demonstrated success in this administrative endeavor. Gronlund also commended the municipal activities of the British government. Britain empowered municipalities through the General Tramway Act of 1870, which owned and operated street railroads to create an affordable, especially for laborers, infrastructure for use, not profit. And like Germany, the various civil servants were experienced citizens who served willingly, staying in "office twenty-five, thirty, forty or even more years" as "heads of departments and directors of public works."[74] What was keeping America from moving in a similar direction to that of Germany and Great Britain was fear of an overreaching state that would undermine personal liberty. But, as mentioned above, the state was the only legitimate power to run such municipal works.

Gronlund included telecommunication services as public utility to be placed under public authority, citing the international examples of Belgium, Holland, and New Zealand. This would have relieved Americans of the expense (31 cents) for telegraph messages as compared to citizens of Europe whose "public dispatches" could be "sent free of charge." In the United States, the cost for using the telegraph benefited the rich, who, Gronlund noted, "probably use it all they wish," as opposed to the poor and even "those in moderate circumstances," forced to pay rates that are "practically prohibitive." This established a dangerous precedent for those who pushed for the expansion of democracy, since the plutocracy would control the movement of information. And the way of initiating the process for each city was to find "men of real ability" to be placed at the head of the "various departments of each one of the great municipal works."[75]

A measure not mentioned in his original "Socializing the State" but added in *New Economy* had to do with large international infrastructural works. Gronlund anticipated the Nicaraguan Canal as a great achievement for

American nationalism.[76] Such a massive project, akin to the transcontinental railroad, would "cement [American citizens] together." The canal would also be an important experiment of nationalized socialism since it would be owned and operated in a democratic manner by the people of the United States. It would not be used for the accumulation of private wealth, and hence government violence would not be used to protect big businesses abroad. And it would also be offered as a means of aid to civilizations around the globe. The building of the canal, from Gronlund's Fabian mindset, would set America on its "glorious mission of educating mankind" toward "a peaceable democratic civilization."[77] Added to this, he believed that the canal was indicative of the movement of "Providence in human affairs." The canal would be a national (or nation-building) project. But this, I believed, reveals a blind spot in Gronlund's thinking, for he failed to see how such an infrastructural work could ever be separated from capitalism and empire. In other words, a canal of this magnitude would accelerate the momentum for production, labor, and the use of resources. It is hard to think how such a project would *not* fuel capitalism. We might also ask whether it is at all possible to effectively separate the modern nation-state from capitalism. One might question whether large infrastructural works can ever stave off capitalist production, accumulation, and empire. These difficult issues were left unanswered. Regardless, Gronlund had faith that once his programs were put in place, American citizens would draw their attention away "from the Filipinos and the Cubans, and come to the conclusion that their own affairs demand all their time and all their efforts."[78]

*State saving banks and loan offices.* The lives of American workers would likewise improve if the state took control of the nation's banking system.[79] In the late 1880s midwestern wheat prices plummeted due to rising yields in Europe, where American wheat had been sold; around the same time, the price of cotton in the sharecropping south fell dramatically. To make matters worse, the railroads were essentially serving the interests of large monopolies, offering significantly lower freight charges while burdening farmers with higher rates. Consequently, to keep their land, farmers had to borrow from the banks at exorbitant interest. The banks, of course, were under the authority of capitalists, and the government, both state and federal, acted at the bidding of these plutocrats. Facing "terrible losses and anguish of mind," American farmers looked for ways, including cooperation, to protect their economic well-being. Since the 1870s, they sought relief by encouraging the increase in the monetary supply. They continued to do so into the 1890s, when new silver mines augmented the country's supply of precious metals. "Free Silver" helped to alleviate the depressed plight of the farmers, especially as depression ravaged the country in the 1890s. But for those who supported the gold standard, a silver-backed monetary supply was still essentially cheap dollars. The capitalist plutocrats demanded gold. When the U.S. government in 1896 faced the reality of bankruptcy, a handful of bankers and investors purchased gold abroad to shore up the finances of the federal government. Not only did this secure the 1896 presidential election for Republicans, the party of big capital, it also enabled the reality that neither the nation nor its government could do much of anything without the approval of big business. Democracy was held hostage by the corporation.[80]

The "Bryan Democrats" had encouraged the government to purchase silver and lend it to farmers. For Gronlund, this would not work over the long term, for such a plan would not change the fundamentals of the monetary system. The complete socialization of America's financial system, whereby the government would "receive deposits" and lend the "moneys which depositors confide to it," was the only and final solution. Gronlund allowed for competitive private banks, but the government banks would "keep aloof from all commercial transactions, of every kind," safeguarding investors' money from commercial investments. The government would then offer loans at moderate interest as a way to help raise revenue for the states in proportion to each states' contribution. This would, "to a great extent," help the country's poor farmers. The loans would be given to the states to create employment. Gronlund anticipated that if such a scheme were to be used in the Presidential campaign among Populist Democrats in 1900, it would have had "a much greater show of success" than what the Bryan Party sought in 1896. The creation and function of a government depository and loan office would increase the popularity of the government and "create a national spirit of solidarity." Gronlund's plan, however, was unacceptable to the members of the People's Party. For years, Gronlund sought to persuade the Populist to substitute their Omaha platform for his. They were not convinced. Why? Gronlund cynically claimed that the Populists cared "not a particle for the government controlling the financial resources of the country"; rather, they cared "more for cheap money and plenty of it."[81]

One remedy to satisfy both the populists and the commonwealth so-cialists, according to Gronlund, would have been to create postal savings banks. Gronlund's banks would provide poorer citizens, many of whom were suspicious of banks to begin with, with a way to secure their earnings, gener-ate modest interest, and finance the public debt. Great Britain, France, Italy, Austria, and France had all adopted such a form. By 1895, the total amount of the deposits transferred into France's postal banks, for instance, was more than $800 million. Italy, Gronlund pointed out, leant savings "exclusively, and as a matter of policy, to her small farmers, at very small interest-charge."[82] Creating a postal savings banking system in 1882, Austria required post of-fices to act as both savings banks and bank depositors. But the best example, according to Gronlund, came from England. Inaugurated by Rowland Hill and William Gladstone in 1861, England's savings banks had become a boon to the citizens of the country:

> [I]n 1886 there were 6,500,000 depositors; in 1896 they had increased to over 11,000,000; in 1886 the value of the postal deposits for the year was $78,500,000; in 1896 these increased to over $160,000,000; the total amount standing to the credit of depositors jumped from $254,000,000 in 1886 to $489,000,000. The cost of each transaction has been about fifteen centers. In that confined empire there are twelve thousand local post-offices that do a savings banks business, they receive deposits of from twenty-five cents to $250 a year, and allow interest of two and half per cent.[83]

Gronlund was confident that this small experiment in what was essentially administrative governance would gain popular approval: "Let us get the mer-est fragment of Government Banking, and without a doubt in a short time all private savings banks will have to wind up their business, and government loans will soon follow, for our farmers will be so persistent in claiming the benefits that would flow from them, that they will be irresistible." When En-gland, just about as individualistic as the United States, introduced postal sav-ings banks, it bid, Gronlund said, "a hearty welcome to the socialistic spirit."[84] These would ensure social security. The American government would evolve into a "General Insurance" office. Something similar could be seen in Ger-many. In the years 1883, 1886, and 1889, the Germans "instituted obligatory insurance of workingmen against sickness, against accidents and against old age." The premiums were paid partly by the worker, "partly by the employer and partly by the state."[85] It was the commitment to "miserable individualism" that kept America from undertaking such a project.

Gronlund may have been harsh when speaking of populist reforms, but he was not insensitive to the plight of America's farm workers. He was especially concerned about large profit-driven bonanza farms. The crop yield of such ventures "during the first years" were much greater in "net production than the small farms," but over time their rate of production would decrease: "each acre of these larges estates gives a much smaller number of bushels of wheat than each acres of the small farms." This was due in part to the environmental impact of bonanza farming, where massive amounts of land were used with little concern for future production. The land would wear out; its soil depleted. This raised another contradiction of capitalism—that expansion of production did not always lead to a greater yield when dependent on natural resources. Such resources were not infinite. Extensive cultivation became "decidedly unprofitable"; eventually, bonanza farms could not "compete with 'intensive' cultivation on small farms." This dilemma pointed to a crisis of capitalism different from mere over-production: the evaporation of natural resources that capitalist agriculture depended upon. An important lesson that Gronlund draws from this is that a farmer should not "tie himself to more land than he is able very carefully to cultivate."[86]

Gronlund called on farmers, many of whom lacked the spirit of cooperation, to work together to achieve greater gains in production and savings. He pointed to the example of French agricultural unions, which were illegal until 1884. French farmers took advantage of the legalization of the unions to create over 1,500 agricultural societies, "of which some have a membership of 8,000 to 10,000 farmers." Such unions "buy and rent machinery in common; they buy in common and of course at wholesale, plants, seeds, and fertilizers." Many American farmers did in fact cooperate to battle the plutocratic elite dominating America's economy. The government would offer further assistance to these framing associations. Gronlund proposed a Department of Agriculture, "a real organ and servant of our farmers," to facilitate cooperation by encouraging agricultural trade unions. Farmers would consider the department a "friend-in-need," an organ to help them purchase "machinery, the fertilizers, the seeds, the breeding animals." It would also eliminate the "gambling hells" characteristic of corn exchanges, produce exchanges, and cotton exchanges by "abolishing all purely speculative sales of 'futures.'" Gronlund pointed to the Canadian system to support his point. Canada's Minister of Agriculture orchestrated a chain of subsidized storage services for products in North America being shipped to ports in Britain:

> The government subsidizes steamships to the extent of paying one-half of the initial cost—about $10,000 per steamer—of providing the best of modern duplex refrigerating machines and insulated compartments. Then, in order that the products, intended for the cold-storage chambers on the steamships, may start in the best possible condition, the government has further subsidized cold-storage buildings at the ports of export for three years, until the trade is sufficiently well established to be sustained entirely by charges on the products. Lastly, the government offers a bonus of $100 to the owner of every creamery who provides a suitable cold-storage room at his creamery, payment to be made only on condition that the cold-storage room is used and kept at a satisfactory temperature.[87]

The U.S. Department of Agriculture would take responsibility for selling the surplus products of American farmers. On this issue, Gronlund examined the significant drop in wheat prices that were hurting farmers in the mid- to late 1880s. Not surprisingly, the decline in prices came from overproduction. Selling surplus wheat was a problem for the US, given the low demand in Europe. One solution was to reduce the surplus, a job that fell to a class of individuals from among the farming community who could regulate production. And, once again, this necessitated cooperative action. Diversifying seed planting was a possible remedy to reduce a surplus, but this would interfere with the commercial demands of large-scale production. But who or what would enforce the diversification of planting to avoid overproduction? It would fall to the Department of Agriculture. During times of plenty, Americans consumed, Gronlund noted, "5.66 bushels of wheat per capita"; during years of difficulty, citizens consumed "less than four bushels" each year, making "an annual difference of more than one hundred million bushels of wheat."[88] A governmental agricultural department would have the authority to monitor America's farm production and help to mitigate the bad times from the good.

The socializing dimensions of agricultural development could not be divorced from the country's transportation infrastructure. "The government must operate the railroads," commented Granger John McArthur, "or the business must be conducted by co-operative associations."[89] Binding the country together would include nationalizing railroad transport fares, significantly reducing the cost of transport. Nationalization would most certainly do away with, as Gronlund said, "unjust discrimination" created by the "unequal rates" in regard to transport as well as the rates imposed on individual companies (not individual people), as in the case of a "traffic-manager making one butcher of one firm of grocers pay a higher rate for the same service than another butcher or another grocer in the same place."[90] Socializing the railroads would no longer favor the wealthy. It would provide U.S. citizens with cheaper transportation, making "the railroads an agent of civilization." It would end "the sickening butcher and piteous maiming of the railway servants [and] all discrimination except the just kind which the difference in locations necessitates." The unjust pricing system of the railroad was not really the result of any one individual but of the competitive system by which every organization was legally compelled to submit. The country's regulating agencies, as in the case of the Interstate Commerce Act (1887), were much too weak to correct such deficiencies. The federal government needed to do more, hence the reason why Gronlund supported a growth in the powers of administration. The government would enforce standardized rates and manage the cost of transport, eliminating the tolls set in secret by a few individuals. Gronlund went so far as to propose a "Railroad Department," headed by a cabinet-level officer who would have the power to dismiss a railroad manager for "persistently disobeying and defying the law." The nation had "a precedent for such legislation in the National Banking Act." Under such an act, when any one bank violated the law, the Comptroller of the Currency would have "the power to appoint a receiver [to] take possession of the books, records, and assets of every description' of such bank."[91]

*Compulsory education of children from four to fourteen years.* Gronlund turned next to education. American socialists, especially by the turn of the nineteenth century, believed that radical change "began with education," according to historian Jason Martinek, "[and] the best way to educate was through print."[92] Throughout the nineteenth century, reformers took as their motto, "Agitation, Organization, Education." Gronlund pushed a different slogan: "Educate, Educate, Educate."[93] Agitation certainly had its place, but Americans in general were not mature (i.e., organized, in Gronlund's sense) enough to do so. The country lacked quality educated leaders who could direct the course of history. Education was needed "to ripen" the American people for the coming cooperative commonwealth.[94] The educational strategy among fellow socialists, Martinek continues, "forged the basis of an oppositional culture at the margins of American society, one that presented mainstream America with an alternative way to live, think and be," encouraging Americans to consider the restructuring of American society from the bottom up.[95]

Gronlund proposed a reconceptualization of late-nineteenth-century education. Young people should be trained as "cooperators in the coming change—each in his or her station, each according to his or her capabilities."[96] The two "leading features" of late-nineteenth-century America were the "Trust and Democracy," yet neither were harnessed in America's educational system. Science and technology created the trust, which, in turn, compelled Americans "in all directions to subordinate themselves to great systems." As the nation's forefathers "laid the foundation for Democracy," science and technology came to assist democratic growth for the creation of "a people of specialists," meaning that not only was democracy growing, but advances in science and technology enabled more comprehensive understandings of the world. But America's educational system of the late nineteenth century ignored the relation between democracy, science, and technology. Sadly, however, education became "a select affair" for the wealthier classes—geared toward the trust, but not democracy. The nation failed to provide an adequate public education for the population, ignoring the preparation needed for the masses to understand their place in the divine plan. And yet even for the select few, liberal education was itself a failure, since it narrowly focused on advancing capitalism. The challenge regarding education in Gronlund's day was how to train young people to be both "capable specialists and all-round men," to combine the sciences and democracy.[97] What he meant was that a young man needed to be trained in something useful for the purpose advancing democracy. True equality, he argued, and an expansion of democracy would occur if educators spent time identifying and cultivating the unique capabilities of every student. Society would function as a highly advanced state, enabling greater freedom for the individual who demonstrated a better grasp of his or her environment. Indeed, for Gronlund, freedom was a matter of increasing a person's power to act on their material conditions. Unfortunately, general education in the United States ignored the potential of each young person and sapped the strength of the national commonwealth.

The curriculum would be more than just the "busy work" of reading, writing, and "ciphering," what he referred to as "the empty wrappers of knowledge."[98] He commended the "New Education" of progressive visionary Joseph Mayor Rice, architect of education research and standardized testing that had been implemented in cities like Minneapolis and Indianapolis. In his 1893 *The Public School System of the United States,* Rice argued that students would study the contents of their disciplines through actively drawing, painting, and modeling—activities that would allow students to form abstract theories through experience, which would furthermore make "visible to the teacher" the knowledge of the children. They would also work together in small groups, around "small square tables," engaging in common work and learning. As students engaged one another through this communal form of education, teachers would have a better opportunity to study their pupils and to identify the specific talents and capabilities of each. Gronlund saw such pedagogy as evolution "made conscious."[99] He also admired the work of American professor of political and social ethics Felix Adler, an advocate of "deed, not creed" and architect of the Ethical Culture movement. Adler held to an ethical theory that encouraged individuals to act toward others in such a way as to bring out the best in those others. Reciprocally, treating someone with respect would draw out the commendable traits of the one being kind to the other. Adler would later develop the ethical maxim: "act as to elicit the unique personality in others, and thereby in thyself."[100] Having each student interact in a communal setting was sharply contrasted with the traditionally individualistic education where educators would simply deposit knowledge into the minds of single individual children. Concern for the "unique personality of others" clashed with the morality of competitive individualism.

In late-nineteenth-century America, young children were constantly subjected to "great demoralization at home and in the street," many abandoned by their parents who were working long hours and thus unable to spend time with them. Gronlund's education would remove children from the competitive dog-eat-dog capitalist world. Kindergartens would provide "gentle but firm discipline" to cultivate character and proper habits. Young children would be free to ask questions about the world, answered by compassionate teachers. Early childhood education would be a learning playroom, where instructors would guide "the play of the children, so that it is made into the most fruitful kind of work."[101] Such structured play would direct students toward the enjoyment of useful work. Happiness contributed to better learning

Gronlund was not suggesting that children be forever sheltered from the public world of labor, however. They would eventually need to enter society and lead the country toward the commonwealth. Here, Gronlund moved to the second level of public education. Older (preteen) children would transfer to manual training schools. Manual training promoted the intellect, reinforced the "inalienable right of every American youth" to have an education, and provided opportunities for students to learn various trades. Young people would be offered a glimpse of "the whole circle of human activities," allowing them to pursue their own "promising career."[102] Most importantly, this phase of education would deepen students' experience in cooperation. Both kindergarten and manual training schools would make cooperation second nature.

The level of education after manual training, during the students' teen years, would focus on history and philosophy. This was for the purpose of developing a young person's moral character. Gronlund commended the study of Greek and Latin writers of antiquity from Homer to Cicero since their work countered selfish competitive individualism and contributed to shaping the virtues of humans in communion with one another. The literary classics would become infinitely more valuable when applied to the cooperative commonwealth. The civilization of the coming commonwealth would revive the universal virtue that prompted humanity to seek "individual welfare through the collective well-being." This stage of education would become "the instrument of the will of the people, working for the enlightenment of all."[103]

Each school would seek out the most qualified instructors, advocating, in particular, for "more male teachers." The majority of teachers in America were "young, untrained girls," who, in Gronlund's judgment, had "entered upon the grand art of teaching simply as a 'business.'" These young women saw their vocation as temporary, a time to earn "a little pocket-money" before entering marriage. But engaging such work in this way sullied the dignity and value of the teaching arts. Such a job "should be the most exalted function," which in Gronlund's chauvinistic mind could not be "expected of women": "men only can be relied upon to make any line of work a profession and devote their whole soul to it." Yet women, not men, were best placed in the kindergartens. Kindergartens "unsex" men, he said: "Hence we must find exceptional women for these positions, women with the true missionary spirit to induce them to accept that function as their life-work."[104]

Funding for this three-tiered system would come from an annual fund—a fund similar to one for veterans ("sailors and soldiers and their dependents") of the war against Spain. Doing so would "lift a whole generation" of Americans "up on a strikingly higher plane of civilization."[105] He called on all American citizens to support this New Education, an education that would create "a more perfect civilization," where young people would alter their social conditions and thereby contribute to the progress of the human nature. American education had been perverted by a pervasive "mercantile spirit," where children were taught to compete with one another, that business was the only "suitable goal for their ambition"—taught a life that would "enable them to 'get the better' of their simpler fellowmen in the struggle for existence and for wealth."[106] The state, therefore, was to act as a protector for the country's children by directing these common schools.

The last portion of *New Economy* called for the creation of an ancillary institution to the state—namely, "Civic Churches." This made sense given his commitment to the divine in history as well as his direct work with liberal religious thinkers in the 1890s. Such churches would be "peculiarly conformable to the American mind." Gronlund understood the practical function of the Christian church, "admirably adapted to concerted efforts." American churches were effective instruments of social mobilization and thus could be used to prepare for the advent of the collectivist commonwealth. Unfortunately, churches in America were complicit in supporting the plutocratic hegemony in the way that they focused on individual salvation, ignoring the redemption of society. His "Civic Churches" were not to be considered as opposition to traditional churches, but as supplements. The former would be places to "prepare for action," with the end goal of making life better on earth, while the latter, as "places for worship and prayer." "Civic Churches," defined not by doctrinal differences, but by "one article of faith": "a belief in the 'Power behind evolution' in the World Spirit."[107] Visitors would attend lectures offered by experts conscious of the fact that they were "acting in unison with the powers and forces" unfolding "the destiny of humanity."[108] Gronlund assumed that the leaders of these churches would encourage citizens "to adopt the measures" proposed in *New Economy*. The churches would raise up competent socialist leaders—leaders "imbued with principles and traditions of the old black Republican party," whose philosophy pointed "straight to Collectivism."[109] Gronlund placed greater hope in the "Civic Churches" to advance the "Power behind evolution" and convince politicians of the need to create a cooperative commonwealth.

Gronlund called on women to encourage their husbands to participate in these churches. Women, he believed, had a "peculiar endowment," a "propelling power" that is "almost divine," that would motivate men toward spiritual action. Indeed, the "dominant influence on the human race" has been "woman's choice," since all patriarchal authority is "due to female selection."[110] More importantly, women had an innate gift for sympathy, intuition, a maternal instinct to care for others, and practical sense from which men could learn. There was another reason behind Gronlund's discussion of the differences between men and women. The failure of the Populist Party, he believed, was caused by women's unchecked "powers of persuasion and stimulation" and the tendency to abandon reason: "the fanaticism and many of the grievous mistakes of the party were due to her, precisely because she was invited to help in framing its policies and defending them in speech and writing." Gronlund admitted that the change of women's conditions in the commonwealth would change their status in society, though it would not change their nature. For Gronlund, a woman's unique strength rested on the fact that she would draw out the power of men—"his strength, his perseverance and his genius"—so that they would decide the necessary course for the betterment of all humanity.

Gronlund never wavered from working to create a new economy. As Seymour Stedman concluded in his reflections on Gronlund, "The peoples of the future will dwell in peace where this hardy pioneer warred with the accumulated prejudice, passions, and ignorance of the ages."[111] At the dawn of the twentieth century, according to Gronlund, humanity would be "able consciously to direct its destiny—to foreordain events."[112] History was the drama of a "mysterious Prompter, the Power behind evolution, the Supreme Reason" that framed the "plots and climaxes" of history. At the same time, it was a power that worked through humans, compelling "men to become its instrument." The great kings and emperors of history believed that they were simply pursuing their own ends, but in reality they served the direction of the

"Supreme Reason." "Exactly the same bait," Gronlund says," is now applied to our capitalists and captains of industry, as well as to our politicians."[113] The true heroes of history represented those whose work aligned with the Power behind evolution. Thus, citizens were to educate themselves and others, organize the state along the lines explicated by Gronlund, "learn to discern and follow the direction in which the finger of the World-Will points," and establish a collective nation. America—and by extension, much of the modern world at the turn of the century—was coming near to "God's hour," as the Power behind evolution prepared for the arrival of his Kingdom.[114]

# WORKING MEN AND WOMEN OF ALL COUNTRIES, COOPERATE!

In a 2015 essay for *The Nation,* historian Eric Foner encouraged then-presidential candidate Bernie Sanders to "embrace" America's socialist heritage rather than appeal to progressive social practices in parts of northern Europe, which, according to Foner, simply reinforced a century-and-a-half belief that "socialism is a foreign import."[1] By presenting the mind of Laurence Gronlund, *American Socialist* recaptures a lost piece of America's history, doing so at a time of serious cultural divisions caused in no insignificant way by economic fragility and historical myopia. The book challenges the way in which the very word *socialism* has been used as a "scare word," as Harry Truman said over a half century ago, "hurled at every advance the people made."[2] Warnings of impending socialism have been used by opponents of social security, farm-pricing, bank deposit insurance, desegregation, civil rights, healthcare, pandemic preventions, and even infrastructural improvements—"almost anything that helps all of the people."[3]

There is a twofold benefit to that noble dream of historical research. First, history confronts ignorance by recovering and preserving the past. Americans seem not only detached from but also irresolutely hostile to history, the result of habits created by neoliberal policies, corporate authoritarianism, and a mnemonically convulsive media ecosystem. Care for the commonwealth, as a result, has been slowed if not completely arrested. Second, knowledge of the past provides direction for how to live in the present. An increasing number of American citizens, especially among the younger generation impacted by the Great Recession, are becoming conscious of the failures of global capitalism. They are, as Gronlund once said, sufficiently motivated to act.

The impact of socialism in America is far more extensive than party organization, movement West, otherworldliness, or the prospects of better living standards under American capitalism.[4] According to Robert Hyfler, socialists effectively introduced "certain social democratic practices in American culture more generally."[5] The radicalism of the past—demonstrated by associationists, collectivists, socialists, communists, and anarchists—has extended beyond a confrontational critique of capitalism. Reformist and radical groups led the way in establishing an eight-hour workday, the eradication of child labor, social security, racial, gender, and sexual equality, commitments that—for the most part—now seem part of everyday life and far from radical. Daniel Pope reminds us that "the history of American radicalism demands a capacity for irony."[6] What may have been considered radical in one age—the abolition of slavery, women's suffrage, the eight-hour workday, social security, workers compensation, weekends, the legal end to segregation—may not be considered so in another. As Pope writes, radicals have often been "forerunners, pressing demands treated as outlandish or subversive at the time, but eventually accepted as practical and just."[7] Certain habits seen as dangerously radical in one period have become common place in another, moving from the fringe to the center. "The waxing and waning" of radicalism, according to Howard Brick and Christopher Phelps, "are best understood by apprehending *margin* and *mainstream* as the constitutive duality of the American radical experience. *Radicals must exist in estrangement from society, in opposition to the whole established order,*" until the establishment is transformed, moving that which was once radical to normal.[8] This fulcrum may account for the difficulties in finding a "tradition" of radicalism in American history. The supposed "failure" of radicalism in its various and often competing forms can easily be confused with the emergence of new ways of living—that is to say, how radical activism can create a new status quo, making the memory of a radical tradition fade considerably. But collective amnesia does not erase historical reality: the specter of radicalism continues to hover over the many accomplishments it has brought to American society. Yet radicalism is never complete; there are always new challenges, setbacks, and defeat. Gronlund acknowledged this reality. Marxist socialism may have been of "negligible importance in the United States," but Gronlund's "somewhat diluted" socialism had "a far-reaching and pervasive influence."[9]

Feeling the lingering effects of the Great Recession, American citizens have become increasingly open to more leftist approaches to the economy, whether reformist or radical. From popular statesmen on down to those marginalized and discriminated against, calls for cooperation spanned the long nineteenth century, reaching a high point in the first quarter of the twentieth century. From the Panic of 1837 to the Great Recession of 2008, citizens have found socialism an increasingly attractive alternative for America.[10] The late Joyce Appleby wrote in *Relentless Revolution: A History of Capitalism*: "Every economic downturn gives critics a change to draft obituaries for capitalism."[11] This may be a bit strong, but economic calamities compel many to rethink their economic commitments, more importantly their everyday habits under capitalism. The words of writers and intellectuals like Bellamy, George, and Gronlund, according to Herbert Schneider, "are every ready helps in time of trouble and are still kept on the great American bookshelf, to be dusted off whenever a major crisis or a periodic depression causes episodic introspection."[12] One consequence of the Great Recession (or any serious economic downturn), according to Marxian historian Eric Hobsbawm, was that "there could no longer be any doubt that [Marx] was back on the public scene."[13] Indeed, sales of Marx's *Capital* boomed after 2008. It is one thing to forget the events of history, it is much harder to disentangle the influence of historical change on society. One can only hope that as Americans face more capitalist crises—which they will, given the tyranny of neoliberalism—they will swing closer to socialism. The question should not be why there is no socialism in America but rather how citizens might anticipate and nurture the recurrence of socialism in the country—harnessing "public sentiment for socialism," writes John Judis, for the purpose of creating "a formidable political movement."[14]

Leftist cooperative efforts have always felt the heavy hand of the establishment. Even in the current world, "whole lines" of Leftist thought have become, according to Steve Fraser, "endangered species, living, if at all, on the margins of public life" that leaves "society defenseless against the predations of a new gilded elite."[15] In his 2019 state of the union address, then-President Donald Trump directly attacked what he perceived as a resurging interest in socialism, suggesting that socialism has always been contrary to all that America was founded upon: "Here, in the United States, we are alarmed by new calls to adopt socialism in our country . . . America was founded on liberty and independence—not government coercion, domination, and control. We are born free, and we will stay free. America will never become a socialist country."[16] Trump and his loyalists might be correct in identifying the renewed popularity of socialism, but they have failed to give its proper rendering.[17] This would require an understanding of history, and no hypernationalist or neofascist has any inclination to take history seriously. The fear of socialism has, today, threatened democracy itself, as militant reactionary forces work to justify voter restrictions and an insurrection against the government. Richard Hofstadter's argument regarding the persistency of the mood of paranoia in American political thought has been largely applied to the reactionary impulses of conservatives. Many contemporary historians, most notably Harvard's Lisa McGirr, have made the case that such an approach to conservativism, which has become a kind of interpretive paradigm to understand the psyche of conservatives, evangelicals, and Republicans, has run its course.[18] But it has revived in recent years. Given the visceral and clamorous support for Trump and the neo-fascism for which he sits at the forefront, "the paranoid style of American politics," Michael Mark Cohen writes, has once again "seized the center of American political power."[19] This renewed reactionary politics has given new life to America's cultural divide.[20] And what fuels this hyper-nationalism is a renewed fear of socialism.

Although not on the same level as the Right, the Left (however "Left" the Left really is) likewise bears responsibility. It is not that members associated with this political end have lacked the courage to stand up to the Right. Part of their ineffectiveness stems from the fact that they, too, for the most part, have forgotten America's socialist legacy, and thus offered partial relief to the needs of society.[21] Those identified as "Left" today have lost sight of the material conditions that perpetuate inequality, making them far from radical Left. Historian Andrew Hartman says that the "Left" today "is a whack-a-mole Left: protest a lumber company here, a trade organization there, police brutality here, Israeli settlement there. Meanwhile, capitalism does what it does—most unabated—and inequality once again becomes the scourge of the time." The contemporary "Left" has, in other words, forgotten "its long-standing Marxist tradition."[22] The material base largely responsible for inequality and marginality is largely ignored. Perhaps such historical amnesia stems from the tacit acceptance of neoliberal authoritarianism, how top-down corporate managerialism has come to reshape key societal spheres. Legislators, for the most part, continue to do the bidding of corporate elites. Institutions like businesses, schools, and governments have adopted a corporate model. The condition of workers in America have been largely brushed aside, especially during the numerous strike waves that have been given very little attention from corporate media outlets. Liberals have rightly concerned themselves with trying to heal a country divided along the lines of class, race, and gender. Yet in their noble pursuits, they have sidelined the conditions that widen such fissures—conditions born of capitalism. I don't mean to sound like a material reductionist, but I will say that very little substantial change will be made to heal America's deep wounds unless citizens look to the material forces that have created such wounds.

Since the postbellum period, the United States has been shaped time and again by a kind of Gilded Age-Progressive Era cycle—an expansion of capitalist wealth and its consolidation in the hands of a few, followed by an economic crisis and a Left-leaning response to regain democracy. The first Gilded Age reached its height in the 1880s–90s, followed by another Gilded Age in the 1920s, then again in the 1950s, 1980s, and 2000s. Along with these gilded periods, new progressive moments appeared in the 1900s, 1930s, 1960s, 1970s, and, of course, after 2008. It bears repeating that from the 1870s to the present, the country has witnessed a handful of economic highs, especially in the late 1940s and 1950s, followed by serious depressions, especially in 1929 and 2008. Each period of largely unrestricted economic growth has brought a celebration of capitalism, while every economic downturn, a condemnation of it. What descriptors beyond *farcical* would Marx use to describe America's third, fourth, and fifth replay of history? It is my hope that reviving the memory of Laurence Gronlund will embolden those who are seriously committed to confronting a nation stuck on repeat.

In a eulogy printed in *The Comrade* in 1905, Eugene V. Debs extolled the humanitarian commitments of Laurence Gronlund, describing him as a "visionary," who willingly and selflessly gave himself "to the battle march of human progress."[23] The memory of Gronlund, Debs believed, would remain through his books, "his eternal monuments." Writing in the same issue of *Comrade,* socialist Leonard Abbott, co-founder of the Stelton Colony in New Jersey, praised Gronlund's "magnificent idealism," which, he continued, became "part of the permanent heritage of humanity."[24] One item of note in Abbott's commemoration was that when "a man of the Gronlund type" dies, his efforts to transform society die with him—that his work "seems to fail." Indeed, I suspect that many in America would see Gronlund's work in a similar way, since those same many are convinced that socialism generally—without a clear definition of what it is or its various forms—represented a disastrous failure. As intimated in parts of the current study, it would be incorrect to say that socialism was a "complete" failure. "If success," say the authors of *We Own the Future*, "means that the United States has become a democratic socialist country, then the movement has certainly failed. But if success means that many Americans now accept ideas that were once considered radical, even socialist, and made the United States a more egalitarian and humane society, then it has accomplished a great deal."[25]

Allow me to entertain for a moment the nature of failure itself. There has hardly ever been a moment of respite in modern history for socialism to flourish on its own. Defenders of capitalism have consistently and aggressively opposed any hint of it. Thus, in this way, socialism fails because it is constantly assailed by its adversary. But let's put aside history for a moment and agree, for the sake of argument, that socialism essentially does not work and is inherently and necessarily violent, repressive, and authoritarian. This is the very nature, supporters of capitalism say, of the socialist system. The principle here is that we should abandon a socioeconomic system not only because of its inherent and irrevocable brokenness but because its failures lead to repressive authoritarianism. If we are to hold consistently to the idea that we should abandon a socioeconomic system because of the brokenness and authoritarianism inherent to it, then we should have abandoned capitalism long ago.

But we can consider the nature of "failure" in a different way. Claims of "failure" might arise because of the way our ideals—thinking in a kind of Platonic manner—regularly evade embodiment. Even if they are materialized, whether in cultural habits or through social institutions, such materiality tends to be ephemeral. Both ideals and the incarnation of those ideals are subject to change given contingencies in our lived experiences. Perhaps we need to humbly accept both the reality and ineffability of ideals themselves. That a practical, cultural, or material instantiation of our ideals may replace an earlier form suggests that the dynamism of reconciling ideals with experience can never be sealed in any final or absolute sense. But this, in no way, means that the pursuit of truth, beauty, and justice are a waste of time. In his 1869 *History of American Socialisms,* John Humphrey Noyes provided an innovative response to those who would dismiss socialism as a complete failure: "If a man's first-born, in whom his heart is bound up dies at six years old, that does not turn the whole affair into a joke . . . or our part we hold that the hopes and predictions [of socialism] were true, and the results were liars."[26] The death of a child does not mean that the importance of establishing a family or having children is a complete waste of time or that the love of a parent has somehow diminished as a result of such a tragedy. The efforts of radicals and reformers are not futile despite their untimely and often tragic departure from this life. Holly Jackson argues that the "history of radical thought must be a history of a certain kind of failure": "we might look not to the perpetuity of [radicals'] outcomes but to the rightness of their principles, their success in prefiguring, at least for a time, a different and better world, and most of all their motivation to act on those principles in the face of failure, to try something when it is easier and safer to do nothing. Devoting their lives to a struggle with no end, they dared to begin"[27] There may even be something inspiring about failure. For Vaneesa Cook, failure fuels radicalism: "the recurring social setbacks and politics failures of leftists movements did not shatter their sense of mission; instead, it radicalized them."[28] The architects of change never outlive the legacy of their heroic efforts. The words and activism of Frederick Douglass, Lydia Maria Child, Lucy Parsons, Eugene Debs, W. E. B. Du Bois, A. J. Muste, or Martin Luther King Jr., to name a small handful, live on. And moments of injustice should not tarnish the legacy of these figures; indeed, they should make America's radical history shine even more. Many of us would not accept the notion that equity and justice *are* failures when instances of inequity and injustice seem strong, though it is very easy for us to become discouraged or disillusioned. "American radicalism," Dan McKanan concludes in *Prophetic Encounters,* "has endured because it has never been thoroughly defeated and because it has never completely triumphed."[29] Eric Foner reminds us that socialism itself "refers not to a blueprint for a future society but to the need to rein in the excesses of capitalism, evident all around us, to empower ordinary people in a political system verging on plutocracy, and to develop policies that make opportunity real for the millions of Americans for whom it is not."[30]

A recurring criticism against Leftists, revived in part after the Occupy Wall Street movement in 2011, is that direct activism lacks a well-worked out plan for a new society. Such criticism, however, is indicative of a lack of knowledge of the history of such activism. One consistent strategy running through radical and reform movements is that of arresting the status quo in order for members of society to reflect on the injustices inherent in economic, political, social, or cultural systems. Moved by the words of Henry David Thoreau, radicals are willing to be "a counter friction to stop the machine," doing so with urgency and without necessarily having a perfectly worked out alternative. At the peak of the Free Speech Movement in 1964, Mario Savio echoed Thoreau when he said that the injustices of the world made people so "sick of heart" that it required placing our bodies "upon the gears and upon the wheels, upon the levers, upon all the apparatus" to make it stop. Martin Luther King Jr. understood that putting one's body on the gears of the machine was necessary to generate a crisis. As he wrote in his "Letter from a Birmingham Jail," "[I]njustice must be exposed, with all the tensions its exposure creates, to the light of human conscience and the air of national opinion *before it can be cured*."[31]

True radicals are not—or *should* not be—mere iconoclasts. A detailed description of a new society *never* precedes crisis, since there is no way to plan every foreseeable detail of the better world desired by radicals. The imagination shapes and is shaped by the various interdependent modes of being. The reality of a new world must grapple with the material, biological, physical, economic, social, aesthetic, logical, and religious modes of being. This is the nature of history, a mind and matter dialectic. Radicals and reformers must recognize their limitations and open themselves up to the contingencies of being. They cannot stubbornly impose their will on the material world. Gronlund rejected the idea of abruptly demolishing the current system to force citizens to comply with a predetermined plan. This is to lose sight of the dynamics of social development and the priority of cooperation. Socialists, Gronlund said, "do not propose to demolish the present order of things, as we tear down an old building, and then compel humanity to rear a new edifice according to any plan that they have drawn."[32] This was exactly Washington Gladden's criticism against Gronlund and the socialists, who seemed to too strong on critique but weak on solutions: "So long as it is content with criticizing the present order it can gain a hearing . . . [But its] advocates are chary of definite information of their plans . . . when they are asked to tell what they would put in the place of the existing system, they at once begin to deal in generalities."[33] The true radical will accept the fact that he or she is motivated by "generalities," Gladden wrote. The late David Graeber asked in his *Democracy Project,* "When has social change ever happened according to someone's blueprint?" Graeber suspects that a detailed vision for social transformation is a "hangover from Enlightenment ideas that have long since faded out virtually everywhere except America":

> We cannot really conceive the problems that will arise when we start actually trying to build a free society. What now seems likely to be the thorniest problems might not be problems at all; others that never even occurred to us might prove devilishly difficult. There are innumerable X-factors . . . What might a revolution in common sense actually look like? I don't know, but I can think of any number of pieces of conventional wisdom that surely need challenging if we are to create any sort of viable free society.[34]

Vaneesa Cook would agree, emphasizing the fact that socialists prefer process over that of the attainment of a "fully fledged structure and operation in a complex world."[35] As A. J. Muste believed, radicals "cannot foresee the society which is to be and we must finally accept the fact that we are dealing with a process and it is in the process that we find our success rather than in the realization of a static plan for society."[36] Radicals understand the contingent nature of life, the inability to control every outcome, but they are nonetheless receptive when penultimate ameliorations come. Those committed to the peaceful uprooting of the sources of injustice and human suffering are willing to do the work necessary to make a *more perfect*—though still *far from* perfect—commonwealth for all. But patience, grace, imagination, and faith must be at the forefront of their minds as a new world is forged, adapting to unforeseeable developments. They should follow the legacy of American Transcendentalists, holding to their convictions while, at the same time, amending their beliefs when new circumstances demand it. This is radical wisdom, and Gronlund understood it. "Socialists have no ready-made plan to lay down for the guidance of those who will be called upon to organize the Coming Commonwealth," he said, "least of all a detailed plan." How could they? "He is a bad architect who cannot plan the building he is required to erect, to the nicest details; who is unable to tell the size of this drawing-room, or the exact location of that closet. Do not demand such details from us."[37] Instead, he likened the socialist to a botanist "able to tell what plant will develop out of a certain seed, but he cannot tell how many leaves it will have."[38] Radicals must be guided "by their own judgment, the [current] condition of affairs, and the temper of the people."[39] They should let ideals—and faith—guide revolutionary change. In his admiration for the Saint-Simonians, John Stuart Mill extolled faithfulness to a sound philosophy even if ultimately unattainable: "the true ideal of a perfect human society . . . which, like any other model of unattainable perfection, everybody is the better for aspiring to, although it be impossible to reach it."[40] Gronlund believed that it was God who willed the coming commonwealth. This did not mean that citizens were to passively stand by; they had a responsibility "to find out" the will of the divine through the implementation of active political and economic reforms.[41]

If the twentieth century "shows anything," write Phelps and Brick, "it is the great danger of conceiving of history's course as fixed." Despite the sharp and contentious differences among radicals and reformers of the past, those in the contemporary world who ache for a better life (and not just for themselves) will find inspiration from the arguments, organizing strategies, and even the sheer will of those who sought to make a better world. "The storehouse of past radicalisms," Brick and Phelps continue, "may provide creative inspiration, although the real yield will surely derive from innovations yet to come."[42] This intellectual biography is an attempt to give a bit of that hope. While it affirms Gronlund's limitations, including parts of his thought that are in today's world passe and outright discriminatory, there remains plenty of his influence to at least raise awareness of what American citizens might be able to achieve. Ralph Waldo Emerson once wrote that a person's words must have an "edge" to them; otherwise, such words ring hollow. It is my hope that the current book will provide an edge, a motivation for readers continuing to live the consequences of one of the worst economic downturns since the Great Depression. A critical study like the present is not just historical; it is also philosophical, but philosophical in a way befitting those sufficiently inspired to act. Both philosophers and historians should do more than simply describe the world; they should seek to change it. They should seek to awaken their readers to action. Historical figures like Laurence Gronlund can motivate and inspire us, moving us to find the edge necessary to change the world for the better.

Today, radicals express, to borrow from Jean-Francois Lyotard, an "incredulity toward metanarratives." The last century has demonstrated how rigid blueprints for society, whether offered from the Right or the Left, can bring great harm. As Michel Foucault noted: "As soon as one 'proposes'—one proposes a vocabulary, an ideology, which can only have effects of domination."[43] This rather strong statement is softened by another one of his: that within the struggle between ideas and practice one may cultivate a faith that "positive conditions [will] emerge."[44] Axel Honneth's position in *The Idea of Socialism* may be appealing to those interesting in making a change: "I make no attempt to draw connections to current political constellations and possibilities for action. I will not be dealing with the strategic question of how socialism could influence current political events, but solely how the original intention of socialism could be reformulated so as to make it once again a source of political-ethical orientation."[45] This does not mean that we should abandon the ideas or strategies of those who sought critical change. Change often comes as a result of an awakened conscience. The undeniable injustices of contemporary global capitalism should be enough to inspire people around the world to act. Many of the challenges that Gronlund addressed in Gilded Age America have remained in the United States today. Consider the economic situation of the United States over the last decade. Peter Edelman, professor at Georgetown University Law and former advisor to Bill Clinton, offered representative numbers of the one percent just before the Great Recession:

> The top 1 percent took-in 9 percent of all personal income in 1979, and that figure skyrocketed to 23.5 percent in 2007. The top fifth took in 53 percent of all after-tax personal income in 2007. The income of the top 1 percent went up a staggering 275 percent between 1979 and 2007, while that of the bottom 20 percent grew just 18 percent in those twenty-eight years. (Income in the middle barely grew either.). The income of the top 0.1 percent (one one-thousandth of the population) increased a staggering 390 percent . . . By 2007, the top 1 percent held a larger share of income than at any time since 1928.[46]

Five years after the Great Recession, unemployment reached its highest level since the Great Depression. The time between unemployment and getting a new job was considerably longer than in previous periods. Yet corporate profits have continued to climb. On the eve of 2008, the salaries of the average CEO increased 400 times that of the average worker. Keep in mind that average worker take-home pay has hovered around 4 percent for nearly half a century. Less than 1 percent of Americans hauled in a bigger percentage of the country's total pre-tax income than at any time since the late 1920s. Less than 1 percent of Americans owned 42 percent of the financial wealth in the country. The top 5 percent owned nearly 70 percent of all the country's wealth. On the eve of the Depression, 5 percent owned 30 percent of the nation's income. Taxes on the nation's highest earners was the lowest it had ever been (25 percent in 1928–29 compared to 35 percent in 2008). And conditions have not substantially improved. The growth in secure, long-term employment has been abysmal. Yes, there has been job growth, but these jobs are largely insecure in relation to long-term benefits for workers. Housing remains a stressed economy. Financial institutions continue to make the same foolish gambles that created the 2008 crisis in the first place. Students are drowning in tuition debt, with little to no help to ameliorate such a burden. Wages continue to be much too low. The health of the environment is continually ignored for the sake of profit.

And a global pandemic has not made the situation any easier. The richest individuals on the planet (3,000 individuals) have had a wealth increase of over $3 trillion. Millions of people have fallen into the category of "extreme" poverty—over 700 million globally. The richest 10 percent of the globe own 76 percent of the entire wealth of the globe. The bottom 50 percent own only 2 percent. The top 10 percent of the globe receive over 50 percent of all income; again, the bottom receives only 8 percent. The wealth of the richest ten men, six of them American, doubled during the pandemic. The collective wealth of just half a dozen Americans went from $700 billion to $1.5 trillion in two years. Indeed, between mid-March and the early weeks of April 2020, when unemployment soared, U.S. billionaires augmented their wealthy by nearly $300 billion. Jeff Bezos, Bill Gates, and Warren Buffett alone own as much as the entire bottom half of Americans. The richest Americans by 2020 were worth 21 times as much as in 1982. The richest 1 percent hold more than half of all stocks and yet less than 5 percent of debt. And these elites seem to live in their own worlds (or outer worlds depending on which one will be going to space next), continuing to conspicuously consume mansions, luxury cars, and superyachts in the midst of widespread human suffering. Wealth disparity in America is wider than in any country, noticeably worse when looking at the lives of minorities, particularly African Americans and Latinx Americans. As Thomas Piketty notes in *Capital in the Twenty-First Century*, the extreme levels of income inequality are "incompatible with the merito-cratic values and principles of social justice fundamental to modern dem-ocratic societies."[47] The drift toward "oligarchy is real," he says.[48] As wealth continues to grow, democracy swiftly withers away, as can be seen in the rise of popular right-wing fascism in the United States, Europe, Australia, and parts of Southeast Asia.

The managerial authoritarianism of neoliberal capitalism has become absolute, the *zeitgeist* of our current age that is nearing full consciousness. And its reach has gone beyond the realm of the public. Employees, Alex Gourevitch concludes in *From Slavery to the Cooperative Commonwealth*, "have lost jobs for expressing or holding political views to which their bosses objected, and employers have used their authority in the workplace to force employees to attend rallies, to listen to and distribute political messages, to influence their votes, and to donate to certain campaigns."[49] Many have been punished for social media comments, supporting unions, failing to fit the image management has for them, or even just questioning management (fail-ing to be "team players," a euphemism for absolute obedience to corporate authority). Even our most private institutions (e.g., the family or religious organizations) cannot escape mimicking the corporate world. Where can we flee from capitalism's presence? If we fly to the heavens, it is there. If we were to make our beds in the depths, it would be there. If we were to rise on the wings of the dawn or settle on the far side of the sea, even there the "invisible hand" of capitalism would snatch us up.

This is not to deny the practical efforts made to deal with the negative consequences of capitalism. One important way is through cooperation. The stubborn commitments of right-leaning individualists and slightly left-of-center statists, according to Bernard Harcourt, have resulted in political, so-cial, and economic gridlock, "pushing many liberal democracies," Harcourt says, "to the brink of civil discord." A key part of the divide stems from the fact that both sides are in the stranglehold of corporate wealth. Harcourt proposes "another path" that relies on cooperation at the ground level, prima facie nonrevolutionary activities that are, nonetheless, latent with very real revolutionary potential. Cooperation, a fundamental tenet of socialism, is entirely ignored by the defenders of competition. Marx dedicated an entire chapter (chapter 13) to cooperation in volume 1 of *Capital*. Cooperation, for him, does two things. First, it "strips off the fetters" of forlorn individuality and contributes to the cultivation of humanity's full potential. Second, it "overcomes" the "antithesis between labor and capital."[50] Later, in his inaugural address at the First International, Marx commended the value of cooperative associations:

> We speak of the cooperative movement, especially of the co-operative factories raised by the unassisted efforts of a few bold 'hands.' The value of these great social experiments cannot be over-rated. By deed, instead of by argument, that have shown that production on a large scale, and in accord with the behest of modern science, may be carried on without the existence of a class of masters employing a class of hands; that to bear fruit, the means of labour need not be monopolized as a means of dominion over, and of extortion against, the labouring man himself; and that, like slave labour, like serf labour, hired labour is but a transitory and inferior form, destined to disappear before associated labour plying its toil with a willing hand, a ready mind, and a joyous heart.[51]

Indeed, cooperation played a vital role in historical development. As Marx argued in volume 3 of *Capital*,

> Co-operative factories show how, at a certain stage of development of the material forces of production, and of the social forms of production corresponding to them, a new mode of production develops and is formed naturally out of the old . . . Capitalist joint-stock companies as much as co-operative factories should be viewed as transition forms from the capitalist mode of production to the associated one, simply that in one case the opposition is abolished in a negative way, and in the other in a positive way.[52]

Gronlund likewise noted the role of cooperation in the stages of history. Even more than Marx, Vladimir Ilyich Lenin stressed the centrality of cooperation. Socialism, for Lenin, equaled cooperation: "the system of civilized cooperators is the system of socialism."[53] What we need to remember in this regard is that Lenin appeared to favor worker cooperative democracy over that of bureaucracy, though he was quite inconsistent with this position given his reliance on party leadership. "Bureaucracy must be abandoned for democracy," he said, "[and] the initiative of the workers and of other employees must be drawn on; they must be immediately summoned to conferences and congresses; a certain proportion of the profits must be assigned to them, provided they institute overall control and increase production."[54]

Notwithstanding the daunting obstacles in its way, cooperative socialism has been and continues to be successful. The growing popularity of democratic cooperation in the economy led the United Nations to declare 2012 the year of the cooperative. Plenty of successful cooperative enterprises have been in existence in a variety of countries around the globe: Argentina, Italy, Spain, Venezuela, Brazil, Canada, England, France, Greece, and the United States. The "most conspicuously successful multinational cooperative," Peter Ranis points out, is Mondragon in Spain, founded by Spanish priest José María Arizmendiarrieta Madariaga.[55] Part of the success of Mondragon over the years has been the result of the "internal cooperative values" of its members as well as the "legal and tax concessions" of the Spanish government.[56] The Great Recession encouraged "social activists and academics of varying ideological positions," writes Ramis, "to rethink and regenerate more community-based forms of economic development, leading to a stakeholder society as opposed to a shareholder society."[57] It is important for those whose self-determination is severely limited by their managerial overlords in the information and digital economy—including Uber drivers, Starbucks employees, Amazon employees, and adjunct faculty at universities around the globe—to reclaim the value that they produce by peacefully and lawfully taking back the means of production by creating their own labor unions and cooperatives. "Worker co-ops are key to socialism's future," argues Marxist economist Richard Wolff: "They criticize socialisms inherited from the past and add a concrete vision of what a more just and humane society would look like. With the new focus on workplace democratization, socialists are in a good position to contest the 21st century's struggle of economic systems."[58] At the same time, cooperatives, according to John Restakis, generally avoid programs of "political control," making such efforts "more durable than Marxism's more militant strategy."[59] One would think that such an observation would nullify the slippery slope argument incessantly raised by anxious reactionaries.

"The grave of Laurence Gronlund," Debs wrote, "is a shrine where Socialist pilgrims may renew their allegiance to the great cause he loved and labored for with all his strength of mind and heart."[60] What is that "great cause" for which citizens of the United States and the world can still engage? First, American citizens can affirm Gronlund's rejection of violence as a necessary component of a cooperative state. Violence is neither a necessary nor inherent tenet of socialist or Leftist activism, though there is no denying the degrees of discipline and violence inherent to capitalism. And Americans can tap into their long history of nonviolent dissent to fight capitalism. Second, speaking of that which is *a priori* or inevitable, there is no innate tension between socialism and religion, whether liberal or conservative. Concern for the well-being of the other falls under the category loving one's neighbor. Christianity, the tradition from which I come, is tied to a religion of selflessness, a faith that gives aid to the poor and confronts the needs of those marginalized and ignored in society regardless of cultural identity.[61] Recognizing the benefits of socialism—*properly understood*—does not require abandoning one's faith. In this last regard, it is my hope that *American Socialist* will cool the politically charged anxiety against socialism felt by committed members of religious communities.

Finally, and most importantly, socialism for Gronlund meant little more than cooperation. Indeed, perhaps American citizens, putting aside partisan commitments and ideologies, can begin the process of change by cooperating. Capitalism has always fractured society, creating and maintaining forlorn individuals divorced from a deep sense of meaning and purpose, cutting life tragically short. Late-nineteenth-century French democratic socialist Louis Blanc illustrated how competitive capitalism created isolated individuals in a way that is destructive to human civilization:

What does competition mean to working men? It is the distribution of work to the highest bidder. A contractor needs a laborer: three apply.

"How much do you ask for your work?"
"Three francs, I have a wife and children."
"Good, and you?"
"Two and a half francs, I have no children, but a wife."
"So much the better, and you?"

"Two francs will do for me; I am single."

"You shall have the work."

With this, the affair is settled; the bargain is closed. What will become now of the other two proletarians? They will starve, it is to be hoped. But what if they become thieves? Never mind, why do have we our police? Or murderers? Well, for them we have the gallows. And the fortunate one of the three; even his victory is only temporary. Let a fourth laborer appear, strong enough to fast one out of every two days; the desire to cut down the wages will be exerted to its fullest extent. A new pariah appears, perhaps a new recruit for the galleys.[62]

In Blanc's scenario, capitalism creates the individual—the kind of individualism that Gronlund likewise challenged. But Blanc goes a bit further than Gronlund. Capitalism works not only to create the individual, but to eliminate it. Furthermore, the system reinforces the sovereignty of the one who holds the power over creation and destruction, of life and death—namely, management. Blanc's words remain true for us today. Corporate media capitalism has intensified hyper-individualism, intensifying feelings of loneliness and isolation. Similar to how it fractures our social world, capitalism continues to create fissures in our psyche. We construct our own virtual world, intentionally avoid reality, and obscure truth, beauty, and goodness. Our splintered minds are further divided as we feed on a diet of tweets and hashtags; we are subconsciously animated by incessant status updates that reinforce the illusion of a universal Platonic self. Yet as we drown in the tumultuous sea of information, as we become complicit in our own alienation through the unreal "selfies" we toss into the digital void, our cognitive ability to make sense of it all atrophies. Like zombies or the "walking dead" (an unsurprisingly popular genre), we mindlessly submit to the dictates of our managerial overlords (e.g., the one in power in Blanc's scenario) and the "inverted totalitarianism" that has created our techno-feudalistic world.[63]

There is no human fulfillment, no meaning in the absence of cooperation, without opening ourselves up to that which is outside us—to others, to the environment, to the divine. Cultivating methods of greater cooperation will assuage the antagonism created by competitive capitalism. And it may not require a well-worked out method, but an attitude—an attitude of openness that does not demand an eradication of principle. Echoing Marx, Henry

George wrote that "men tend to progress just as they come closer together, and by co-operation with each other increase the mental power that may be devoted to improvement."[64] "Civilization is co-operation," he wrote:[65]

> The great extension of association—not along in the growth of larger and denser communities, but in the increase of commerce and the manifold exchanges which knit each community together and link them with other though widely separated communities; the growth of international and municipal law; the advances in security of property and of person, in individual liberty, and towards democratic government—advances in short towards the recognition of the equal rights to life, liberty, and the pursuit of happiness—it is these that make our modern civilization so much greater, so much higher, than any that has gone before. It is these that have set free the mental power which has rolled back the veil of ignorance which hid all but a small portion of the globe from men's knowledge; which has measured the orbits of the circling spheres and bids us see moving, pulsing life in a drop of water; which has opened to us the ante-chamber of nature's mysteries and read the secrets of a long buried past.[66]

Meaning, including self-meaning, requires cooperation. The relations of the planets in the cosmos, words that structure sentences, numbers that function with other numbers, true love, and self-identity all require forms of cooperation for the purpose of creative and substantial meaning. There is no meaning without cooperation. "Cooperation is our specie's superpower," writes Nichola Raihani, "the reason that humans managed not just to survive but to *thrive* in almost every habitat on Earth."[67] The collapse of civilization comes from our failure to cooperate. One does not need a well-worked-out philosophical argument to understand this. Healing begins with caring associations. If members of society refuse to work together, refuse to confront the conditions that create social and psychological isolation, refuse to open up to each other, and refuse to love each other, the result will be, as it was in the Gilded Age, a "petrification"—to borrow from Henry George—of human development. Through cooperation, we can break our chains; through cooperation, we can win the world.

WORKING MEN AND WOMEN OF ALL COUNTRIES, COOPERATE!

# NOTES

## INTRODUCTION

1. Barker, *British Socialism: An Examination of its Doctrines, Policy, Aims and Practical Proposals*, 6; "Gronlund Talks: Discusses the Future of Socialism," *Morning Call* (San Francisco) 4 January 1895, https://www.newspapers.com/image/92930549; "Socialism Analyzed: Laurence Gronlund on Its Present and Future," *The Boston Globe,* 20 February 1888.

2. "Laurence Gronlund, The Great Socialist is Now in Our City," *Sacramento Bee,* 29 May 1895, https://www.newspapers.com/image/623383514.

3. "Leader of Socialism: Famous Laurence Gronlund Arrives in the City," *Seattle Post-Intelligencer,* 1 August 1895, https://www.newspapers.com/image/332951377.

4. A. B. Edler, "Obituary of Laurence Gronlund," *Appeal to Reason,* 25 November 1899, https://www.newspapers.com/clip/2487704/obituary-of-laurence-gronlund-1846.

5. Helen Sumner, "Laurence Gronlund," *The Comrade* 4, no. 2 (February 1905), 28.

6. "Leader of Socialism," https://www.newspapers.com/image/332951377.

7. Whitman, *American Reformers,* 383.

8. Edwards, *New Spirits: Americans in the 'Gilded Age,' 1865–1905,* 1.

9. Calhoun, *The Gilded Age,* 2. Further works on the Gilded Age include: Fink, *The Long Gilded Age: American Capitalism and the Lessons of a New World Order;* Trachtenberg, *The Incorporation of America: Culture and Society in the Gilded Age;* Levy, *Freaks of Fortune: The Emerging World of Capitalism and Risk in America;* Levy, *Ages of American Capitalism: A History of the United States;* Beatty, *Age of Betrayal: The Triumph of Money in America, 1865–1900;* Brands, *American Colossus: The Triumph of Capitalism, 1865–1900.*

10. *The Dawn* 7, no. 9 (October 1895), 4; Persons, introduction to 1965 edition, *The Cooperative Commonwealth* by Laurence Gronlund, x; *Boston Globe,* 20 February 1888.

11. Gronlund, "Nationalism," *Arena* 1 (December 1889): 154. Debs, *The American Movement,* 24.

12. Shore, *Talkin' Socialism: J. A. Wayland and the Role of the Press in American Radicalism, 1890–1912;* Crunden, *Ministers of Reform: The Progressives' Achievement in American Civilization;* Lipow, *Authoritarian Socialism in America: Edward Bellamy and the Nationalist Movement;* Errol Wayne Stevens, "Los Angeles: Harrison Gray Otis and Job Harriman," *California History* 86, no. 3 (2009): 44–64; Johnpoll, *Pacifist's Progress: Norman Thomas and the Decline of American Socialism;* Egbert and Persons, *Socialism and American Life,* Vol. 2; Salvatore, *Eugene V. Debs: Citizen and Socialist;* Ginger, *The Bending Cross: A Biography of Eugene V. Debs;*

Buhle, *Women and American Socialism 1870–1920,* 80; An acquaintance of Gronlund, Willard's commitment to socialism intensified when Gronlund recommended that she read Bellamy's *Looking Backward* over his own "dry" *Co-operative Commonwealth.* Jacob Dorn, "The Social Gospel and Socialism: A Comparison of the Thought of Francis Greenwood Peabody, Washington Gladden, and Walter Rauschenbusch," *Church History* 62, no. 1 (March 1993): 82–100; Persons, "Preface" to Gronlund, *The Co-operative Commonwealth,* rep. 1965, p. xi; Bell, *Marxian Socialism in the United States,* 17.

13. William Dean Howells, review of *Cooperative Commonwealth, Harper's Magazine,* LXXVI (April 1888): 801–802.

14. Hugh O. Pentecost, who considered *Looking Backward* as *Co-operative Commonwealth* "rewritten," testified that he had once read a letter from Edward Bellamy admitting that "school children of the future would be taught to revere the name of Lawrence Gronlund [*sic*]." Pentecost, "State Socialism Defined," *Twentieth Century,* 1 June 1889, https://babel.hathitrust.org/cgi /pt?id=wu.89096693429&view=1up&seq=205&q1=Gronlund.

15. Gronlund's works were also read by intellectuals in Austria, Poland, and Russia; Gemorah, "Laurence Gronlund's Ideas and Influence, 1877–1899," 275ff.

16. Jones, "Henry George and British Socialism," 484.

17. Mallock quote in Owen, *Integral Co-operation,* 219. He also spent two weeks with authors William Morris and H. M. Hyndman, *Social Democratic Herald,* 4 November 1889.

18. Hill, *Principles and Fallacies of Socialism,* 97, https://babel.hathitrust.org/cgi/pt?id=uiug .30112087839285&view=1up&seq=101&q1=Gronlund.

19. Persons, introduction to *The Cooperative Commonwealth,* xi.

20. Grant Allen, "Gronlund," in *Social Democracy Red Book: A Brief History of Socialism in America,* 101; Florence Kelley shared a similar concern. In a letter to Henry Demarest Lloyd in 1896, Kelley rejected "the practice of expelling everyone who can speak English from the Socialist Party." Quoted in Young, *Dissent: Explorations in the History of American Radicalism,* 258; Some, like Frederic Heath, found the SLP not as radically democratic as they had hoped. Heath wrote about the SLP in Milwaukee: "The Socialism present by the Socialist Labor Party soon grew to be repugnant to me. I could not square it with my love of democracy"; Frederic Heath, "How I Became a Socialist" *The Comrade* 2, no. 7 (April 1903):154–55; Phelps and Vandome, *Marxism & America: New Appraisals,* 9.

21. Maher, "Laurence Gronlund: Contributions to American Socialism," 622.

22. Gemorah, "Laurence Gronlund's Ideas and Influence, 1877–1899," 251.

23. Stromquist, *Reinventing "The People,"* 49.

24. Gronlund, *The New Economy,* 81.

25. In *Laissez Faire and the General-Welfare State,* author Sidney Fine notes that in his letter to Ely, on April 16, 1891 (Ely Papers, State Historical Society of Wisconsin), Gronlund added that qualification for membership would "exclude followers of Henry George and Herbert Spencer." Fine, *Laisse Faire and the General-Welfare State,* 332, footnote #112.

26. Hillquit, *History of Socialism in the United States,* 293. For Hillquit, the American Fabian organizations were "short-lived" but "left their mark on the political life of the nation" (293); Bliss, *The Encyclopedia of Social Reforms,* 578.

27. *American Fabian* 1 (February 1895), 5.

28. Thomas Jenkins, "The American Fabian Movement," *Western Political Quarterly* 1, no. 2 (June 1948): 115.

29. Laurence Gronlund, "For and By the People," *Harrison Press Journal* (Harrison, Nebraska), 11 May 1899, https://www.newspapers.com/image/556693416.

30. May, *Protestant Churches and Industrial America*, 259.

31. Gemorah, "Laurence Gronlund's Ideas," 271. Stow Persons's introduction, *Cooperative Commonwealth*, xi; Evans, *Social Gospel in American Religion*, 128.

32. Evans, *The Social Gospel in America*, 128.

33. Barton, *J. Stitt Wilson*. "Socialism is Applied Christianity," Kindle.

34. Janine Giordano Drake, "The Other Social Gospelers: The Working-Class Religious Left, 1877–1920" in Leilah Danielson, Marian Mollin, and Doug Rossinow, eds., *The Religious Left in American America: Doorkeepers of a Radical Faith* (London: Palgrave/Macmillan, 2018), 21.

35. "Leader of Socialism: Famous Laurence Gronlund Arrives in the City," *The Seattle Post-Intelligencer*, 1 August 1895, https://www.newspapers.com/image/332951377. In a letter to Commissioner of Labor Carol D. Wright, Gronlund informed Wright that he had "married *again*." The subject of the letter was to inquire as to whether Wright could provide Gronlund with work in the department. Apparently, Gronlund had left and later came back to Wright; Gemorah, "Laurence Gronlund's Ideas," 8.

36. "Laurence Gronlund: The Great Socialist, Is Now in This City," *Sacramento Bee*, 25 May 1895, https://www.newspapers.com/image/624086849.

37. A. B. Edler, *Appeal to Reason*, 25 November 1899.

38. Clarence B. Bagley, *History of Seattle: From the Earliest Settlement to the Present Time:* Vol. 2 (Chicago: S.J. Clarke Publishing Co., 1916), 642.

39. Persons, "Introduction," xxiv.

40. Pittenger, *American Socialists and Evolutionary Thought, 1870–1920*, 46.

41. Laurence Gronlund, "The Sugar Beet from the Standpoint of National Economy," *Ranch and Range* 15, no. 35 (August 3, 1899), 3, https://www.newspapers.com/image/78716341.

42. A. B. Edler, *Appeal to Reason*, 25 November 1899; "Death of Laurence Gronlund," *Evening Star* (Washington, D.C.), 18 October 1899, https://www.newspapers.com/image/145544677.

43. Gustav Bang, "Socialism in Denmark" *The Comrade* 2 (1 October 1902), 11; Ely, *The Strengths and Weaknesses of Socialism*, 65.

44. Owen, *Two Discourses on a New System of Society; As Delivered in the Hall of Representatives at Washington*.

45. Gronlund, "Le Socialisme Aux Etats-Unis," 116.

46. Kruger, *The St. Louis Commune of 1877*, 6.

47. Burbank, *Reign of Rabble*, 184; Pittenger, *American Socialists and Evolutionary Thought, 1870–1920*, 45; Bellesile, *1877: America's Year of Living Violently*; Bruce, *1877: Year of Violence*; Gronlund was charged with the "unlawful purpose of preventing men from plying their lawful avocations" through the means of "terrorism, intimidation, etc." Quoted in Mark Kruger, *St. Louis Commune: Communism in the Heartland*, 240. In reality, the authorities had nothing on which to convict Gronlund and his associates. Kruger writes: "Authorities in St. Louis were

clearly more concerned with removing strikers from the streets than with seriously punishing them . . . [They] desired the return of order to the city, the kind of order that was in effect when they controlled the city's businesses and government" (241).

48. "Leader of Socialism," 1

49. Gronlund, "Why I Am a Socialist," 5–6.

50. Ibid., 5.

51. Marinek, *Socialism and Print Culture in America, 1897–1920,* 1.

52. Ibid., 2. It is worth imagining the correlation between high literacy and progressivism—even radicalism.

53. Heath, *Social Democracy Red Book,* 101. Among the works that turned him to socialism, according to William Baily, was a pamphlet by Ferdinand Lasalle. William Bailey, "The Coming Socialism," *Dublin University Review* 1, no. 7 (December 1885): 343. Lassallean socialism was distinct from Marxian socialism. The former preferred political action as the means of implementing a socialist commonwealth. The latter, however, believed strongly that political change would mean very little—if anything—if workers did not become conscious of their plight and, on their own initiative, take back the means of production. Given his opposition to the emphasis on class warfare among German socialists, his prioritizing the leadership of an intellectual and religious elite, and his involvement in several political organizations, Gronlund certainly reflected more of a Lassallean socialism than that of the Marxian brand.

54. "The Populists Meet," *Salt Lake Herald,* 12 October 1894, https://www.newspapers.com/image/80974433.

55. Goldmann, *The Human Sciences and Philosophy,* 28.

56. Michael Löwy preface to Goldmann's *Hidden God: A Study of Tragic Vision in the* Pensees *of Pascal and the Tragedies of Racine,* 301.

57. Goldmann, *The Hidden God,* 301. See also Traverso, *Revolution: An Intellectual History,* 38.

58. Cohen, *The Wager of Lucian Goldmann.*

59. Gronlund, "Why I Am a Socialist," 6.

60. Shaw, *Fabian Essays in Socialism,* 25.

61. Wallerstein, *Historical Capitalism,* 7–8.

62. Marx, *A Contribution to the Critique of Political Economy,* 11–12.

63. Judis, *The Socialist Awakening,* 21.

64. Gronlund, "Nationalization of Industry," 33–36; Gronlund, *Commonwealth,* 63. See also Marx and Engels, *Community Manifesto:* "What the bourgeoisie, therefore, produces, above all, is its own gravediggers" (483).

65. Luxemburg, "Social Reform or Revolution," *The Rosa Luxemburg Reader,* 147.

66. Recognizing the power of cooperation for both capital and labor was not first realized in the Gilded Age. The editors of the *New York Evening Post,* William Cullen Bryant and William Leggett, wrote in the 1830s how the rich tended to "act upon a common interest," suggesting that the laboring poor should act in a similar way for the "preservation of their rights." The only "bulwark behind which mechanics and laborers may safely rally to oppose a common enemy" was the principle of combination. See Schneider, *A History of American Philosophy,* 113–112.

67. Rockefeller's goal was to avoid what looked like a monopoly. He brought together many companies that would appear to remain independent but would essentially do the bidding of Rockefeller. When the trust was identified by progressive lawmakers as a monopoly under a different name, Rockefeller changed the "trust" into a holding company.

68. Gronlund, "A Lesson of Trusts," 4.

69. Gronlund, *The Co-Operative Commonwealth in Its Outlines,* 2.

70. In volume 1 of *Capital,* Marx argued that cooperation was far from an anomaly to capitalism, but rather fundamental to it: "Simple co-operation has always been, and continues to be, the predominant form in those branches of production in which capital operates on a large scale, but the division of labour and machinery play only an insignificant part . . . Co-operation remains the fundamental form of the capitalist mode of production, although in its simple shape it continues to appear as one particular form alongside the more developed ones"; *Capital,* 454.

71. Edward Bellamy, *Looking Backward, 2000–1887,* Edited with an Introduction and Notes by Matthew Beaumont (Oxford: Oxford University Press, 2007), 33.

72. Edward Bellamy, "Plutocracy or Nationalism—Which?" *Nationalist Extra* 1, 31 May 1889, 9.

73. Imogen Fales, "The Organization of Labor," *Journal of United Labor* IV, no. 5 (September 15, 1883): 557.

74. *The National Economist Almanac* (Washington: The National Economist Print, 1890), 10.

75. "The Reform Press," *The National Economist,* 11 April 1891.

76. "A Point Well Taken," *The New Nation,* 18 April 1891.

77. Levy, *Ages of American Capitalism.*

78. Plenty of socialists both in the U.S. and Europe were drawn to Darwinian evolution. See John Hoffman, *Marxism and Theory of Praxis: Selected Correspondence, Marx to Engels, 19th December 1860* (New York: International Publishers, 1975), 55. Indeed, Marx believed that Darwin's theory mirrored his own dialectical method. Darwin's work was "epoch-making," Marx wrote in *Capital* 1, 461. Socialist conservative and economist Richard Ely, a prolific intellectual responsible for turning a number of American citizens to socialism, wrote that Marx and Darwin were the "two great intellectual lights" of the nineteenth century. See Ely, *The Strengths and Weaknesses of Socialism,* 74.

79. Hofstadter, *Social Darwinism in American Thought,* 96; Pittenger, *American Socialists,* 47.

80. Gronlund, *Commonwealth,* 88.

81. Spencer, *The Principles of Ethics,* 46.

82. Gronlund, *Our Destiny,* 61. He would use the phrase again in his essay, "Why I Am a Socialist," 5–6, https://theanarchistlibrary.org/library/laurence-gronlund-why-i-am-a-socialist For Gronlund, the "struggle for life" was not one of individual competition and ultimate domination of one over another, but rather a fight to preserve life. The struggle for life, he says, "applies to the animal world and savages, [but] it does not apply—was never intended to apply—to civilized men." He then redefines the statement: "Let it, then, be clearly understood, that when we want to destroy competition, it is this *struggle for life,* for existence, we want to abolish forever, while we desire to foster *emulation.*" Richard Hofstadter appeared to be one of the first to

associate robber-baron capitalists with the competitive struggle of social Darwinism. Yet the literature within the last few decades has exonerated thinkers like Herbert Spencer and William Graham Sumner from advocating "the law of the jungle" to human society. Robert Bannister challenges the idea that the "survival of the fittest operated in modern society." He continues: "Social Darwinism itself is what one might term the *myth of social Darwinism;* the charge, usually unsubstantially or quite out of proportion to the evidence, that Darwinism was widely and wantonly abused by forces of reaction. While not a deliberate deception, this myth was important in itself. And as a prelude to the 'correct' readings of Darwin, it invariably prefaced the many varieties of so-called reform Darwinism." See Bannister, *Social Darwinism: Science and Myth in Anglo-American Social Thought,* 9, 47; Hayashi, *Hunting Down Social Darwinism,* 22; and Howard L. Kaye, *The Social Meaning of Modern Biology: From Social Darwinism to Sociobiology* (London: Routledge, 2017).

83. Gronlund, *Our Destiny,* 66.

84. Levy, *Ages of American Capitalism,* Kindle.

85. Geoffrey Hawthorn, *Enlightenment in Despair: A History of Sociology* (Cambridge: Cambridge University Press, 1976), 91.

86. Levy, *Ages,* Kindle.

87. Spencer, *First Principles,* 216, 219.

88. Ibid., 497.

89. Gronlund was not the only early socialist to believe in a divine agent. Influential thinkers like James Bates Clark and Richard Ely did so as well. See Pittenger, *American Socialists,* 29.

90. Indeed, an argument could be made that capitalism has survived *because* its supporters have worked against its very nature. The illusion of capitalism is also its greatest irony—namely, that the only way for it to thrive is to disobey it.

91. "Campaign Notes," *Salt Lake Herald,* 11 October 1894. https://www.newspapers.com/image /12659414/; Laurence Gronlund, "Reply to Dr. Heber Newton," 158–161.

92. Gronlund quoted in Harris, *A Discourse of the Prospects, Dangers, Duties and Safeties of the Times,* n.p. A few intellectuals like Richard Ely noted that socialism in America and England was not as rigidly materialistic as German socialism. In *Strengths and Weaknesses of Socialism,* Ely wrote, "Socialism in England and America can be appreciated in its full strength only when it becomes entirely emancipated from the materialistic conception of history advanced by Karl Marx . . . to make everything depend upon economic forces, is shutting one's eyes to other forces . . . Religion is an independent force, often sufficient to modify and even to shape economic institutions" (Ely, *Strengths,* 175).

93. "Proletarian Literature," *Pall Mall Gazette* (London) September 5, 1888, 5., www.newspapers .com/image/392709036/.

94. "Gronlund Talks."

95. Gemorah, "Laurence Gronlund: Utopian or Reformer," 450.

96. Schneider, *History of American Philosophy,* 202. Whatever is rational, Gronlund says in his only explicit reference to Hegel in *Commonwealth,* "necessarily conforms to the innermost nature of things" (108). See Gemorah, "Laurence Gronlund—Utopian or Reformer?" 448; Taylor, *Hegel,* 438.

97. "Moral Regeneration Not Impossible: Laurence Gronlund's Lecture on the Meaning of Rational Socialism," *San Francisco Chronicle,* 16 January 1895, https://www.newspapers.com /image/27598319/?terms=Laurence%20Gronlund&match=1; "Commended by Leo Tolstoy: Laurence Gronlund, the Socialist, in the City," *Los Angeles Herald,* March 8, 1895, https://www .newspapers.com/image/80567150/.

98. Stow Persons introduction, xxiii.

99. Gronlund, "Why I Am a Socialist," 6.

100. Gronlund, *Co-operative Commonwealth,* 2.

101. Judis, *The Socialist Awakening,* 17.

102. Schneider, *A History of American Philosophy,* 91; Robert Owen, "First Discourse on a New System of Society," in *Socialism in America: From the Shakers to the Third International, A Documentary History,* ed. Albert Fried (Garden City, NY: Anchor, 1971), 94–111.

103. Jacob H. Dorn, "The Social Gospel and Socialism: A Comparison of the Thought of Francis Greenwood Peabody, Washington Gladden, and Walter Rauschenbusch," *Church History* (March 1993): 82–100.

104. Friedrich Engels, "Description of Recently Founded Communist Colonies Still in Existence" (1844), in *Marx and Engels on the United States* (Moscow: Progress Publishers, 1979), 33.

105. Gronlund, *Cooperative Commonwealth,* 102.

106. Hillquit, *Socialism in Theory and Practice,* 11.

107. Quoted in Ely, *The Strength and Weakness of Socialism,* 23.

108. Kirkup, *Inquiry into Socialism,* 11–12; See also Kirkup's *History of Socialism* (New York: Macmillan, 1909) and *A Primer of Socialism* (First edition 1908; London: A&C Black). Gronlund's socialism aligned with the British Fabians. William Clarke, from the Fabian Society of England, defined a socialist as "one who believes that the necessary instruments of production should be held and organized by the community, instead of by individuals, or groups of individuals, within or outside of the community" (quoted in Ely, *Strength and Weakness,* 24). Another Fabian, Graham Wallas, wrote that socialists "work for the owning of the means of production by the community and the means of consumption by individuals" (Ely, *Strength and Weakness,* 24). See also Gronlund, *Commonwealth* (1891), 147. The means of production extended beyond the mere use of tools. It included ownership of the self. Part of the means of production included labor, which originated in the self. To take away a person's labor would be to take away their humanity. Not to distract too much from the current study, it is interesting to note how American socialism gained much from the antislavery tradition, especially the arguments offered by Frederick Douglass and Wendell Phillips, the latter of whom exhibited socialistic tendencies when suggesting that ex-slaves as well as workers should collectively own the means of production. Belief in the ownership of self likewise shares a resemblance to Marx's concept of "alienation." But we need not discuss this here, since Gronlund says nothing about it, though we can draw out the implications. As we will see in the next chapter (Chapter 1), value is inextricably tied to labor, which means that the value of a human being is lost when divorced from labor. What is more, labor is likewise tied to time. Value is the combination of both labor and time. The tragedy of capitalism was that owners claimed the entire person of the laborer. "Your time is mine," Gronlund lamented: "Your body is mine . . . your actions are

mine for so many hours of the twenty-four." Workers were bound to obedience: "What in the name of reason is that but slavery?"

109. Judis, *The Socialism Awakening*, 19.

110. In fact, Gronlund, according to Jessie Wallach Hughan, "proposed that capitalists be compensated merely with annuities terminable with their lives or those of their children"— annuities that would "allow a standard of living not far from what they formerly enjoyed." See Jessie Hughan, *American Socialism of the Present Day*, 126; F. M. Sprague likewise notes Gronlund's "annuities" for capitalists in *Socialism from Genesis to Revelation* (Boston: Lee and Shepard, 1893), 334, 336.

111. Quoted in Bliss, *What is Christian Socialism?* 20, https://babel.hathitrust.org/cgi/pt?id=nnc1.cu56775105&view=1up&seq=22

112. Ibid., 22.

113. Quint, *Forging of American Socialism*, 174.

114. Fink, *Workingmen's Democracy*, 7; Voss, *The Making of American Exceptionalism*, 89; Leikin, *The Practical Utopians*, 158; Rodgers, *Atlantic Crossings*, 343; Hofstadter, *The Age of Reform*.

115. Nelson, "People's Capital," 51.

116. Levy, *Freaks of Fortune*, 192; Witt, *The Accidental Republic*, 78.

117. "Letter from the Knights of Labor General Executive Board," 28 May 1884, Hoboken, NJ; John Samuel Papers, Wisconsin Historical Society, Madison, WI.

118. Hofstadter, *Social Darwinism in American Thought*, 114.

119. Gemorah, "Laurence Gronlund's Ideas and Influence, 1877–1899."

120. Gemorah, "Laurence Gronlund—Utopian or Reformer," 446–458.

121. Tsuzuki, "Laurence Gronlund and American Socialism," 17–25.

122. Pittenger, *American Socialists*, 62; Edward Spann likewise offers an entire chapter on Gronlund (along with Bellamy) in his *Brotherly Tomorrows: Movements for a Cooperative Society in America, 1820–1920*, Chapter 11.

123. May, *Protestant Churches and Industrial America*, 259.

124. Gronlund, *The Co-operative Commonwealth*, 2, 257.

125. Burbank, *When Farmers Voted Red*; Bisset, *Agrarian Socialism in America*; Drake, "Between Religion and Politics."

126. Gronlund, *Commonwealth* (1884), 2.

127. Gemorah, "Laurence Gronlund—Utopian or Reformer?" 448.

128. "Laurence Gronlund's Rejoinder," *Spokesman-Review*, 2 December 1895, https://www.newspapers.com/image/566377981/.

129. J. S. Mill, *Principles of Political Economy*, Books IV and V (Harmondsworth, 1985), 360, 366; Raimund Ottow, "Why John Stuart Mill Calls Himself a Socialist," *History of European Ideas* 17, no. 4 (January 2012): 479–483.

130. Gronlund, "Socializing a State," in *A Primer on Socialism*, ed. G.C. Clemens (Terre Haute, Indiana: Debs Publishing Company, 1900), 15, https://babel.hathitrust.org/cgi/pt?id=mdp.39015068648099&view=1up&seq=15.

131. Wade Matthews argues that both Marx and Engels were often stuck between a "politics of revolution" and a "science of capitalism" and that "it was never clear to Marx and Engels how

a transition to socialism would be effected at all—oscillating as they did between a conception of the transition as the product of the will of the working class and as a consequence (at times inevitable) of the development of productive forces"; See Matthews, "The Poverty of Strategy: E. P. Thompson, Perry Anderson, and the Transition to Socialism," *Labour/Le Travail,* 50 (Fall 2002), 217.

132. Gronlund, *Commonwealth,* x.

133. Ibid., 257.

134. Levy, *Freaks of Fortune,* 14.

135. Gronlund, *Commonwealth,* 178.

136. Burbank, *Reign of Rabble,*196; Gronlund, *Commonwealth* (1891), 16.

137. In his *Social Aspects of Christianity* (1889), Richard Ely argued that the state was the necessary agent in ushering in the will of the divine "and," writes Gary Dorrien, "no less sacred than faith and the church." Dorrien, *American Democratic Socialism,* 71.

138. Gourevitch, *From Slavery to the Cooperative Commonwealth,* 167.

139. Ibid., 185.

140. Quoted in Gemorah, 226.

141. Ibid., 227.

142. Kates, *The French Revolution,* 4; Juares, *A Socialist History of the French Revolution;* Mathiez, *The French Revolution;* LeFebvre, *The Coming of the French Revolution;* Soboul, *The French Revolution, 1787-1799;* Vovelle, *The Fall of the French Monarchy, 1787-1791;* Furet, *Interpreting the French Revolution.*

143. Tendler, "Alphonse Aulard Revisited," 649-669. It is enough to say that Gronlund stood between Aulard and the Marxist School. Thus, there is no need to delineate further the historiography on the French Revolution. Suffice it to say, however, that the current historiography of the French Revolution, Gary Kate writes, is an "almost total collapse of the orthodox Marxist interpretation" (Kates 4).

144. Jack R. Censer, "Biography and the French Revolution, *International Labor and Working-Class History,* no. 14/15 (Spring 1979): 9-15.

145. Samuel Bernstein, "The Danton-Robespierre Controversy Today" *Science & Society* 23, no. 3 (Summer 1959): 221-232, p. 222; Bernstein argued that attitudes toward Danton were relative to the historical period in France.). See also Jonathan Israel, *The Enlightenment that Failed: Ideas, Revolution, and Democratic Defeat, 1748-1830* (Oxford: Oxford University Press, 2019), 482.

146. Mathiez, 228.

147. Bernstein, "The Danton-Robespierre Controversy Today," 221-232.

148. Hampson, *Danton,* 81.

149. Gronlund, *Ça Ira,* ix.

150. Hook, *The Hero In History,* 48.

151. *Commonwealth* (1884), 10.

152. Eric Foner, *Who Owns History: Rethinking the Past in a Changing World* (New York: Hill & Wang, 2002), e-book.

153. "Gronlund Talks."

154. Gronlund, *Commonwealth,* 254.

155. Ibid., 257.

156. Robertson, *The Last Utopians,* 27.

157. Gronlund, *Commonwealth,* 284.

158. Lenin, *Imperialism,* 1999.

159. Pittenger, *American Socialists,* 55, 59.

160. "Essay on Lincoln by Carl Schurz," in *The Papers and Writings of Abraham Lincoln: Biographies, Speeches and Debates, Civil War Telegrams, Letters, Presidential Orders & Proclamations* (7 volumes), vii.

161. Fink, *The Long Gilded Age,* 10.

162. Nelson, "People's Capital," 54.

163. This would become the position of V. I. Lenin: "The history of all countries shows that the working class, exclusively by its own efforts, is able to develop only trade-union consciousness . . . The theory of Socialism, however, grew out of the philosophic historical and economic theories that were elaborated by the educated representatives of the propertied classes, the intellectuals." See Lenin, *What Is to Be Done?* (New York: International Publishers, 1931), 32–33. Like Thomas Skidmore and Wilhelm Weitling, not all socialists agreed that the intellectual elite were the ones who should lead the revolution.

164. Gemorah, "Utopian or Reformer," 261–262

165. Wolin, *Democracy Incorporated,* xxiv.

## 1. NO ORDINARY BOOK

1. Ginger, *The Bending Cross,* 155–56.

2. Debs, *Report on the Chicago Strike of June–July, 1894,* 129–180. Debs was also greatly impressed—more so than even Gronlund—with the writings of evolutionary socialist Karl Kautsky. Debs not only readily grasped Kautsky's argument but also "the spirit of his socialist utterance." See Eugene V. Debs, "How I Became a Socialist," *The Comrade* (April 1902), https://www.americanyawp.com/reader/20-the-progressive-era/eugene-debs-how-i-became-a-socialist-april-1902/; Salvatore, *Eugene V. Debs,* 151; Ginger, *The Bending Cross,* 173.

3. Bliss, *New Encyclopedia of Social Reform,* 564.

4. J. H. West, *The New Ideal* 3 (1890), 140.

5. *Christian Socialist* vol. 3, no. 25 (June 1885): 7. Gronlund set aside three dollars of his ten-dollar weekly salary to defray the cost of publication. See Fred Harrison, "Gronlund and Other Marxists" in Anderson, *Critics of Henry George,* 197.

6. Thomas Harris Lake, *A Discourse of the Prospects, Dangers, Duties and Safeties of the Times* (Santa Rosa, CA: Fountain Grove Press, 1891), 40.

7. Lee, *When Sunflowers Bloomed Red,*16.

8. Quoted in Gemorah, 177–78.

9. Edward Aveling, review of *Co-operative Commonwealth, Commonweal* 1 (September 1885), 85.

10. Gustave Rouanet, "Henry George et Laurence Gronlund," *La Revue Socialists* (August 1887), 192.

11. Quint, *Forging of American Socialism*, 28.

12. Heath, *Social Democracy Red Book*, 42.

13. Bellamy's biographer Arthur Morgan disagreed. Morgan, New Deal intellectual and founding director of the TVA, argued that Bellamy's ideas had been presented in lectures that he had given years earlier. See Morgan, *Plagiarism in Utopia*, 7. Sylvia Brown agreed with Morgan. There is no evidence that Bellamy read Gronlund "until after the publication of *Looking Backward*." See Bowman, *Edward Bellamy Abroad: An American Prophet's Influence* (New York: Twayne Publishers, 1962), 50.

14. Arthur Morgan disagrees. See William Dean Howells, *Harper's Magazine* LXXVI (April 1888), 801–02, https://babel.hathitrust.org/cgi/pt?id=hvd.hnv11x&view=1up&seq=275&q1=Gronlund.

15. Shurter quoted in Morgan, *Plagiarism in Utopia*, 6.

16. Bell, "Background and Development of Marxian Socialism in The United States," In *Socialism and American Life*, ed. Donald Egbert and Stow Persons (Princeton 1952), 1:229; Heath, *Social Democracy Red Book*, 4.

17. Admittedly, there is scant historical evidence to determine such a question with a strong degree of certainty. Gronlund eventually favored Bellamy's book over his own. He compelled his publisher to "stop the sale" of *Commonwealth*, since *Looking Backward* was "doing a lot [more] for socialism." See Morgan, *Plagiarism in Utopia*, 9; Bowman, *Year 2000*, 116, 119; Gronlund would later offer a harsh criticism against Bellamy's *Equality* (1897).

18. Goldstene, *The Struggle for America's Promise*, 160.

19. Gronlund, *The Co-operative Commonwealth in its Outlines*, 7. Gronlund, *Co-operative Commonwealth*, 9.

20. Gronlund, *Co-operative Commonwealth*, x, 6.

21. Lloyd, *Wealth Against Commonwealth*, 2; Smith, *Urban Disorder and the Shape of Belief*, 253; Edwards, *New Spirits*, 194.

22. Gronlund, *Co-operative Commonwealth*, vii.

23. Gourevitch, *From Slavery to the Cooperative Commonwealth*, 99.

24. Terence Powderly, *The Path I Trod: The Autobiography of Terence V. Powderly*, ed. Harry J. Carman, Henry David, and Paul Guthrie (New York: Columbia University Press, 1940), 269.

25. Gourevitch, *From Slavery to the Cooperative Commonwealth*, 66, 118.

26. Ibid., 185.

27. Gemorah, "Laurence Gronlund," 227.

28. Trachtenberg, *The Incorporation of America*, xi.

29. Francis, *Herbert Spencer and the Invention of Modern Life*, 45.

30. Gronlund, *Commonwealth*, 16, 95.

31. Ibid., ix, xiv.

32. Gronlund, *Commonwealth*, 15, 20.

33. Ibid., 26.

34. Marxists place a high premium (excuse the market terminology) reserved only for the capitalist—laziness or simply time off work. As Leon Trotsky once wrote, "man is a rather lazy animal. It is on this quality, essentially, that all human progress is founded, to a considerable extent, because, if man did not strive to expend his energy economically, did not try to obtain the largest possible quantity of goods in return for a small quantity of energy, there would have been no development of technique or any social culture. Thus, from this standpoint, human laziness is a progressive force." Trotsky, *The Military Writings and Speeches of Leon Trotsky*, 3:99. It bears repeating: progress rests on time off work.

35. Marx, *Capital* Vol. 1: 300, 325.

36. Gronlund, *Commonwealth*, 27, 29.

37. Ibid., 22, 59.

38. In his response to Gronlund's *Commonwealth*, Joseph Rickaby, writing in the December 1885 edition of *Christian Socialist*, argued that supply and demand determined value. *Christian Socialist* 3, no. 31 (1885): 100–4; 3, no. 32 (1886): 120–2; 3, no. 33 (1886): 133–8.

39. Gronlund, *Commonwealth* (1884), 25. In his exposition of Marx's *Capital*, Ernest Untermann agreed with Gronlund that supply and demand could only "modify" value, never determine it. Untermann, *Marxian Economics*, 167.

40. Gronlund, *Commonwealth* (1884), 14.

41. Marx, *Capital* Vol. 1: 128.

42. Ibid., 128. Emphasis mine.

43. Georg Simmel, "The Metropolis and Mental Life," in *The Sociology of Georg Simmel*, trans., ed., with introduction by Kurt H. Wolff (Glencoe, IL: Free Press, 1950), 414.

44. Gronlund, *Commonwealth*, 140.

45. Hadas Thier, *A People's Guide to Capitalism: An Introduction to Marxist Economics* (Chicago: Haymarket Books, 2020) e-book. See also Harvey, *Companion to Marx's Capital*, 39–40.

46. Marx, *Capital* Vol. 1: 163.

47. In our age of information capitalism, the hackneyed idiom of "controlling the narrative," appropriated from corporate advertisement jargon, has made its way into the mouths of educational administrators, religious autocrats, and political leaders.

48. Gronlund, *Commonwealth*, 14. While we may distinguish, as Marx does, abstract from concrete labor in relation to value, value is always tied to labor. He writes in volume 1 of *Capital* that "the value of a commodity represents human labor pure and simple." Marx, *Capital* Vol. 1, 134.

49. Gronlund, *Commonwealth*, 21–22.

50. Ibid., 140.

51. Morton, *The Life and Ideas of Robert Own*,115.

52. Gronlund, *Commonwealth*, 137.

53. Gronlund, *Commonwealth*, 134; "Gronlund in Debate: The Socialist Crosses Swords with the Populists," *Seattle Post-Intelligencer*, 10 August 1895.

54. Gronlund, *Commonwealth*, 142.

55. Ibid., 136.

56. Ibid., 29.

57. Marx, *Capital*, 1:742.

58. Gronlund, *Commonwealth* (1885), 24.

59. Ibid., 55; Marx and Engels, *Collected Works* Vol. 6: 487; Gronlund, *Commonwealth*, 42.

60. Ibid., 43.

61. Paul Ehrman, "L.A. 1562 v. Co-Operation," *Journal of United Labor.* September 1883; Robert Gabriel Nelson, "The People's Capital: The Politics of Popular Wealth in the Gilded Age" (PhD diss., University of California, Berkeley, 2019), 52; Clarke, *Marx's Theory of Crisis,* 16.

62. Gronlund, *Commonwealth*, 48.

63. Ibid., 49–50.

64. Gronlund, "Nationalization of Industry," 33–36.

65. Imogen Fales, "The Organization of Labor," *Journal of United Labor* IV, no. 5 (September 15, 1883): 557.

66. Gronlund, *Commonwealth* (1884), 97.

67. Gronlund incorporated the distinction between coercive and voluntaristic cooperation from Spencer's *Principles of Sociology.* As society "assumes a higher" state of being, "labor becomes less coercive": "Here we reach a form in which the coerciveness has diminished to the smallest degree consistent with combined action. Each member is his own master in respect of the work he does; and is subject only to such rule, established by majority of the members, as are needful for maintaining order." See also Spencer, *Principles of Sociology* Vol. 3: 562–563.

68. Ibid., 57.

69. Gronlund, *Commonwealth* (1884), 57.

70. Ibid., 58. Gronlund did not focus on slavery, but I think that the transition from slavery to a kind of serfdom in America illustrates his point well. After the Civil War, African slaves transitioned, essentially, into peasant serfs, bound to the land of their former masters, who now transitioned to landlords. Former slaves had little freedom to association (i.e., cooperate) with others. They had only regained two sources of the means of production—themselves and their labor time. Yet, in most cases, this was short-lived. As is often the case in history, masters will impose new systems of dependence under different titles—from "owner" to "landlord," imposing restrictions on former slaves that were tantamount to the earlier form of slavery. Former slaves turned into contract laborers. And conditions were imposed in which such contractual relationships became less and less voluntary. This is where ex-slaves, nominally free, entered a serf-like stage, where they continued to be dependent on the authority of their former owners, whether landlords, managers, or both. In most cases, Gronlund argues, the new serf—as in the case of a former slave within a sharecropping system—was tied down to the land and the landlord. Those African Americans who gained work in the factories experienced no less liberation as they, like whites, fell under the dictates of capitalists.

71. Ibid., 151.

72. Laurence Gronlund, "The Wage System Tottering," *Salina Herald* (Salina, KS) 24 January 1890, https://www.newspapers.com/image/484657760/.

73. Gourevitch, *From Slavery to the Cooperative Commonwealth,* 113.

74. "Co-operation," *Journal of United Labor,* IV, no. 6 (October 15, 1883), 580.

75. McNeill quoted in Gourevitch, 113.

76. Gronlund, *Commonwealth*, 60.

77. Pittenger, *American Socialists*, 111.

78. Gemorah, "Utopian or Reformer," *Science & Society* vol. 33, no. 4 (Fall–Winter 1969): 446–458.

79. Ibid., 451.

80. Gronlund, *Commonwealth* (1884), 98.

81. Ibid., 59.

82. Gronlund, *Commonwealth*, 63; Wienen, *American Socialist Triptych*, 112

83. Kloppenberg, *Uncertain Victory*, 206.

84. Gronlund, *New Economy*, 63.

85. Gronlund, *Commonwealth*, 34.

86. Fraser, *Mongrel Firebugs and Men of Property: Capitalism and Class Conflict in American History* (London: Verso, 2019), 22. Fraser writes: "It is the nature of capitalism to reproduce maladies and calamities. They are, one might say, its second nature" (22).

87. Gronlund, *Commonwealth*, 35

88. Ibid., 93. Marx challenged the universality of violence. He dealt with this at the First International Meeting in Amsterdam: "I must not be supposed to imply that the means to this end [socialist revolution] will be everywhere the same. We know that special regard must be paid to the institutions, customs, and traditions of various lands; and we do not deny that there are certain countries, such as the United States and England, in which the workers may hope to secure their ends by peaceful means. If I mistake not, Holland belongs to the same category. Even so, we have to recognize that in most continental countries, force will have to be the lever of revolution. It is to force that in due time the workers will have to appeal if the dominion of labor is at long last to be established." Marx quoted in Oakley Johnson, *Marxism in the United States History Before the Russian Revolution* (New York: Humanities Press, 1974), Kindle, Ch. 1.

89. Gronlund, *New Economy*, 53.

90. Ibid., 53.

91. Gronlund, *Commonwealth* (1884), 96.

92. Gronlund, *New Economy*, 53.

93. One can appreciate Gronlund's desire for peace among classes, but it is unfortunate that he ignored the violence inherent to capitalist production itself. There is no denying the violence of primitive accumulation that made for capitalism (slavery, enclosure, vagrancy laws, etc.). But we deceive ourselves if we conclude that because slavery, the enclosure movement, or laws for vagabondage ended (which in each case is highly contestable given the continued appropriations of land, legal protections of capitalism, and modes of labor exploitation around the globe) that violence and capitalism are no longer inextricably tied. There is no capitalism without violence. Of course, we need to clarify what we mean by violence. Violence comes in degrees, from overt brutal violence to coercive and latent disciplinary habits that workers face daily. "The Roman slave," Marx wrote, "was held by chains; the wage-laborer is bound to his owner by invisible threads." Marx, *Capital*, Vol. 1:719, 896–897. One only needs to read Frederick Winslow Taylor's *Principles of Scientific Management* to see the disciplinary methods at work in modern capitalism. Yet the source of the violence is not completely "invisible." There is no

denying that workers are under the dictatorship of the capitalist. As Taylor writes, "When [the capitalist] man tells you to walk, you walk; when he tells you to sit down, you sit down, and you don't talk back at him." Taylor, *Scientific Management* (New York: Harper & Row, 1947 [1911]), 46. Not much is different from the corporate dictatorship of our own day.

94. Gronlund, *Commonwealth*, 63-64. Quint, *American Socialism*, 29.

95. Ibid., 65.

96. Ibid., 66; Fink, *Workingmen's Democracy*, xii.

97. Gronlund, *Commonwealth* (1891), 67.

98. Gronlund, *Commonwealth*, 70.

99. Ibid., 44; Green, *Grass-Roots Socialism*.

100. Hine and Faragher, *The American West*; Shannon, *The Farmer's Last Frontier*.

101. Lee and Cox, *When Sunflowers Bloomed Red*, 16.

102. Sreenivasan, *Utopias in American History*, 339.

103. Gronlund, *Commonwealth* (1891), 64. This is not in the original 1884 publication.

104. Gronlund quoted in Quint, *Forging American Socialism*, 82; Gronlund, *Commonwealth* (1891), 64; Miller, *This Radical Land*; W. Carey Jones, "The Kaweah Experiment in Co-operation," *The Quarterly Journal of Economics* 6, no. 1 (October 1891): 47–75, https://booksc .org/ireader/26026623; Robert F. Zeidel, review of Jay O'Connell, *Co-operative Dreams: A History of the Kaweah Colony, California History* 79 (January 2000), https://booksc.org/book/27219311 /6b3243; Postel, *The Populist Vision*, 226.

105. Theodore Kallman, *The Kingdom of God is at Hand: The Christian Commonwealth in Georgia, 1896–1901* (Athens: University of Georgia, 2021), 6.

106. Gronlund, *Co-operative Commonwealth*, 49.

107. Gronlund, *Commonwealth* (1891), 67.

108. Ibid., 92.

109. This portion of Gronlund's *Commonwealth* comes from Chapter 3. In the original, this chapter was titled, "The Darkest Hour." In later editions, the title was changed to "Culmination." "Culmination" refers to the "dark hour" of economic crisis that would lead to the end of capitalism. Gronlund is warning that markets will eventually dry up and that overproduction will "involve capitalists and labourers in one common ruin" (76). The "culmination," mentioned in the previous chapter refers to the collapse.

110. Gronlund, *Commonwealth* (1891), 77; Ely, *Monopolies and Trusts*, 59.

111. Gronlund, *Commonwealth*, 88.

112. Ibid., 78, 82. Nature would, through competition, select stronger species to subdue or even eradicate weaker ones. This was the assumed law of nature. Interfering with the dictates of nature was, by definition, unnatural. Such liberal ideology, the "hands-off" approach, became, in the opinion of Hofstadter, the backbone of the conservative ideology of wealthy elites who held power in the country, a position challenged in recent scholarship. See Hofstadter, *Social Darwinism*, 5; Bannister, *Social Darwinism*; Mike Hawkins, *Social Darwinism in European and American Thought, 1860–1945: Nature as Model and Nature as Threat* (Cambridge: Cambridge University Press, 1997); Peel, *Herbert Spencer*.

113. Gronlund, *Commonwealth*, 96.

114. Ibid., 97.

115. Gemorah, "Laurence Gronlund," 145.

116. Gronlund, *Commonwealth* (1884), 41.

117. Gourevitch, *Slavery to Cooperation*, 106.

118. Ibid., 39.

119. Ibid., 85.

120. Daniel Raymond, *Thoughts on Political Economy* (Baltimore: Fielding Lucas, Jr., 1820), 219–21.

121. "Campaign Notes," *Salt Lake Herald*, 11 October 1894, https://www.newspapers.com/image /12659414/.

122. Gemorah "Laurence Gronlund," 157.

123. *Salt Lake Herald*, 11 October 1894.

124. Gronlund did not always maintain a clear distinction between the administrative state and the State organism.

125. Gronlund, *Commonwealth* (1891), 81.

126. Joseph Labadie, "To the Readers of the Journal," *Journal of United Labor,* June 1882.

127. Gronlund, *Commonwealth*, 81. Other socialists understood the organism of the State differently. Christian Socialist William Dwight Porter Bliss, founder of the Church of the Carpenter, expressed concern that however large the state became it was imperative that it be democratic: "The expansion of the State is Socialistic only when the State is the people, a true democracy, the organic unity of the whole people." Quoted in Dorrien, *American Social Democracy,* 83. See also Bliss, "What is Christian Socialism?" *The Dawn* (January and February 1890). It was possible—and certainly worrisome—to have a State organism that was anti-democratic.

128. Elisha Mumford, *The Nation: The Foundations of Civil Order and Political Life in the United States* (New York: Hurd and Houghton: 1870), 10.

129. Burnette G. Haskell, "Why I Am a Nationalist," *Twentieth Century* 4, no. 20 (May 15, 1890): 5–7.

130. Ely, *Socialism: An Examination of its Nature, Its Strengths and Its Weakness, with Suggestions* (New York: Thomas Y. Crowell & Co., 1894), 3.

131. Vail, *Modern Socialism,* 439.

132. Gronlund, *Commonwealth*, 105.

133. Ibid., 83.

134. Ibid., 104; Edward Bellamy, *Looking Backward, 2000–1887* (Boston: Houghton, Mifflin and Company, 1889), 67.

135. Gronlund, *Commonwealth*, 107.

136. Laurence Gronlund, "A Reply to Herber Newton," *The Nationalist* 1, no. 5 (September 1889): 159; Smith, *Urban Disorder and the Shape of Belief,* 211.

137. Gronlund, *Commonwealth*, 107, 140, 149.

138. Ibid., 115, 147–48, 158–59.

139. Ibid., 113.

140. Ibid., 148–49.

141. Ibid., 126, 145.

142. Ibid., 117.

143. Ibid., 119.

144. Foster, *Marx's Ecology*, Epilogue, e-book.

145. Hegel quoted in Frederick Copleston, *A History of Philosophy: Modern Philosophy, Fichte to Hegel* (New York: Double Day, 1963), 7: 257.

146. Hawthorn, *Enlightenment in Despair*, 48.

147. Gronlund, *Commonwealth*, 160, 162, 165.

148. Ibid., 165.

149. Ibid., 110, 164–5, 167, 172, 179, 200. Gronlund was critical of Bellamy's suggestion that the composition of the board of administrators would be made up of "retired functionaries." While common sense would favor experience, Gronlund did not restrict leadership to retired individuals.

150. Ibid., 126.

151. Ibid., 124.

152. McArthur and Bellamy quoted in Nelson, "People's Capital," 59.

153. Gronlund, *Commonwealth*, 127.

154. Ibid., 129. Statistics would be used to gain knowledge of the condition of workers. See Porter, *Trust in Numbers*. African American intellectuals believed that statistical analysis would be the "great lever" for greater social equality.

155. Gronlund, *Commonwealth*, 173, 175, 183.

156. Ibid., 175; Ely, *The Strengths and Weaknesses of Socialism*, 31. Ely mentions the system in Switzerland and adds to the popularity of the initiative and referendum proportional representation, "a third political reform which meets with general favor on the part of socialists."

157. Gronlund, *Commonwealth*, 177.

158. Ibid., 179, 182, 184.

159. Ibid., 193–94.

160. Ibid., 202, 204–5. Gronlund defended the opportunity of women to become doctors but not surgeons, offering no explanation as to why.

161. Postel, *The Populist Vision*, 96.

162. In relation to electing the leaders of government, Gronlund assumed America's standard for voting at the time—universal male suffrage.

163. Gronlund, *Commonwealth*, 177.

164. Ibid., 206. Spencer too expressed that "with a universal distribution of votes the larger class will inevitably profit at the expense of the smaller class." See Spencer, *The Principles of Ethics* Vol. 2:192.

165. Ibid., 206.

166. Ely, *Strengths and Weaknesses of Socialism*, 43–44, 48.

167. Gronlund, *Commonwealth*, 211.

168. Ibid., 206–207, 214.

169. Ibid., 228.

170. Bok, *Higher Education in America*; Mattingly, *American Academic Cultures*; Thelin, *A History of American Higher Education*; Barrow, *Universities and the Capitalist State*; Menand, *The Metaphysical Club*.

171. Gronlund, *Commonwealth*, 221.

172. Ibid., 231, 229, 234.

173. Ibid., 223, 224, 225.

174. VanOverbeke, *The Standardization of American Schooling*; Gronlund, *Commonwealth* (1891), 225.

175. Ibid., 224.

176. Gronlund, *Commonwealth* (1900), 257, 282.

177. *San Francisco Call*, 7 May 1895.

178. Gronlund, *Commonwealth*, 241, 239.

179. Ibid., 236–37, 251.

180. Ibid., 247–48, 251, 254, 258.

181. Debs, *Report on the Chicago Strike*.

182. Debs, "Letter to the American Railway Union," *Railway Times* (1 January 1897).

183. Gronlund, *Commonwealth*, 263.

184. Ibid., 263; "Laurence Gronlund," *Topeka Daily Press*, 23 December 1893.

## 2. OH, IT GOES . . . GOD WILLS IT

1. Gronlund, *Commonwealth*, 263.

2. "Lawrence Gronlund on Trusts and Collectivism: Single Tax Idea Attacked," *Los Angeles Herald*, 18 March 1895, https://www.newspapers.com/image/80568104/; Marx and Engels, *Collected Works of Karl Marx and Frederick Engels* Vol. 10, 122.

3. Gronlund, *Ça Ira*, 236.

4. "When Trusts are a Boon to Humanity: Laurence Gronlund, the Socialist, Says [Trusts] are Good Things as Means to an End," *Los Angeles Times*, 18 March 1895, https://www.newspapers.com/image/378338135/.

5. "The Problem Solved: Laurence Gronlund Tells How the Social Problem May Be Solved Peaceably and Gradually," *Daily News Advertiser* (Vancouver, British Columbia), 30 September 1897, https://www.newspapers.com/image/774954022; "When Trusts Are a Boon to Humanity," *Los Angeles Times*, 18 March 1895. The Protestant Reformation, for instance, demonstrated the slow natural evolution with that decisive moment inaugurated by Martin Luther in 1517. The "great outburst" created by Luther nailing his 95 theses on the church door at Wittenberg was preceded by a century of evolutionary preparation. The same held true for the world-changing event in the French Revolution that began in 1789 as well as the abolition of slavery in the United States in the 1860s. And in Gronlund's own day, the trust represented that "revolutionary" and "decisive point of evolution" that cut at the root of competition, giving birth to socialism.

6. Hegel, *Phenomenology of Spirit*, 6–7.

7. "Edinburgh University: Social Reform Society Report," *The Christian Socialist* 3, no. 37 (June 1886): 198–99, https://babel.hathitrust.org/cgi/pt?id=mdp.39015074740377&view=1up&seq =445&q1=Gronlund.

8. Grant Allen, "Gronlund," in *Social Democracy Red Book: A Brief History of Socialism in America*, ed. Frederick Faries Heath (Terre Haute: Debs Publishing Co., 1900), 101.

9. Gronlund, *Ça Ira*, 244. Associates of Gronlund understood the French Revolution in a similar way. In his reflections on the Paris Commune, George Herron summarized the revolution in the following manner: "[The French Revolution] was essentially a middle class overthrow of the feudal class. But it was the peasant who did the fighting and owned the victories; and it was Rousseau, whose heart and motive were with the peasant, who furnished the revolution's philosophy and dynamic. Upon the victories of the long-starved peasants capitalism laid its secure foundations." George Herron, "From Revolution to Revolution" *The Comrade* 2, no. 12 (September 1903): 267–273; Henry Heller, *The Bourgois Revolution in France (1789–1815)* (New York: Berghan Books, 2006), 12.

10. "Literary Notes," *Indianapolis News*, 12 February 1887, 3, https://www.newspapers.com /image/34510667.

11. Quoted in Schneider, *History of Philosophy in America*, 166.

12. Wirzbicki *Fighting for the Higher Law*, 244.

13. Quoted in Schneider, *History of Philosophy in America*, 166.

14. Philip S. Foner, *The Workingmen's Party of the United States: A History of the First Marxist Party in the Americas* (Minneapolis: University of Minnesota, 1984), 68. Foner quoted in Mark Kruger, *St. Louis Commune: Communism in the Heartland* (Lincoln: University of Nebraska Press, 2021), 200.

15. Phillips quoted in David Burbank, *Reign of Rabble: The St. Louis General Strike of 1877* (New York: August M. Kelley, 1966), 197.

16. Gourevitch, 106.

17. Kruger, *St. Louis Commune*, 9, 82.

18. Ibid., 204.

19. Gronlund quote in Burbank, *Reign of Rabble*, 197. Burbank might be overplaying Gronlund's negative—at least for Burbank—attitude toward the "poor and weak," including the laboring masses.

20. Ibid., 197.

21. Kruger, *St. Louis Commune*, 194, 196.

22. "New Books," *St. Albans Daily Messenger* (Vermont), 10 December 1887, https://www .newspapers.com/image/444179307.

23. Gemorah, "Laurence Gronlund—Utopian or Reformer," 450; Pittenger, *American Socialists and Evolutionary Thought, 1870–1920*, 46.

24. In many ways, the consolidation of the middle class and its political authority came as a result of the political weakness of both the nobility and the monarchy. William Doyle writes: "France under Louis XVI was governed not by the nobility, but by a plutocracy in which the majority of nobles had no share. Half or more of the nobility were no better off than the average

bourgeois, and many were a good deal poorer." William Doyle, *The Oxford History of the French Revolution.* 2nd ed. (Oxford: Oxford University Press, 2002), 29.

25. Gronlund, *Ça Ira,* 4.

26. Ibid., 1.

27. Ibid., 3. Gronlund might be closer to Albert Mathiez's interpretation than that of Aulard. Bertel Nygaard, "Constructing Marxism: Karly Kautsky and the French Revolution," *History of European Ideas* 35, no. 4 (2009): 450–464.

28. Gronlund, *Ça Ira,* 3; Preface to Aulard, *Histoire politique de la Révolution française* (four volumes, Paris, 1901); *The French Revolution: A Political History, 1789–1804* (four volumes, London, 1910); Joseph Tendler, "Alphonse Aulard Revisited," *European Review of History—Revue europeenne d'histoire* 20, no. 4 (2013): 649–669. It is enough to say that Gronlund stood between Aulard and the Marxist School. Thus, there is no need to delineate further the historiography of the French Revolution. It is important to note that the current historiography of the French Revolution, Gary Kate writes, is "almost total collapse of the orthodox Marxist interpretation" (Kates 4).

29. The French Revolution, according to George Lefebvre, stood as an "episode in the general rise of the bourgeoisie." Lefebvre, *The French Revolution from 1793 to 1799,* 360. The conflict that inspired the Revolution did not revolve strictly around conflicts between the crown and the nobility, though there were certainly tensions and frustrations between the two, but between the nobility and the rising number of middling individuals who constituted the class of the bourgeois. From the perspective of the bourgeoisie, the nobility was more of an impediment to social, economic, and political reform. For Albert Soboul, the revolutionary contest revolved around a maturing bourgeoisie "confronted by a decadent aristocracy holding tenaciously to its privileges." Quoted in T. C. W. Blanning, *The French Revolution: Aristocrats Versus Bourgeois?* (Atlantic Highlands, NJ: Humanities Press, 1987), 9. Revisionists have challenged the Marxist interpretation. On the eve of the Revolution, Paris did not have a clearly defined nor conscious bourgeoisie class. Post-revisionists like Timothy Tackett have likewise challenged arguments that focused on the maturation of Enlightenment ideas as the main driver of the Revolution.

30. Gronlund, *Ça Ira,* 4.

31. Jean Juares quoted in Doyle, *The Oxford History of the French Revolution,* 448.

32. Juares, *A Socialist History of the French Revolution;* Mathiez, *The French Revolution;* Doyle, *Origins of the French Revolution;* Tackett, *Becoming Revolution;* Tackett, *When the King Took Flight;* Tackett, *The Coming of the Terror in the French Revolution.*

33. "Book Reviews," *Nebraska State Journal,* 30 October 1887, https://www.newspapers.com/image/313774815.

34. Gronlund, *Ça Ira,* 5, 11. Gronlund adopted Thomas Carlyle's view that great men—"heroes"—represented the movers of history. History, Carlyle said, "is but the Biography of great men." Thomas Carlyle, "Of Heroes and Hero Worship," *Works of Thomas Carlyle* (London: Chapman and Hall, 1869): 12: 285.

35. Gronlund, *Ça Ira,* 11.

36. Ibid., 12–13.

37. Gronlund, *Ça Ira,* 13–14.

38. Karl Marx, *The Poverty of Philosophy* (New York: International Publishers, 1963), 111. "Slavery is just as much the pivot of bourgeois industry and machinery, credits, etc. Without slavery you have no cotton; without cotton you have no modern industry . . . Thus slavery is an economic category of the most importance."

39. This is my addition. Gronlund does not speak of primitive accumulation. I include it, however, because I think it helps complete Gronlund's argument.

40. Gronlund, *Ça Ira*, 14.

41. Linebaugh and Rediker, *The Many-Headed Hydra*.

42. Gronlund, *Ça Ira*, 15; Henry Heller, *The Bourgeois Revolution in France (1789–1815)* (New York: Berghan Books, 2006), 11.

43. Gronlund, *Ça Ira*, 16; Clark, "Early Capitalism and Invention," *The Economic History Review* vol. 6, no. 2 (April 1936): 143–156.

44. Marx and Engels, *Collected Works of Karl Marx and Frederick Engels*, Vol. 29: 262–64.

45. Of course, we can run philosophical circles around the question of whether ideas can ever be divorced from ideology.

46. Gronlund, *Commonwealth* (1890), 105.

47. Gronlund, *Ça Ira*, 17. Richard Ely made a distinction between German and English socialists, especially the Fabians, in that the latter did not hold to a strict "materialist conception of history," but gave "room for the play of conscience." See Ely, *The Strengths and Weaknesses of Socialism*, 80. American socialism, in general, and thanks to the influence of Gronlund, seemed closer to the English Fabians on this point than the Germans.

48. Wirzbicki, *Fighting for the Higher Law*, 6.

49. Traverso, *Revolution*, 47. Traverso continues on this point: "The entanglements of causality and agency, structural determinism and political subjectivity—two explanatory keys that tend to remain separated in Marx's writings—has produced the best achievements of Marxist historiography, from Trotsky's *History of the Russian Revolution* (1930–32) to C.L.R. James's *The Black Jacobins* (1938); Daniel Guerin's *Bourgois and 'Bras Nus'* (1947) to Adolfo Gilly's *The Mexican Revolution* (1971)."

50. "History is," Marx and Engels wrote in *The Holy Family*, "nothing but the activity of man pursuing his aims." Marx and Engels, *Collected Works of Karl Marx and Frederick Engels*, Vol. 4: 93.

51. Gronlund, *Ça Ira*, 19.

52. Gronlund, *Ça Ira*, 10; Fraser, *Mongrel Firebugs and Men of Property: Capitalism and Class Conflict in American History*, 519.

53. Gronlund, *Commonwealth* (1891), 74.

54. McGrath, *Reformation Thought: An Introduction*, 220–221.

55. Ibid., 221.

56. Gronlund, *Ça Ira*, 18.

57. Gronlund, *Commonwealth* (1890), 104.

58. Gronlund, *Ça Ira*, 19.

59. Jonathan Israel, *A Revolution of the Mind* (Princeton University Press, 2010), 224.

60. Gronlund, *Ça Ira*, 19, 25.

61. Ibid., 21–23.

62. Ibid., 30, 33, 36, 44–5, 46–7, 53; Heller, *Bourgeois Revolution in France (1789–1815)*, 29.

63. Ibid., 36.

64. Gronlund, *Ça Ira*, 36–37, 39. Emphasis in the original unless noted otherwise. See also Heller, *Bourgeois Revolution*, 11; Furet, *Marx and the French Revolution*, 37, 48, 189.

65. Gronlund, *Ça Ira*, 42.

66. Ibid., 41.

67. Gronlund, *Ça Ira*, 52; Tackett, *Coming of the Terror in the French Revolution*, 84.

68. Ibid., 53.

69. Ibid., 64.

70. Ibid., 66–67, 68–69.

71. Spencer quoted in Hook, *Hero in History*, 54.

72. Gronlund, *Ça Ira*, 28.

73. Popkin, *A New World Begins*, 378.

74. Juares, *Socialist History of the French Revolution*, 181.

75. Gronlund, *Ça Ira*, 58.

76. Doyle, *Oxford History of the French Revolution*, 228.

77. Gronlund, *Ça Ira*, 55–56.

78. Ibid., 60.

79. Gronlund, *Ça Ira*, 61; Tackett, *When the King Took Flight*.

80. Gronlund, *Ça Ira*, 62.

81. Doyle, *Oxford History of the French Revolution*, 154.

82. Gronlund, *Ça Ira*, 63.

83. Ibid., 70.

84. Tackett, *Coming of the Terror*, 183–184; Terry Pinkard, *German Philosophy, 1760–1860: The Legacy of Idealism* (Cambridge: Cambridge University Press, 2002), 84.

85. Gronlund, *Ça Ira*, 77.

86. Doyle, *Oxford History of the French Revolution*, 190, 251.

87. Gronlund, *Ça Ira*, 78.

88. Ibid., 80, 82, 84–85, 87.

89. Popkin, *A New World Begins*, 288; Doyle, *Oxford History of the French Revolution*, 221.

90. Gronlund, *Ça Ira*, 89.

91. Ibid., 94. Doyle, *Oxford History of the French Revolution*, 422.

92. Gronlund, *Ça Ira*, 95.

93. Doyle, *Oxford History of the French Revolution*, 202.

94. Gronlund, *Ça Ira*, 96.

95. Doyle, *Oxford History of the French Revolution*, 201.

96. Gronlund, *Ça Ira*, 97.

97. Ibid., 123. This would influence Gronlund's nationalism over that of international communism. As he learned from studying the French Revolution, Gronlund came to the position that before revolution could spread to other parts of the world, there was a prior need to establish socialism in one country. This was also a priority of Fabian Socialism.

98. Tackett, *Coming of the Terror*, 233, 241; Gronlund, *Ça Ira*, 98.

99. Doyle, *Oxford History of the French Revolution*, 200.

100. Gronlund, *Ça Ira*,103, 105.

101. Ibid., 108.

102. Gronlund, *Ça Ira*, 111; Israel, *Revolutionary Ideas*, 505.

103. Gronlund, *Ça Ira*, 108, 114.

104. Ibid., 113; Doyle, *Oxford History of the French Revolution*, 227.

105. Gronlund, *Ça Ira*, 128, 132.

106. Ibid., 133. See also Wahnich, *In Defense of the Terror*, 33.

107. Gronlund, *Ça Ira*, 136; Tackett, *Coming of the Terror*, 320.

108. Gronlund, *Ça Ira*, 129, 137, 138; Tackett, *Coming of the Terror*, 195.

109. Gronlund, *Ça Ira*, 115–117; Tackett, *Coming of the Terror*, 270

110. Gronlund, *Ça Ira*, 118.

111. Ibid., 119, 123–125.

112. Ibid., 141–143.

113. Tackett, *Coming of the Terror*, 28.

114. Gronlund, *Ça Ira!*, 144–145, 147.

115. Ibid., 148.

116. Heller, *Bourgeois Revolution*, 92.

117. Ibid., 141, 150–153.

118. Ibid., 155, 157.

119. Ibid., 160–63.

120. Tackett, *Coming of the Terror*, 313.

121. Gronlund, *Ça Ira!*, 172.

122. Ibid., 164.

123. Ibid., 164–167.

124. Ibid., 174.

125. Ibid., 175.

126. Ibid., 142.

127. Ibid., 176, 178. This was an important lesson that Americas needed to bear in mind. There was a similar division in late nineteenth-century American, Gronlund cited, between anarchists and individualists, "between John Most on the one side, and Hebert Spencer and Auberon Herbert on the other." Hebert perpetuated his own "federalism," which divided France into "autonomous communes" and eliminated the supremacy of the State. In Gronlund's mind, the anarchists were regressive in the way they pushed for "small, voluntary, 'autonomous' groups" that would dissolve the organic unity of the State.

128. Gronlund, *Ça Ira*, 177.

129. Ibid., 177, 179.

130. Gronlund, *Ça Ira*, 204.

131. Ibid., 205, 211–212.

132. Gronlund, *Ça Ira*, 183.

133. Israel, *Revolutionary Ideas*, 52.

134. Gronlund, *Ça Ira*, 183.

135. Ibid., 184; Tackett, *Coming of the Terror*, 328.

136. Gronlund, *Ça Ira*, 185.

137. Ibid., 186–187.

138. Ibid., 187.

139. Tackett, *Coming of the Revolution*, 340.

140. Gronlund, *Ça Ira*, 188.

141. Israel, *Revolutionary Ideas*, 554.

142. Gronlund, *Ça Ira*, 189.

143. Ibid., 190, 197, 199.

144. Doyle, *Oxford History of the French Revolution*, 274.

145. Gronlund, *Ça Ira*, 192.

146. Ibid., 193, 195.

147. Tackett, *Coming of the Terror*, 330; Israel, *Revolutionary Ideas*, 556; Most historians of the French Revolution remained puzzled as to the motivations behind Danton's trial and execution. William Doyle writes: "Few episodes in the Revolution are harder to interpret than the fall of Danton and Desmoulins, for reliable evidence about the motivation of those involved is almost completely lacking . . . Their execution, in fact, marked the beginning of a new phase in the Terror, when people would die for their potential as much as for specific crimes, and sometimes merely for their failure to match some ideal moral standard." Doyle, *Oxford History*, 274.

148. Gronlund, *Ça Ira*, 196.

149. *Christian Socialist* (June 1886), 199.

150. Gronlund, *Ça Ira*, 202–203.

151. Tackett, *Coming of the Revolution*, 336, 340.

152. Gronlund, *Ça Ira*, 206–207.

153. Ibid., 208.

154. Ibid., Heller, *The Bourgeois Revolution*, 109, 112.

155. Popkin, *New World Begins*, 466, 476.

156. Gronlund, *Ça Ira*, 217. See also Laura Mason, *The Last Revolutionaries: The Conspiracy Trial of Gracchus Babeuf and the Equals* (New Haven: Yale, 2022).

157. Gronlund, *Ça Ira*, 218.

158. Ibid., 218.

159. Ibid., 219.

160. Ibid., 221.

161. Ibid., 226.

162. Heller, *The Bourgeois Revolution*, 22.

163. Gronlund, *Ça Ira!*, 228.

164. Ibid., 229, 230–31.

165. Ibid., 243.

166. Ibid., 244. Ely, *Strength and Weaknesses of Socialism*, 33. Characteristic of socialism in America and Europe is "the general desire, on the part of socialists, to reduce the functions of government to a minimum."

167. Gronlund, *Ça Ira,* 235.

168. Ibid., 236.

169. Ibid., 237.

170. Ibid., 238.

171. Ibid., 239, 241, 252.

### 3. STONE-BLIND IN ONE EYE

1. Gronlund, *The Co-Operative Commonwealth,* vii; Richard Ely would later agree as he wrote in *Strengths and Weaknesses of Socialism:* "Socialism is known wherever modern industrial civilization exists" (71).

2. Bryson, *The Economics of Henry George;* Barker, *Henry George;* Steven Cord, *Henry George: Dreamer or Realist,* 2nd edition (New York: Robert Schalkenback Foundation, 1984); Hellman, *Henry George Reconsidered;* Moss, *Henry George;* O'Donnell, *Henry George and the Crisis of Inequality.*

3. Henry George Jr., *The Life of Henry George* (NY: Doubleday and McClure Company, 1900), 191.

4. Henry George, *Progress and Poverty: An Inquiry into the Cause of Industrial Depressions and of Increase of Wealth with Increase of Wealth* (New York: Sterling Publishing Company, 1879), 266.

5. Ibid., 266.

6. Isenberg, *The Destruction of the Bison.*

7. George, *Progress and Poverty,* 264.

8. Ibid., 266.

9. Ibid., 213.

10. Leo Tolstoy was moved by George's remedy. Sun Yat-sen incorporated George's single-tax scheme into his "Three Principles of the People." Wasserstraum, *Oxford Illustrated History of Modern China,* 130.

11. George Warren Arms, "Further Inquiry into Howells's Socialism," *Science & Society* 3, no. 2 (Spring 1939): 245–248; Gronlund said the same in *Ça Ira:* George's scheme would not constitute a revolution but "downright robbery" (242).

12. Marx quoted in Bell, *Marxian Socialism in the United States,* 28.

13. Marx quoted in Johnson, *Marxism in United States History Before the Russian Revolution (1876–1917),* 47.

14. Friedrich Engels, *The Condition of the Working Class in England* in the *Collected Works of Karl Marx and Frederick Engels* Vol. 4 (New York: International Publishers, 1975), 438–439.

15. Gronlund, *Cooperative Commonwealth* (1884), 27; O'Donnell, *Henry George and the Crisis of Inequality,* 272; Gronlund, *Insufficiency,* 1–2; Gronlund, *Ça Ira,* 175.

16. Gemorah, "Laurence Gronlund," 283.

17. Geiger, *The Philosophy of Henry George,* 255. To be fair, Geiger also includes A.M. Simons's *Single Tax Versus Socialism* (Chicago 1899); Gronlund, *Co-operative Commonwealth* (1891), 86; Andelson, *Critics of Henry George* Vol. 1; Hudson, "Henry George's Political Critics,"

1–46. Hudson identifies twelve political criticisms against George's reform efforts: "(1) his refusal to join with other reformers to link his proposals with theirs, or to absorb theirs into his own campaign; (2) his singular focus on ground rent to the exclusion of other forms of monopoly income, such as that of the railroads, oil and mining trusts; (3) his almost unconditional support of capital, even against labor; (4) his economic individualism rejecting a strong role for government; (5) his opposition to public ownership or subsidy of basic infrastructure; (6) his refusal to acknowledge interest bearing debt as the twin form of *rentier* income alongside ground rent; (7) the scant emphasis he placed on urban land and owner-occupied land; (8) his endorsement of the Democratic Party's free-trade platform; (9) his rejection of an academic platform to elaborate rent theory; (9) his rejection of an academic platform to elaborate rent theory; (10) the narrowness of his theorizing beyond the land question; (11) the alliance of his followers with the right wing of the political spectrum; and (12) the hope that full taxation of ground rent could be achieved gradually rather than requiring a radical confrontation involving a struggling over control of government." Unfortunately, as Fred Harrison notes, there is no existing copy of Simons's work.

18. Gronlund says in his response to George's comments on socialism after the election of 1886 that George "should do him the honor of reading my forthcoming book, *Danton in the French Revolution*" (*Ça Ira* 33).

19. Fred Harrison, "Gronlund and Other Marxists" in *Critics of Henry George,* ed. Robert V. Andelson (Madison, NJ: Fairleigh Dickinson University Press, 1979): 197.

20. Gronlund, *Insufficiency of Henry George's Theory.*

21. Gronlund, *Insufficiency,* 1.

22. De Mille, *Henry George,* 2.

23. Webb, *Socialism in England,* 20–21.

24. Gronlund, *Commonwealth* (1891), 86.

25. Gronlund, *Insufficiency,* 18.

26. "Not Fighting George: Socialists Contemplate the Perfection of the United Labor Party," *St. Louis Post-Dispatch,* 24 June 1887, https://www.newspapers.com/image/138121774.

27. Gronlund, *Cooperative Commonwealth* (1890), 86–87.

28. Gronlund, *Socialism vs. Tax Reform: An Answer to Henry George.*

29. John L. Thomas *Alternative America: Henry George, Edward Bellamy, Henry Demarest Lloyd and the Adversary Tradition* (Cambridge: Harvard/Belknap Press, 1983); Philip S. Foner, *History of the Labor Movement in the United States: From Colonial Times to the Founding of the American Federation of Labor,* 2 vols., (New York: International Publishers, 1947).

30. Maher, "Laurence Gronlund: Contributions to American Socialism," 618–624; O'Donnell, *Henry George and the Crisis of Inequality,* 51–52.

31. Maher, "Laurence Gronlund," 622.

32. Gronlund, *Cooperative Commonwealth* (1884), 34.

33. Gronlund, *Ça Ira,* 175.

34. Gronlund, "Reply to Dr. Heber Newton: Critic of Nationalism," 158–161

35. O'Donnell, *Henry George and the Crisis of Inequality,* 260.

36. Henry George quoted in O'Donnell, 260.

37. Gronlund, *Socialism v. Tax Reform*, 3; Henry George, *The Standard*, no. 4 (July 30, 1887), 1.

38. Henry George, *The Condition of Labor: An Open Letter to Pope Leo XIII*. In *The Complete Works of Henry George* Vol. 3: *The Land Question* (New York: Doubleday Page and Co, 1891), 60–61.

39. Gronlund, *Socialism vs. Tax Reform*, 3.

40. Gronlund likewise challenged the way socialism had been "continually and unjustly confounded with Communism," which distributes all things equally to the citizenry regardless of labor, a system in which "the man who loafs gets as much as the man who works." See "Socialists to the Front: Eager to Convert the Rest of the United Labor Party, *New York Sun*, 24 June 1887, https://www.newspapers.com/image/78262561 (interview with Gronlund).

41. George, "The Condition of Labor: An Open Letter to Pope Leo XIII" in *The Complete Works of Henry George*, Vol. 3: *The Land Question* (NY: Doubleday Page and Co., 1891), 61.

42. Gronlund, *Insufficiency*, 19.

43. Gronlund, *Socialism vs. Tax Reform*, 13; McCann, Jr., "Apprehending the Social Philosophy of Henry George," 67–88.

44. Gronlund, *Socialism vs. Tax-Reform*, 30.

45. Gronlund, *Socialism vs. Tax-Reform*, 30.

46. Ibid., 31.

47. Gronlund, *Insufficiency*, 13.

48. *Cigar Makers'* quote in O'Donnell, 259.

49. Gronlund, *Insufficiency*, 3.

50. Ibid., 7.

51. Gronlund interview, *New York Sun*, 24 June 1887.

52. Gronlund, *Insufficiency*, 7.

53. Ibid., 7.

54. Gronlund, *Socialism vs. Tax Reform*, 18.

55. Ibid., 19.

56. Ibid., 20.

57. Ibid., 21.

58. Gronlund, *Insufficiency*, 20.

59. Maher, "Laurence Gronlund: Contributions to American Socialism," *Western Political Quarterly* 15, no. 4 (Dec. 1962): 618–624.

60. Gronlund, *Socialism vs. Tax Reform*, 21.

61. George *Progress and Poverty*, 51; Gemorah, "Laurence Gronlund," 148.

62. Gronlund, *Insufficiency*, 27.

63. Ibid., 28.

64. Gronlund, *Socialism vs. Tax Reform*, 25.

65. Ibid., 16.

66. Henry George, *The Science of Political Economy* (New York: Robert Schalkenbach Foundation, 1898 [1962]), 391.

67. Gronlund, *Socialism vs. Tax Reform*, 25.

68. O'Donnell, *Henry George*, 265.

69. Gronlund, *Socialism vs. Tax Reform*, 25.

70. Hillquit, *History of Socialism in the United States*, 279.

71. Gronlund, *Socialism vs. Tax Reform*, 34.

72. Ibid., 18.

73. Ibid., 27.

74. Ibid., 26.

75. Gronlund, *Socialism vs. Tax Reform*, 28.

76. Henry George, *Progress and Poverty* (New York: D. Appleton and Company, 1880), 284.

77. Ibid., 416.

78. George, *Progress and Poverty*, 457.

79. O'Donnell, *Henry George and the Crisis of Inequality*, 55.

80. Ibid., 56.

81. Gronlund, *Socialism vs. Tax Reform*, 12.

82. Daniel Gaido, "*The American Worker* and the Theory of Permanent Revolution: Karl Kautsky on Werner Sombart's *Why Is There No Socialism in the United States*," *Historical Materialism* 11, no. 4 (December 2003): 79–123.

83. Karl Kautsky, "Unsere amerikanischen Berichte," *Die Neue Zeit* 8 (1895): 183–5.

84. Gronlund interview. *New York Sun*, 24 June 1887.

85. Gronlund, *Socialism vs. Tax Reform*, 24.

86. Gronlund, *Socialism vs. Tax Reform*, 25.

87. *St. Louis Post-Dispatch*, June 24, 1887.

88. Gronlund, *Socialism vs. Tax Reform*, 12.

89. Ibid., 31.

90. Ibid., 32.

91. Ibid., 18.

92. Gronlund interview. *New York Sun*, 24 June 1887.

93. Gronlund, *Insufficiency*, 17.

94. Gronlund, *Socialism vs. Tax Reform*, 35.

## 4. RESTORATION OF A BROKEN BOND

1. "Commended by Leo Tolstoy"; Tolstoy's letter to Gronlund also published in "A Noted Lecturer: Laurence Gronlund Calls Himself a Collectivist," *Salt Lake Herald*, 11 October 1894, https://www.newspapers.com/image/80974360.

2. *Salt Lake Herald*, 11 October 1894, https://www.newspapers.com/image/80974360; Emile Laveleye wrote to Gronlund expressing his concern about the success of *Our Destiny*, given, wrote Laveleye, that it would "seem too radical for some and too religious for others." "Gronlund Talks: discusses the Future of Socialism," *Morning Call* (San Francisco), January 4, 1895, https://www.newspapers.com/image/92930549.

3. "Commended by Leo Tolstoy."

4. Blau, "The Cooperative Commonwealth as Secular Apocalypse," 216.

5. Gronlund, *The Co-operative Commonwealth* (1884), 257. Spencer recognized the issue on logical rather than pragmatic grounds: "Unless a real Non-relative Absolute be postulated, the Relative itself becomes absolute, and so brings the argument to a contradiction. See Spencer, *First Principles*, 99.

6. Ibid., 178; Gronlund, *The Co-operative Commonwealth* (1884). See also the American editions between 1884 and 1903.

7. "Edinburgh University: Social Reform Society Report," *The Christian Socialist* 3, no. 37 (June 1886): 199, https://babel.hathitrust.org/cgi/pt?id=mdp.39015074740377&view=1up&seq=445&q1=Gronlund. Gronlund's lecture was entitled "Personal Views."

8. Gronlund, *Ça Ira*, 12.

9. Karl Marx, *A Contribution to the Critique of Hegel's Philosophy of Right*, ed. J. O'Malley and trans. by A. Jolin (Cambridge: Cambridge University Press, 1970).

10. This quotation came from Marx's dissertation, *The Difference between Democritean and Epicurean Philosophies of Nature*; Grayling, *The History of Philosophy*, 353.

11. Religious belief does not diminish the radicalism of socialist activism. There is a rich tradition in Liberation Theology, which combines leftist thinking with Christianity, for instance. Scholars have acknowledged the galvanizing nature of faith, especially Christianity, among socialists despite the sharp differences they may have held over political engagement, social strategies, or the application of scientific theories. See Burbank, *When Farmers Voted Red;* Bisset, *Agrarian Socialism in America;* Janine G. Drake, "Between Religion and Politics: The Working Class Religious Left, 1880–1920," (PhD diss., University of Illinois at Urbana-Champaign, 2014); McKanan, "The Dialogue of Socialism."

12. McCarraher, *The Enchantments of Mammon*,187.

13. Quoted in Grayling, *History of Philosophy*, 356. I would modify Marx's words. It is not the case that religion is illusory in its very essence, but it nonetheless *can* be so. Thus, I would agree that an illusory religion should be dismantled not solely for the purpose of providing happiness, but for the sake of truth.

14. Klay and Lunn, "The Relationship of God's Providence to Market Economies," 541–564. Numerous evangelical conservatives have returned to defending or redeeming the relationship between Christianity and capitalism. See Richards, *Money, Greed, and God;* Barnes, *Redeeming Capitalism.*

15. Gronlund, *Our Destiny,* v.

16. Ibid., 135.

17. Guarneri, "The Associationists," 36–49.

18. Dorn, *Socialism and Christianity in Early Twentieth-Century America,* 11.

19. McKanan, *Prophetic Encounters,* 146.

20. Barton, *J. Stitt Wilson,* 110.

21. Bliss quoted in Dombrowski, *The Early Days of Christian Socialism in America,* 100; Nichola Paine Gilman, *Socialism and the American Spirit* (Boston and New York: Houghton, Mifflin, and Company, 1893), 230.

22. "Religion that is pure and undefiled before God the Father is this: to visit orphans and widows in their affliction, and to keep oneself unstained from the world" (James 1:27 ESV).

23. Howison quoted in Kuklick, *A History of American Philosophy*, 113; George Holmes Howison, *The Limits of Evolution and Other Essays: Illustrating the Metaphysical Theory of Personal Idealism*, 2nd. ed. (New York: Macmillan Company, 1905), xv.

24. Kuklick, *A History of Philosophy in America*, xii.

25. Indeed, as to Europe, Gronlund thought that no two thinkers had a greater impact in the 1890s than Hegel and Marx, https://www.newspapers.com/image/92930549.

26. Anderson and Fisch, *Philosophy in America*, 443.

27. Hegel, *Lectures on the Philosophy of History*, trans. J. Sibree (London: George Bell and Sons, 1884), 90. Goetzmann, *The American Hegelians*, 20.

28. Goetzmann, *The American Hegelians*, 3; Lloyd D. Easton, "Hegelianism in Nineteenth-Century Ohio," *Journal of the History of Ideas* 23, no. 3 (July–September 1962): 355–378.

29. Flower and Murphy, *A History of Philosophy in America* Vol. 2:471.

30. Goetzmann, *American Hegelians*, 6.

31. Flower and Murphey, *History of Philosophy in America* Vol. 2:469.

32. Gemorah, "Laurence Gronlund," 101. Gemorah writes: "Hegel's system is a philosophy of evolutionary idealism. It is evolutionary in an historical sense, with time left out . . . His doctrine of the existence of a corporate social consciousness, presupposed the existence of some objective universal mind."

33. Gronlund, *Our Destiny*, 169. Gronlund's tone toward Spencer in *Commonwealth*, even with his qualifications (rejecting individualism and complementing Spencer's organicism, was much more positive. His references to Spencer in *Our Destiny*, however, seemed much more critical.

34. Gemorah, "Laurence Gronlund," 102.

35. Gronlund, *Commonwealth*, 88; Hofstadter, *Social Darwinism in American Thought*, 96.

36. Laurence Gronlund, *The New Economy*, 59; Spencer, *The Study of Sociology* Vol. 2:607.

37. Gronlund, *Our Destiny*, 28, 37.

38. Royce quoted in Trevor Pearce, *Pragmatism's Evolution: Organism and Environment in American Philosophy* (Chicago: University of Chicago, 2020), 181.

39. Samuel Alexander, "Hegel's Conception of Nature," *Mind* 11 (1886): 518.

40. David George Ritchie, "Darwin and Hegel," *Proceedings of the Aristotelian Society* 1 (1891): 63–64.

41. Kuklick, *American Philosophy*, 108.

42. Davaney and Frisina, *The Pragmatic Century*, 9; John Dewey, "From Absolutism to Experientialism"; John Dewey, *The Later Works, 1925–1953*, ed. Jo Ann Boydston, 15 vols. (Carbondale: Southern Illinois University Press, 1984) Vol. 2:153; Beiser, *The Cambridge Companion to Hegel*, 184.

43. John Scott Haldane, "Life and Mechanism," *Mind* 9 (1884): 32–33. See also Haldane, *Organism and Environment as Illustrated by the Physiology of Breathing* (New Haven: Yale University Press, 1917).

44. Alexander, *Moral Order and Progress*, 271–72.

45. Everett, *Religion in Economics*, 23.

46. Gemorah, "Laurence Gronlund," 100–101.

47. Gronlund, *Co-operative Commonwealth* (1900), 277.

48. Edward Caird quoted in Pearce, *Pragmatism's Evolution*, 175. It is interesting that Caird identified Kant's philosophy as a "first stage, though a necessary stage, in the transition of philosophy to higher forms of Idealism." Caird, *A Critical Account of the Philosophy of Kant, With an Historical Introduction* (Glasgow: J. Maclehose, 1877), 667.

49. Spencer, *First Principles*, 46.

50. Schneider, *American Philosophy*, 284; Pearce, *Pragmatism's Evolution*, 72.

51. David Watson, "The Neo-Hegelian Tradition in America," *Journal of American Studies* 14, no. 2 (August 1980): 219–234; Watson, 226.

52. Herbert Spencer, *First Principles* 6th ed. (London: Williams & Norgate, 1928), Vol. 1:83.

53. Spencer's quote in Taylor, *The Philosophy of Herbert Spencer*, 137.

54. Gronlund, *Commonwealth*, 16, 95 (American and British editions 1891).

55. Walter Mueder and Laurence Sears, *The Development of American Philosophy: A Book of Readings* (Boston: Houghton-Mifflin, 1940), 219.

56. Spencer, *First Principles*, 37.

57. Charles Hodge, *What Is Evolution?* (New York: Scribner, Armstrong, and Company, 1874), 177. About Spencer, Hodge claimed: "Mr. Spencer, therefore, in accounting for the origin of the universe and all its phenomena . . . rejects Theism, or the doctrine of a personal God, who is extramundane as well as antemundane, the creator and governor of all things; he rejects Pantheism [and] he rejects Atheism . . . He contents himself with saying we must acknowledge the reality of an unknown something which is the cause of all things—the noumenon of all phenomena . . . We doubt not Mr. Spencer would indignantly reject the imputation of atheism; nevertheless, in the judgment of most men, the difference between Antitheist [Spencer's rejection of traditional beliefs on God] and Atheist is a mere matter of orthography" (19–20).

58. John Fiske, *The Idea of God as Affected by Modern Knowledge* (Boston and New York: Houghton, Mifflin and Company, 1887): 149–50, 166–67.

59. Hegel, *The Logic of Hegel*, 43.

60. Hegel, *Science of Logic*, 87, 101.

61. John McTaggart, *Studies in the Hegelian Dialectic* (Cambridge: J. and C. F. Clay at the University Press, 1896), 69.

62. Anderson and Fisch, *Philosophy in America*, 408.

63. Gemorah notes the similarities in dialectical methodology in Hegel and Marx. Yet there was a distinction. Hegel's structure contained an obvious "religious motif" different from the "activistic atheism" of Marx's system. Gronlund favored the religious over the atheistic. Gemorah, "Laurence Gronlund," 100.

64. Gronlund, *Our Destiny*, 34.

65. Ibid., 36.

66. Ibid., 29. The relationship between individuals was much more amicable than that of Hegel. While he posited that an individual's being cannot be constituted without another, Hegel argued that the initiate encounter between self and other was one of antagonism and even elimination, a contradiction which is eventually overcome. This is the so-called Master-Slave dilemma.

67. Laurence Gronlund, "Our Destiny" in *Nationalist* Vol. 2, *Radical Periods in the United States, 1890–1960* (New York: Greenwood Reprint Corporation, 1968), 2; https://babel.hathitrust.org/cgi/pt?id=uc1.b3785638&seq=190&q1=Gronlund.

68. Hegel, *Phenomenology of Spirit*, 110; Taylor, *Hegel*, 481.

69. Gronlund, *Our Destiny*, 29, 36.

70. Ibid., 3, 29, 46, 75, 78–79.

71. Gronlund, *Commonwealth*, 106.

72. Gronlund, *Ça Ira*, 17, 19.

73. Dorn, "The Social Gospel and Socialism," 84.

74. Gronlund, *Our Destiny*, 1.

75. Ibid., 68–69; Schneider, *American Philosophy*, 202

76. Gronlund, *Our Destiny*, 45.

77. Ibid., 32.

78. Ibid., 83.

79. Ibid., 105.

80. Ibid., 78.

81. "Moral Regeneration Not Impossible."

82. Taylor, *The Philosophy of Herbert Spencer*, 2.

83. Gronlund, *Our Destiny*, 61.

84. Gronlund, "A New Interpretation of Life," 351–361.

85. "Moral Regeneration Not Impossible."

86. Gronlund, *Our Destiny*, 76.

87. Ibid., 77. See also Burns, *The Life and Death of the Radical Historical Jesus*.

88. Gronlund, *Co-operative Commonwealth* (1900), 258.

89. Gronlund, *Our Destiny*, 21.

90. Ibid., 45.

91. Ibid., 67, 111, 113.

92. Ibid., 50, 54, 59.

93. Taylor, *Hegel*, 447.

94. Gronlund, *Our Destiny*, 88.

95. Ibid., 45, 47, 84.

96. Ibid., 43–44.

97. Ibid., 29.

98. Ibid., 27, 30, 130, 284.

99. Ibid., 21, 127, 129, 134, 138.

100. Ibid., 118–119, 120–121, 142, 144, 145.

101. Cook, *Spiritual Socialists*, 12.

102. Gronlund, *Our Destiny*, 157.

103. Gronlund, *Commonwealth* (1900), 256.

104. Gronlund, *Our Destiny*, 147, 148.

105. Ibid., 149–150.

106. Ibid., 153–155, 157, 159, 166.

NOTES TO PAGES 151–155

107. Janet, *La Morale,* iv; W. T. Harris, "Paul Janet and Hegel," *The Journal of Speculative Philosophy* 1, no. 4 (1867): 250–256.

108. Gronlund, *Our Destiny,* 166.

109. Ibid., 97–98.

110. Ibid., 13.

111. Ibid., 19–20.

112. Tsuzuki, "Lawrence Gronlund and American Socialism," 20–23. Yet it was not only industrialization that contributed to mental regression. Planned communities often had a similar effect. Gronlund mentions his experience with Jean-Batiste Andre ́ Godin's Familistere in Guise, France, "the only successful instance of the practical application of Fourierism to business" (Tsuzuki 22). This commune, at which Gronlund spent a few months, provided a minimum wage, a sick fund, and an old age pension fund. But there was a significant problem. There were "no social gatherings, no clubs, no literary or debating societies among them, as one would naturally expect; and the reason is a simple one; the material success as well as the failures are due to the character of the found." While studying the *Familistere,* Gronlund came to the irrevocable conclusion, as other like-minded socialists, "that material well-being is not sufficient for a people and must not be an end" (Tsuzuki 23).

113. Gronlund, "Why I Am a Socialist," 5–6.

114. Gronlund, *Our Destiny,* 167.

115. Ibid., 169–170. Gronlund supported an eight-hour day, but not as a partial means to alleviate the conditions of workers. A complete overhaul of capitalism was necessary.

116. Laurence Gronlund, "Les Socialisme Aux Etats-Unis," *Revue d'economic politique,* vol. 1 (March–April 1887), 121.

117. Laurence Gronlund, "What to Do?" 5.

118. Hofstadter, *Social Darwinism in American Thought,* 114–115.

119. Dorrien, *American Democratic Socialism,* 78.

120. Robert T. Handy, "George D. Herron and the Kingdom Movement" 19, no. 2 (June 1950): 97–115.

121. George Herron, *The Christian State* (New York: Thomas Y. Crowell Co., 1895), 18.

122. George Herron, *The New Redemption* (New York: Thomas Y. Crowell Co., 1893), 14.

123. Gronlund mentions Gladden throughout his book. The two interacted at the Labor Congress held at the Chicago Exposition in 1893. Shelton Stromquist, *Reinventing "The People"* 49.

124. Rauschenbusch, *A Theology for the Gospel,* 110–111; Lambert, *Religion in American Politics,* 98; McGerr, *A Fierce Discontent,* 66; Kloppenberg, *Uncertain Victory,* 209; Interestingly, however, Gladden offers a harsh criticism of Gronlund's commonwealth in *Applied Christianity:* "Coming as this does, in the course of a conjectural discussion of the ways in which socialism may be realized, it is little better than fiendish." See footnote in Gronlund, *Co-operative Commonwealth* (rev. ed., 1900), 302.

125. Gladden, *Applied Christianity,* 85, 90

126. Gladden quoted in Lambert, *American Politics,* 98.

127. Ibid., 98.

128. Herron, "Why I Am a Socialist," 9.

129. Vail, *Modern Socialism*, 5, 23.

130. Quoted in Evans, *The Social Gospel in America*, 135.

131. McKanan, *Prophetic Encounters*, 139.

132. McGarrahar, *Enchantments of Mammon*, 290.

133. McKanan, *Prophetic Encounters*, 145.

134. Persons, introduction to *The Cooperative Commonwealth* (1965), xxiii.

135. Ibid., xxv.

136. McKanan, *Prophetic Encounters*, 8.

137. Ibid., 3.

138. Ibid., 4.

139. Ibid., 49.

140. Cantor, "Radicalism, Religion, and the American Working Class," 17–33.

141. Danielson, Mollin, and Rossinow, *The Religious Left in Modern America: Doorkeepers of a Radical Faith*, vii.

142. Ibid., viii.

143. McKanan, *Prophetic Encounters*, 112.

144. Ibid., 137.

145. Fones-Wolf, *Struggle for the Soul of the Postwar South*, 114.

146. Ibid., 44.

147. McDonald quoted in Cook, *Spiritual Socialists*, 1.

148. Judis, *The Socialist Awakening*, 47.

149. Eugene V. Debs, "Laurence Gronlund" *Comrade* 4, no. 2 (February 1905), 28; Kirk, 185–206.

150. Gronlund, *Ça Ira*, 212.

## 5. SOMETHING, INDEED, MUST BE DONE

1. Gronlund, "A Weak Argument," 1–2.

2. Ibid., 2.

3. Gronlund, *The New Economy*, 361.

4. Gronlund, "A Weak Argument," 3.

5. Ibid., 2.

6. Gronlund, *Ça Ira*, 240.

7. Seymour Stedman, "Laurence Gronlund," *Social Democratic Herald* 2, no. 19 (October 1899), 2.

8. Tsuzuki, "Laurence Gronlund," 25. Author Henry D. Lloyd and Hull House architect Jane Adams offered financial support to Gronlund during this time.

9. Gronlund, *The New Economy*, 12.

10. Gronlund, *The New Economy*, 359; Aronoff, *We Own the Future*, 43; Bender, *A Nation of Nations*; Smith, *American Empire*; Hobsbawm, *The Age of Empire, 1875–1914*; Perez Jr., *The War of 1898*.

11. Gronlund, "Nationalization of Industry," 33–36.

12. Karl Marx and Friedrich Engels, *Communist Manifesto*, ch. 5.

13. Herron quoted in Dorrien, *American Social Democracy*, 117.

14. Lenin, *Imperialism*, 91.

15. Gronlund, *Commonwealth*, 62.

16. Fink, *The Long Gilded Age*; Katz, *Gangsters of Capitalism*; Patnaik and Patnaik, *Capital and Imperialism*; Hiltzik, *Iron Empires*.

17. Gronlund, *New Economy*, 360.

18. Ibid., 4.

19. Ibid., 359. Yet some wars—including the Civil War as Gronlund mentions—were necessary, righteous even. The Civil War was "like a thunderstorm" for it reconstituted a nation without slavery. The war created "a social sentiment; and rouses the social spirit in a people to pursue the loftiest ideal of a race" (8). Righteous wars, he believed, were part of the Power behind evolution, representing stages in human social evolution, where the deaths of some many Americans, so many brothers, cultivated sympathy for the dead and by extension the human family.

20. Herron, "Why I Am a Socialist," 1–10.

21. Gronlund, *New Economy*, 1.

22. Laurence Gronlund, "For and By the People," *Sioux County Journal-Harrison Press-Journal* (Harrison, Nebraska), 11 May 1899, https://www.newspapers.com/image/840309578.

23. Webb quoted in Gemorah, *Gronlund*, 163. See also Harry W. Laidler, *Social Economic Movements* (New York: Thomas Y. Crowell Company, 1944), 219–220.

24. Gemorah, *Gronlund*, 164.

25. Gronlund, *New Economy*, 52–53. The Paris Commune, in Gronlund's mind, represented the failure of both internationalism and class violence. He viewed the commune as a brief reactionary movement that effectively divided the country and hurt efforts to create a unified commonwealth.

26. Gronlund quoted in Quint, *Forging American Socialism*, 89.

27. Hegel, *Philosophy of Right*, 247.

28. Gronlund, *New Economy*, 17.

29. Ibid., 20.

30. Ibid., 61–62.

31. Ibid., 22–23, 27.

32. Ibid., 15, 25, 29.

33. Gronlund, "For and By the People," *Harrison Press Journal*, 11 May 1899.

34. Gronlund, *New Economy*, 49.

35. Not everyone agreed with Gronlund's simple solution to a just wage. William Graham, for instance, was skeptical of how compensation would be determined in a just society. See William Graham, *Socialism New and Old* (London: Kegan Paul, Trench, Trubner & Co., 1890), ch. 10 and the note on Gronlund (p. 156).

36. Gronlund, *New Economy*, 96.

37. Ibid., 103.

38. Ibid., 102.

39. Ibid., 89.

40. Ibid., 64.

41. Ibid., 70.

42. Gronlund, *New Economy*, 69; Again, Elisha Mulford communicated in a similar way in *The Republic of God*: "The ethical relation of man gives to social law and the development of history an element that is universal . . . It will verify itself through the life of the Spirit in the history of the world; and as the skepticism of men must meet it there, so the faith of men shall there have its strength . . . There is henceforth the conviction of the world. There is henceforth the realization of the kingdom of heaven on earth." Elisha Mulford, *Republic of God,* 132.

43. Ibid., 60, 71. Gronlund capitalizes "Providence," opaquely referring to its nature as a divine agent.

44. Hegel's quote Mulford, *Republic of God*, 86.

45. Gronlund, *New Economy*, 74.

46. Ibid., 75.

47. Ibid., 78.

48. Ibid., 115, 119.

49. Edward W. Bemis, review of *Socialism and the American Spirit*, by N.P. Gilman, *Journal of Political Economy* 1, no. 3 (June 1893): 480–482. Gilman was also critical of a tenet of Gronlund's vision for the government: "The governing powers in America need purification today rather than an enlargement of their field." Nicholas Gilman, *Socialism and the American Spirit* (Boston and New York: Houghton, Mifflin and Co., 1893), viii.

50. Gilman, *Socialism*, viii, 236. See also Gilman's *Profit Sharing Between Employer and Employee: A Study in the Evolution of the Wages System* (Boston and New York: Houghton, Mifflin and Company, 1889).

51. Ibid., 120.

52. Ibid., 124.

53. Ibid., 127–28.

54. Hegel quoted in Charles Taylor, *Hegel* (Cambridge: Cambridge University Press, 1975), 445–446.

55. Gronlund, *New Economy*, 358.

56. Ibid., 115; Gronlund was well aware of the indomitable power of capitalism as he recounted his experience witnessing the violence against the "moans from the starving miners" at Spring Valley, Illinois, in 1895. When the Spring Valley mines shut down, the entire United States monitored the experience of the miners, who were eventually violently coerced back to work. Gronlund tried to use a church to address the workers, but the Protestant pastor of the town refused. This, of course, suggested to Gronlund that established religion was in league with business elites and the power of the state. Unfortunately, Gronlund did not consider the racial violence among the miners, the animosity between white miners and the influx of new Black miners. The oppressive labor of the mines contributed to interracial tension among the working class, spilling over into a full-fledged race riot. Caroline Waldron Merithew, "Making the Italian

Other: Blacks, Whites, and the In between in the 1895 Spring Valley, Illinois, Race Riot" (2003), *History Faculty Publications*, https://core.ac.uk/download/pdf/232827815.pdf.

57. Gronlund, *New Economy*, 138.

58. Ibid., 139.

59. Ibid., 168.

60. Ibid., 143.

61. Ibid., 144–45.

62. Gronlund, "Socializing a State," *Three In One: A Trinity of Arguments on Socialism* (Chicago: The Social Democracy, 1898), 4. He added a section on larger infrastructural works and changed heading sections. For example, he changed "State Saving Banks and Loan Offices" to "National Banks of Deposit and Banks of Loan."

63. Ibid., 150.

64. Ibid., 159, 173.

65. Ibid., 174.

66. Gronlund, *New Economy*, 180.

67. Ibid., 182.

68. "To Locate Debs' Colony," *Pittsburg Daily Headlight*, 7 July 1897. https://www.newspapers.com/image/101681443.

69. Ibid., 155.

70. Ibid., 163.

71. Ibid., 209.

72. Ibid., 210.

73. Ibid., 214.

74. Ibid., 194–97, 200.

75. Ibid., 205, 207, 235, 240.

76. Plans for a canal through Nicaragua were abandoned in the early twentieth century when the U.S. turned to the construction of a canal in Panama. Discussions between nations over the construction of a Nicaraguan canal have continued well into the twenty-first century. The latest agreement came between the Nicaraguan government and the Hong Kong Nicaragua Canal Development Group (HKND). Construction was to begin in 2014, but no major work has been done as of yet and the HKND folded in 2018, though current law allows for the expropriation of land.

77. Gronlund, *New Economy*, 224.

78. Gronlund, "For and By the People," *Sioux County Journal: Harrison Press-Journal*, 11 May 1899.

79. Gronlund, *New Economy*, 224.

80. Young, *Dissent*, 248–253; Eric Foner, *Give Me Liberty: An American History* (New York: W.W. Norton, 2011), 687–88; Kazin, *American Dreamers*, 103–104.

81. Gronlund, *New Economy*, 244, 246–47, 280.

82. Ibid., 253–54.

83. Ibid., 254. Gronlund mentions the efforts of Charles Emory Smith, Postmaster General during the McKinley administration, and John Wanamaker, Postmaster General under

Harrison, for Congress to create postal saving banks. Incidentally, Wanamaker also supported government management of telegraph and telephone communications. The U.S. created its first postal savings system in 1911, but it was later discontinued in 1966. In 2024, Bernie Sanders, Elizabeth Warren, and Kristen Gillibran supported such a plan. A new Postal Banking Act was announced in in the fall of 2020.

84. Ibid., 258.

85. Ibid., 260.

86. Ibid., 283–84.

87. Ibid., 278, 288, 291–93.

88. Ibid., 295.

89. Nelson, "The People's Capital," 41.

90. Gronlund, *New Economy,* 264–65. Gronlund avoided discussions about racial discrimination and its connection to capitalism. He said nothing about the *Plessy* v. *Ferguson* case, decided two years before the publication of *New Economy,* which constitutionally protected Jim Crow segregation on public transportation.

91. Ibid., 266, 272, 277.

92. Jason D. Martinek, *Socialism and Print Culture in America, 1897–1920* (London: Routledge, 2016), 1.

93. Gronlund, *New Economy,* 343.

94. Ibid., 299.

95. Martinek, *Socialism and Print Culture,* 1.

96. Gronlund, *New Economy,* 299, 302.

97. Ibid., 303–304.

98. Ibid., 309.

99. Ibid., 310–11.

100. A. B. Adler, *An Ethical Philosophy of Life* (New York and London: D. Appleton and Company, 1918), 222.

101. Gronlund, *New Economy,* 312.

102. Ibid., 324.

103. Ibid., 327, 336.

104. Ibid., 333–34.

105. Ibid., 337.

106. Ibid., 326.

107. Ibid., 348.

108. Ibid., 350.

109. Ibid., 352.

110. Ibid., 354–55, 358.

111. Seymour Stedman, "Laurence Gronlund," *Social Democratic Herald* 2, no. 19 (28 October 1899), 2.

112. Gronlund, *New Economy,* 360.

113. Ibid., 363–64.

114. Ibid., 11, 364.

## CONCLUSION

1. Eric Foner, "How Bernie Sanders Should Talk About Democratic Socialism," *The Nation* (21 October 2015), https://www.thenation.com/article/archive/how-bernie-sanders-should-talk-about-democratic-socialism; Judis, *The Socialist Awakening*, 69.

2. Harry Truman, "Rear Platform and Other Informal Remarks in New York," Gerhard Peters and John T. Woolley, *The American Presidency Project*, https://www.presidency.ucsb.edu/node/233393.

3. Ibid. It never surprises me the ways in which right-wing reactionaries have demonstrated their ignorance about Martin Luther King Jr. in their misappropriation of his words to support their anti-socialist and pro-capitalist agenda. In 1961, King said, "Call it democracy, or call it democratic socialism, but there must be a better distribution of wealth within this country for all God's children." King quoted in Aronoff, *We Own the Future*, ch. 1 "How Socialists Changed America," (New York: The New Press, 2020) e-book. See also Cornel West, ed., *The Radical King* (Boston: Beacon, 2015).

4. Buhle, *Encyclopedia of the American Left*; Buhle, *Marxism in the United States*; Diggins, *The Rise and Fall of the American Left*; Foner, *The Story of American Freedom*; Howe, *Socialism and America*; Lasch, *The Agony of the American Left*; Rorty, *Achieving Our Country*.

5. Hyfler, *Prophets of the Left*, 72

6. Pope, *American Radicalism*, 8.

7. Ibid., 9.

8. Brick and Phelps, *Radicals in America*, 7. Emphasis mine.

9. Persons, "Introduction," *Co-operative Commonwealth*, ix.

10. Judis, *The Socialist Awakening*, 38.

11. Appleby, *The Relentless Revolution*, 422.

12. Schneider, *History of American Philosophy*, 178.

13. Hobsbawm, *How to Change the World*, 6.

14. Judis, *Socialist Awakening*, 14.

15. Fraser, *Age of Acquiescence*, 382.

16. Trump, not one to learn from the past, was obviously ignorant of the overwhelmingly positive reception of Robert Owen's socialism when he presented to the same institutional body that included not just congressmen but Supreme Court justices and presidents in 1825. Michael Kazin, "American Socialism," in Kevin M. Kruse and Julian E. Zelizer, eds., *Myth America: Historians Take on the Biggest Legends and Lies about the Past* (Basic Boos, 2022), 117.

17. Phelps and Vandome, *Marxism & America*, 13. Phelps and Vandome offer an important response to Trump's American exceptionalism: "claims of an essentially capitalist America implacable to any Marxist influence and inured to all theory are overdone" (13).

18. McGirr, *Suburban Warriors: The Origins of the New American Right*, Introduction.

19. Cohen, *The Conspiracy of Capital*, xv.

20. I make a distinction between the culture of popular conservatism and its more intellectual threads represented in the work of George Wills or Robert George.

21. Nichols, *The "S" Word*, 240.

22. Andrew Hartman, "Beyond the Whack-a-Mole Left," *Jacobin,* https://www.jacobinmag .com/2016/06/radicals-in-america-brick-phelps-cpusa-race-class-left-vietnam. See also Haberski and Hartman, *American Labyrinth,* ch. 9; Brick and Phelps, *Radicals in America,* 275.

23. Eugene V. Debs, *Comrade* (February 1905), 28, https://www.marxists.org/history/usa /pubs/comrade/v04n02-feb-1905-The-Comrade.pdf.

24. Leonard Abbott, *Comrade* (February 1905), 28, https://www.marxists.org/history/usa /pubs/comrade/v04n02-feb-1905-The-Comrade.pdf

25. Aronoff, Dreier, and Kazin, *We Own the Future,* ch. 1 "How Socialists Changed America" (New York: The New Press, 2020) e-book.

26. John Humphrey Noyes, *History of American Socialisms* (Philadelphia: J.B. Lippincott & Co., 1870), 108, 228;

27. Jackson, *American Radicals,* 316 (Kindle).

28. Cook, *Spiritual Socialists,* 8.

29. McKanan, *Prophetic Encounters,* 276.

30. Foner, "Bernie Sanders," *The Nation.*

31. Martin Luther King, Jr., "Letter from a Birmingham Jail," http://www.africa.upenn.edu /Articles_Gen/Letter_Birmingham.html.

32. Gronlund, *The Co-operative Commonwealth in its Outlines* (1884), 101.

33. Gladden, *Applied Christianity,* 86.

34. Graeber, *The Democracy Project,* 282–84.

35. Cook, *Spiritual Socialists,* 12.

36. Muste quoted in Cook, *Spiritual Socialists,* 17.

37. Gronlund, *Commonwealth* (1884), 130; Barker, *British Socialism,* 6; Brown, *Studies in Modern Socialism and Labor Problems,* 50.

38. Gronlund, *Commonwealth* (1884), 130.

39. Gronlund, *Commonwealth* (1891), 188.

40. John Stuart Mill, "Fontana and Prati's St. Simonism in London," (1986) *Collected Works of John Stuart Mill* 23, edited J. M. Robson, 33 vols (Toronto: University of Toronto Press, 1962–91), 678.

41. Laurence Gronlund, "Economics of Socialism III: Co-Operation," *Christian Socialist,* 5, no. 47 (April 1887), 49–51.

42. Brick and Phelps, *The U.S. Left since the Second World War,* 321.

43. Michel Foucault, "Confinement, Psychiatry, Prison," interview by David Cooper, et al., 178–210, in *Politics, Philosophy, Culture: Interviews and Other Writings, 1977–1984,* ed. Lawrence Kritzman, trans. Alan Sheridan. (New York: Routledge, 1988), 197.

44. Foucault, "Confinement, Psychiatry, Prison," 97.

45. Alex Honneth, *The Idea of Socialism: Towards a Renewal* (Cambridge: Polity Press, 2017), 5.

46. Edelman, *So Rich, So Poor,* 33.

47. Piketty, *Capital in the Twenty-First Century,* 34.

48. Ibid., 662.

49. Gourevitch, *Slavery to Cooperation,* 175.

50. Karl Marx, *Capital* Vol. 1:329, 387.

51. Quoted in Jossa, *Political Economy of Cooperatives,* 2–3; Printed as a pamphlet in *Inaugural Address and Provisional Rules of the International Working Men's Association,* along with the "General Rules" (London, 1864).

52. Karl Marx, *Capital,* 3:570–71.

53. Vladimir Ilyich Lenin, "On Cooperation," *Pravda* (no. 115–116) (26–27 May 1923); From Lenin's *Collected Works,* 2nd English edition (Moscow: Progress Publishers, 1965) Vol. 33:467–75, https://www.marxists.org/archive/lenin/works/1923/jan/06.htm.

54. Vladimir Ilyich Lenin, *The Impending Catastrophe and How to Combat It* (1917), 802, 810–11.

55. Ranis, *Cooperatives Confront Capitalism,* 34, 143.

56. Ibid., 145.

57. Ibid., 151.

58. Richard Wolff, "Ten Things You Should Know about Socialism," https://www.open democracy.net/en/transformation/ten-things-you-should-know-about-socialism.

59. Restakis, *Humanizing the Economy,* 46.

60. Debs, *Comrade,* 28.

61. Aronoff, et al., *We Own the Future,* 49.

62. Louis T. Moore, J. M. Burnam, and H. G. Hartmann, eds., *University of Cincinnati Studies* (Cincinnati, 1911), Series II, Vol. 7:15–16.

63. Wolin, *Democracy Incorporated;* Yanis Varoufakis, *Another Now* (Brooklyn: Melville House, 2021); Yanis Varoufakis, "Techno-Feudalism is Taking Over" (7 September 2021), https://diem25.org/techno-feudalism-taking-over.

64. George quoted in O'Donnell, *Henry George and the Crisis of Inequality,* 56.

65. Henry George, *Progress and Poverty* (New York: D. Appleton and Company, 1880), 471.

66. Ibid., 472.

67. Raihani, *The Social Instinct,* 2.

# BIBLIOGRAPHY

WORKS BY LAURENCE GRONLUND

*Books*

*The Co-operative Commonwealth in Its Outlines: An Exposition of Modern Socialism.* Boston: Lee and Shepard, 1884.

*The Co-operative Commonwealth in Its Outlines: An Exposition of Modern Socialism.* London: The Modern Press, 1885.

*The Co-operative Commonwealth in Its Outlines: An Exposition of Modern Socialism.* 2nd edition. Boston: Lee & Shepard, 1890.

*The Co-operative Commonwealth in Its Outlines: An Exposition of Modern Socialism.* London: Swan Sonnenschein, Le Bas & Lowre, 1891.

*Ça Ira! Or Danton in the French Revolution.* Boston: Lee and Shepard, 1887.

*Insufficiency of Henry George's Theory.* New York: New York Labor News Co., 1887.

*Socialism vs. Tax Reform: An Answer to Henry George.* New York: New York Labor News Co., 1887.

*Our Destiny: The Influence of Socialism on Morals and Religion: An Essay in Ethics.* London: Swan Sonnenschein & Co., 1890.

*The New Economy: A Peaceable Solution of the Social Problem.* Chicago, IL: Herbert St. Stone & Co., 1898.

*Three in One: A Trinity of Arguments in Favor of Social Democracy.* With G. C. Clemens and G. A. Hoehn. Chicago: Social Democracy of America, 1898.


*Other Works by Laurence Gronlund*

"The Work Before Us." *The Commonweal*, no. 1 (July 1885): 61–2.

"Les Socialism Aux Etats-Unis." *Revue d'economic politique,* no. 1 (March–April 1887): 109–24.

"A Lesson of Trusts." *The Leader.* 26 July 1887.

"The Nationalization of Industry." *The Nationalist* 1, no. 2 (June 1889): 33–6.

"Christian Socialism in America." *The Christian Register* LXVII (13 June 1889): 4.

"Reply to Dr. Heber Newton." *The Nationalist* 1, no. 5 (September 1889): 158–61.

"Nationalism." *The Arena* 1, no. 2 (January 1890): 153–65.

"Godin's Social Palace." *The Arena* 1 (May 1890): 691–99.

"Why I Am a Socialist." *Twentieth Century* 4, no. 19 (8 May 1890).

"Le Socialism Comme Probleme Moral Et National." *Revue d'economic politique,* no. 6 (February 1892): 261–67.

"What to Do?" *Twentieth Century,* no. 13 (August–December 1894): 5.

"Studies in Ultimate Society: A New Interpretation of Life." *The Arena* 18 (1897): 351–61.

"A Weak Argument: Berger's Platform Analyzed and Its Defects Pointed Out," *The Social Democrat* 5, no. 24 (June 23, 1898): 1.

"Socializing a State." In *A Primer on Socialism,* no. 13, *Progressive Thought,* edited by G. C. Clemens, 16–22. Terra Haute, IN: Debs Publishing Company, 1900.


SECONDARY SOURCES

Alexander, Samuel. *Moral Order and Progress: An Analysis of Ethical Conceptions.* London: Trubner, 1889.

Alter, Thomas II. *Toward a Cooperative Commonwealth: The Transplanted Roots of Farmer-Labor Radicalism in Texas.* Urbana: University of Illinois Press, 2022.

Amini, Babak. "A Brief History of the Dissemination and Reception of Karl Marx's Capital in the United States and Britain." *World Review of Political Economy* 7, no. 3 (Fall 2016).

Andelson, Robert V., ed. *Critics of Henry George: An Appraisal of Their Strictures on Progress and Poverty.* Vol. 1. Hoboken, NJ: Wiley-Blackwell, 2003.

Anderson, Benedict. *Imagined Communities: Reflections on the Origin and Spread of Nationalism.* Rev. ed. London: Verso, 1998.

Anderson, Paul Russell, and Max Fisch. *Philosophy in America: From the Puritans to James.* New York: D. Appleton-Century Company, 1939.

Appleby, Joyce. *The Relentless Revolution: A History of Capitalism.* New York: W.W. Norton, 2011.

Aronoff, Kate, Peter Dreier, and Michael Kazin, eds. *We Own the Future: Democratic Socialism—American Style.* New York: New Press, 2020.

Aulard, Francois Victor Alphonse. *Histoire politique de la Révolution française [The French Revolution: A Political History], 1789–1804.* 4 vols. London, 1910.

Bailey, William. "The Coming Socialism." *Dublin University Review* 1, no. 7 (1885): 20.

Banner, Lois W. "Biography as History." *The American Historical Review* 114, no. 3 (June 2009).

Bannister, Robert C. *Social Darwinism: Science and Myth in Anglo-American Social Thought.* Philadelphia: Temple University Press, 1979.

Barker, Charles Albro. *Henry George.* New York: Oxford University, 1955.

Barker, J. Ellis. *British Socialism: An Examination of its Doctrines, Policy, Aims and Practical Proposals.* London: Smith, Elder and Co., 1908.

Barnes, Kenneth J. *Redeeming Capitalism.* Grand Rapids: Eerdmans, 2018.

Baron, Hal S. *Mixed Harvest: The Second Great Transformation in the Rural North, 1870–1930.* Chapel Hill: University of North Carolina Press, 2000.

Barrow, Clyde W. *Universities and the Capitalist State: Corporate Liberalism and the Reconstruction of American Higher Education, 1894–1928.* Madison: University of Wisconsin Press, 1990.

Barton, Stephen E. *J. Stitt Wilson: Socialist, Christian, Mayor of Berkeley.* Berkeley: Berkeley Historical Society, 2020.

Beatty, Jack. *Age of Betrayal: The Triumph of Money in America, 1865–1900.* New York: Vintage, 2008.

Beisner, Frederick C. *The Cambridge Companion to Hegel.* Cambridge: Cambridge University Press, 1993.

Bell, Daniel. *Marxian Socialism in the United States.* With a new introduction by Michael Kazin. Ithaca: Cornell University Press, 1996.

Bellamy, Edward. *Looking Backward, 2000–1887.* Edited with an Introduction and Notes by Matthew Beaumont. Oxford: Oxford University Press, 2007.

Bellesiles, Michael. *1877: America's Year of Living Violently.* New York: New Press, 2012.

Bender, Thomas. *A Nation of Nations: America's Place in World History.* New York: Hill & Wang, 2006.

Bensel, Richard. *The Political Economy of American Industrialization, 1877–1900.* Cambridge: Cambridge University Press, 2000.

Berlin, Isaiah. *Two Concepts of Liberty.* London: Oxford University Press, 1958.

Bernstein, Eduard. *Evolutionary Socialism: A Century and Affirmation.* Translated by Edith C. Harvey. New York: B.W. Huebsch, 1909.

Bernstein, Samuel. "The Danton-Robespierre Controversy Today." *Science & Society* 23, no. 3 (Summer 1959).

Bisset, Jim. *Agrarian Socialism in America: Marx, Jefferson, and Jesus in the Oklahoma Countryside, 1904–1920.* Norman: University of Oklahoma Press, 1999.

Blackhawk, Ned. *Violence Over the Land: Indians and Empires in the Early American West.* Cambridge: Harvard University Press, 2006.

Blanning, T. C. W. *The French Revolution: Aristocrats Versus Bourgeois?* Atlantic Highlands, NJ: Humanities Press, 1987.

Blau, Joseph L. "The Cooperative Commonwealth as Secular Apocalypse." *Transactions of the Charles S. Peirce Society* 12, no. 3 (Summer 1976).

Bliss, William Dwight Porter. *Handbook of Socialism*. London: Swan Sonnenschein; New York: Charles Scribner, 1895.

———. *New Encyclopedia of Social Reform* (1897).

———. *Socialism in the Church of England*. Boston: n.p., 1888.

———. *What is Christian Socialism?* Boston: Society of Christian Socialists, 1890.

Bok, Derek. *Higher Education in America*. Rev. ed. Princeton: Princeton University Press, 2015.

Brailsford-Bright, J. "Theosophy and Modern Socialism." *Theosophical Siftings* 11, no. 7 (1892).

Brands, H. W. *American Colossus: The Triumph of Capitalism, 1865–1900*. New York: Anchor Books, 2011.

Brick, Howard, and Christopher Phelps. *The U.S. Left since the Second World War*. Cambridge: Cambridge University Press, 2015.

Brody, David. *In Labor's Cause: Main Themes on the History of the American Worker*. Oxford: Oxford University Press, 1993.

———. *Steelworkers in America: The Nonunion Era*. 1998.

Brown, T. Edwin. *Studies in Modern Socialism and Labor Problems*. New York: D. Appleton and Company, 1886.

Bruce, Robert V. *1877: Year of Violence*. Indianapolis: Bobbs Merrill Co., Inc., 1959.

Bryson, Phillip J., *The Economics of Henry George: History's Rehabilitation of America's Greatest Early Economist*. New York: Palgrave/Macmillan, 2011.

Buhle, Mary Jo. *Women and American Socialism, 1870–1920*. Urbana: University of Illinois Press, 1981.

Buhle, Mary Jo, Paul Buhle, and Dan Georgakas, eds., *Encyclopedia of the American Left*. New York: Oxford University Press, 1998.

Buhle, Paul. *Marxism in the United States: A History of the American Left*. 3rd ed. London: Verso, 2013.

Burbank, David. *Reign of Rabble: The St. Louis General Strike of 1877*. New York: Augustus M. Kelley, 1966.

Burbank, Garin. *When Farmers Voted Red: The Gospel of Socialism in the Oklahoma Countryside, 1910–1924*. Westfield: Praeger, 1977.

Burns, David. *The Life and Death of the Radical Historical Jesus*. Oxford: Oxford University Press, 2013.

Caldemeyer, Dana. *Union Renegades: Miners, Capitalism, and Organizing in the Gilded Age*. Urbana: University of Illinois Press, 2021.

Calhoun, Charles W. *The Gilded Age: Perspectives on the Origins of Modern America*. Lanham: Rowman & Littlefield, 2006.

Calhoun, Craig. *The Roots of Radicalism*. Chicago: Chicago University Press, 2012.

Cantor, Milton. "Radicalism, Religion, and the American Working Class" *Irish Journal of American Studies* 1 (December 1992).

Carter, Heath W. *Union Made: Working People and the Rise of Social Christianity in Chicago*. Oxford: Oxford University Press, 2015.

Carter, Paul. *The Decline and Revival of the Social Gospel*. Ithaca: Cornell University Press, 1954.

Censer, Jack. "Historians Revisit the Terror—Again," *Journal of Social History* 48, no. 2 (Winter 2014)

Chandler, Alfred. *The Visible Hand: The Managerial Revolution in American Business*. Cambridge: Harvard University Press, 1977.

Clark, G. N. "Early Capitalism and Invention" *The Economic History Review* 6, no. 2 (April 1936).

Clarke, Simon. *Marx's Theory of Crisis*. New York: Saint Martin's Press, 1994.

Cohen, Michael Mark, *The Conspiracy of Capital: Law, Violence, and American Popular Radicalism in the Age of Monopoly*. Amherst: University of Massachusetts Press, 2019.

Cohen, Mitchell. *The Wager of Lucian Goldmann: Tragedy, Dialectics, and a Hidden God*. Princeton: Princeton University Press, 1994.

Commons, John. *History of Labour in the United States*. 2 vols. New York: MacMillan, 1918.

Comninel, George C. *Rethinking the French Revolution: Marxism and the Revisionist Challenge*. London: Verso, 1991.

Cook, Vaneesa, *Spiritual Socialists: Religion and the American Left*. Philadelphia: University of Pennsylvania, 2019.

Cord, Steven. *Henry George: Dreamer or Realist*. Philadelphia: University of Pennsylvania Press, 1965.

Cronon, William. *Nature's Metropolis: Chicago and the Great West*. New York: W.W. Norton and Company, 1991.

Cross, Ira. *The Essentials of Socialism*. New York: Macmillan, 1912.

Crunden, Robert M. *Ministers of Reform: The Progressives' Achievement in American Civilization*. New York: Basic Books, 1982.

Danielson, Leilah. *The Religious Left in Modern America: Doorkeepers of a Radical Faith*.

Davaney, Sheila Greeve, and Warren G. Frisina, eds. *The Pragmatic Century: Conversations with Richard Bernstein*. New York: SUNY Press, 2006.

Debs, Eugene V. *The American Movement*. Chicago: Charles H. Kerr & Company, 1900.

———. "How I Became a Socialist." *The Comrade* (April 1902).

———. "Letter to the American Railway Union." *Railway Times* (1 January 1897).

———. *Report on the Chicago Strike of June–July, 1894, by the United States Strike Commission. Appointed by the President July 26, 1894, Under the Provisions of Sec-*

*tion 6 of Chapter 1063 of the Laws of the United States with Appendices Containing Testimony, Proceedings, and Recommendations.* Washington, DC: Government Print Office, 1895.

Debs, Eugene V., and Leonard Abott. "Laurence Gronlund," *Comrade* (1905).

Degler, Carl N. *In Search of Human Nature: The Decline and Revival of Darwinism in American Social Thought.* New York and London: Oxford University Press, 1991.

De Leon, Daniel. *The Socialist Reconstruction of Society.* New York: New York Labor News, 1905.

De Mille, Anna George. *Henry George: Citizen of the World.* Chapel Hill: UNC Press, 1950.

Diggins, John Patrick. *The Rise and Fall of the American Left.* New York: W.W. Norton, 1992.

Dombrowski, James. *The Early Days of Christian Socialism in America.* New York: Columbia University Press, 1936.

Dorn, Jacob, ed. *Socialism and Christianity in Early Twentieth-Century America.* Westport: Greenwood, 1998.

Dorn, Jacob. "The Social Gospel and Socialism: A Comparison of the Thought of Francis Greenwood Peabody, Washington Gladden, and Walter Rauschenbusch." *Church History* 62, no. 1 (March 1993).

———. *Socialism and Christianity in Early Twentieth-Century America,* Westport, CT: Praeger, 1998.

Dorrien, Gary. *American Democratic Socialism: History, Politics, Religion, and Theory.* New Haven: Yale, 2021.

Doyle, William. *Origins of the French Revolution.* 3rd ed. Oxford: Oxford University Press, 1999.

———. *The Oxford History of the French Revolution.* 2nd ed. Oxford: Oxford University Press, 2002.

Draper, Theodore. *The Roots of American Communism.* New York: Viking Press, 1957.

Dressner, Richard B. "William Dwight Porter Bliss's Christian Socialism," *Church History* 47 (March 1978).

Durey, Michael. *Transatlantic Radicals and Early American Republic.* Lawrence: University of Kansas, 1997.

Eagleton, Terry. *Why Marx was Right.* New Haven: Yale University Press, 2011.

Edelman, Peter. *So Rich, So Poor: Why It's So Hard to End Poverty in America.* New York: New Press, 2012.

Edwards, Rebecca. *New Spirits: Americans in the "Gilded Age," 1865–1905.* New York: Oxford, 2015.

Egbert, Donald Drew, and Stow Persons, *Socialism and American Life.* Princeton: Princeton University Press, 1952.

Ely, Richard. *French and German Socialism in Modern Times.* New York: Harper and Brothers, 1883.

———. *Ground Under Our Feet: An Autobiography.* New York: Macmillan, 1938.

———. *The Labor Movement in America.* New York: Thomas Y. Crowell, 1886.

———. *Monopolies and Trusts.* New York: Macmillan Company, 1906.

———. *Socialism: An Examination of Its Nature, Its Strengths and Its Weakness, with Suggestions.* New York: Thomas Y. Crowell & Co., 1894.

———. *Strengths and Weakness of Socialism.* New York: The Chautauqua Press, 1894.

Evans, Christopher. *The Social Gospel in American Religion: A History.* New York: NYU Press, 2017.

Everett, John Rutherford. *Religion in Economics: A Study of John Bates, Richard T. Ely, and Simon N. Patten.* New York: King's Crown Press, 1946.

Fink, Leon. *The Long Gilded Age: American Capitalism and the Lessons of a New World Order.* Philadelphia: University of Pennsylvania Press, 2015.

———. *Workingmen's Democracy: The Knights of Labor and American Politics.* Urbana: University of Illinois Press, 1983.

Finnegan, David, and Ariel Hessayon, eds., *Varieties of Seventeenth and Early Eighteenth Century English Radicalism in Context.* London: Routledge, 2016.

Flacks, Richard. *Making History: The American Left and the American Mind.* New York: Columbia University Press, 1988.

Flower, Elizabeth, and Murray Murphy. *A History of Philosophy in America.* New York: Capricorn Books, 1977.

Foner, Eric. *Battles for Freedom: The Use and Abuse of American History.* London and New York: I.B. Tauris and *The Nation.* 2017.

———. *The Story of American Freedom.* New York: W.W. Norton, 1999.

Foner, Philip S. *The Great Labor Uprising of 1877.* New York: Pathfinder, 1977.

———. *History of the Labor Movement in the United States.* New York: International Publishers, 1947.

———. "Marx's *Capital* in the United States." *Science & Society* 31, no. 4 (Fall 1967): 461-66.

Fones-Wolf, Elizabeth A. and Ken Fones-Wolf, *Struggle for the Soul of the Postwar South: White Evangelical Protestants and Operation Dixie.* Urbana: University of Illinois Press, 2015.

Foster, John Bellamy. *Marx's Ecology: Materialism and Nature.* New York: Monthly Review Press, 2000.

Fraser, Steve. *The Age of Acquiescence: The Life and Death of American Resistance to Organized Wealth and Power.* New York: Little, Brown, and Company, 2015.

———. *Mongrel Firebugs and Men of Property: Capitalism and Class Conflict in American History.* London: Verso, 2019.

Fried, Albert. *Socialism in America.* Garden City, NY: Anchor/Doubleday, 1970.

Furet, Francois. *Interpreting the French Revolution.* Translated by Elborg Forster. Cambridge: Cambridge University Press, 1981.

———. *Marx and the French Revolution.* Chicago, 1988.

Gaido, Daniel. "*The American Worker* and the Theory of Permanent Revolution: Karl Kautsky on Werner Sombart's '*Why Is There No Socialism in the United States?*'" *Historical Materialism* 11, no. 4 (December 2003).

Geiger, George Raymond. *The Philosophy of Henry George.* Introduction by John Dewey. NY: Macmillan, 1933.

Gemorah, Solomon. "Laurence Gronlund's Ideas and Influence, 1877–1899." PhD diss., New York University, 1965.

———. "Laurence Gronlund—Utopian or Reformer?" *Science & Society* 33, no. 4 (Fall/ Winter, 1969).

Ginger, Ray. *The Bending Cross: A Biography of Eugene V. Debs.* Introduction by Mike Davis. Chicago: Haymarket Books, 2007.

Gladden, William. *Applied Christianity: Moral Aspects of Social Questions.* Boston and New York: Houghton, Mifflin and Company, 1891.

Goetzmann, William H. *The American Hegelians: An Intellectual Episode in the History of Western America.* New York: Knopf, 1973.

Goldmann, Lucian. *Hidden God: A Study of Tragic Vision in the Pensees of Pascal and the Tragedies of Racine.* London: Verso, 2016.

———. *The Human Sciences and Philosophy.* London: Jonathan Cape, 1973.

Goldstene, Claire. *The Struggle for America's Promise: Equal Opportunity at the Dawn of Corporate Capital.* Jackson: University Press of Mississippi, 2014.

Goodwyn, Lawrence. *Democratic Promise: The Populist Movement in America.* New York: Oxford University, 1976.

Gourevitch, Alex. *Labor and Republican Liberty in the Nineteenth Century.* Cambridge, 2015.

Goyens, Tom, *Beer and Revolution: The German Anarchist Movement in New York City, 1880–1914.* Urbana: University of Illinois Press, 2007.

Graeber, David. *The Democracy Project: A History, A Crisis, A Movement.* New York: Spiegel & Grau, 2013.

Grayling, A. C. *The History of Philosophy.* New York: Penguin, 2019.

Green, James R. *Death in the Haymarket: A Story of Chicago, the First Labor Movement and the Bombing that Divided Gilded Age America.* NY: Anchor Books, 2006.

———. *Grass-Roots Socialism: Radical Movements in the Southwest, 1895–1943.* Baton Rouge: Louisiana State University Press, 1978.

Greenberg, Edward S. *Workplace Democracy: The Political Effects of Participation.* Ithaca: Cornell University Press, 1986.

Guarneri, Carl. "The Associationists: Forging a Christian Socialism in Antebellum America." *Church History* 52, no. 1 (March 1983).

———. *The Utopian Alternative: Fourierism in Nineteenth-Century America.* Ithaca: Cornell University Press, 1991.

Gutman, Herbert. *Power & Culture: Essays on the American Working Class.* 1987.

———. *Work, Culture and Society in Industrializing America.* 1977.

Haberski, Raymond, and Andrew Hartman, *American Labyrinth: Intellectual History for Complicated Times.* Cornell University Press, 2018.

Haldane, John Scott. *Organism and Environment as Illustrated in the Physiology of Breathing.* New Haven: Yale, 1917.

Hampson, Norman. *Danton.* London: Blackwell, 1988.

Handy, Robert T., ed. *The Social Gospel in America, 1870–1920.* New York: Oxford University Press, 1966.

Harcourt, Bernard E. *Cooperation: A Political, Economic, and Social Theory.* New York: Columbia University Press, 2023.

Hardt, Michael, and Antonio Negri. *Empire.* Cambridge: Harvard University Press, 2000.

Harrington, Michael. *Socialism: Past and Future.* New York: Arcade Publishing, 1989.

Harris, Thomas Lake. *A Discourse of the Prospects, Dangers, Duties and Safeties of the Times.* Santa Rosa, CA: Fountain Grove Press, 1891.

Hartz, Louis. *The Liberal Tradition in America: An Interpretation of American Political Thought Since the Revolution.* San Diego: Harcourt Brace & World Co., 1955.

Harvey, David. *Companion to Marx's Capital.* London: Verso, 2018.

———. *The Enigma of Capital and the Crisis of Capitalism.* New York: Oxford University Press, 2010.

Hayashi, Stuart K., *Hunting Down Social Darwinism: Will This Canard Go Extinct?* Lanham: Lexington Books, 2015.

Heath, Frederick Faries. *Social Democracy Red Book: A Brief History of Socialism in America.* Terre Haute: Debs Publishing Co., 1900.

Hegel, G. W. F. *Lectures on the History of Philosophy.* 3 vols. Translated by E. S. Haldane and Frances H. Simson. London: Routledge and Kegan Paul, 1894.

———. *Phenomenology of Spirit.* Translated by A.V. Miller. Oxford: Oxford University Press, 1977.

———. *The Philosophy of Right.* Translated by T. M. Knox. Oxford: Clarendon Press, 1942.

———. *Science of Logic.* Translated by A. V. Miller. New York: Humanity Books, 1969.

Heller, Henry. *The Bourgeois Revolution in France (1789–1815).* New York: Berghan Books, 2006.

Hellman, Rhoda. *Henry George Reconsidered.* Carlton Press, 1987.

Herreshoff, David. *American Disciples of Marx: From the Age of Jackson to the Progressive Era.* Detroit: Wayne State University Press, 1967.

Herron, George, "Why I Am a Socialist: Address at a Mass Meeting of the Social Democratic Party at Central Music Hall, Chicago." Published as no. 20 in the Pocket Library of Socialism series. Chicago: Charles H. Kerr & Co., 1900.

Hill, David J. *Principles and Fallacies of Socialism.* New York: John W. Lovell & Company, 1885, 97.

Hillquit, Morris. *Socialism in Theory and Practice.* New York: Macmillan, 1913.

Hiltzik, Michael. *Iron Empires: Robber Barons, Railroads, and the Making of Modern America.* Boston: Houghton Mifflin Harcourt, 2020.

Hine, Robert V. *California's Utopian Colonies.* New York: W.W. Norton, 1973.

Hine, Robert V., and John Mack Faragher. *The American West.* New Haven: Yale University Press, 2000.

Hinson-Hasty, Elizabeth. *Beyond the Social Maze: Exploring Vida Dutton Scudder's Theological Ethics.* New York: T & T Clark, 2006.

Hobsbawm, Eric. *The Age of Empire, 1875–1914.* New York: Vintage, 1989.

———. *The Age of Extremes: A History of the World, 1914–1991.* New York: Vintage, 1996.

———. *Echoes of the Marsellaise: Two Centuries Look Back on the French Revolution.* New Brunswick: Rutgers University Press, 1990.

———. *How to Change the World: Reflections on Marx and Marxism.* New Haven: Yale, 2011, 6.

Hofstadter, Richard. *The Age of Reform: From Bryan to F.D.R.* New York: Vintage Books, 1955.

———. *Social Darwinism in American Thought.* Philadelphia: University of Pennsylvania Press, 1944.

Hook, Sidney. *From Hegel to Marx.* New York: John Day, 1936.

———. *The Hero in History: A Study in Limitation and Possibility.* Boston: Beacon Press, 1945.

Howe, Irving. *Socialism and America.* New York: Harcourt, 1985.

Hudson, Michael. "Henry George's Political Critics" *American Journal of Economics and Sociology* 67, no. 1 (January 2008).

Hughan, Jessie Wallace. *American Socialism of the Present Day.* New York: John Lane Company, 1911.

Hunt, Lynn. *Politics, Culture, and Class in the French Revolution.* 20th Anniversary Edition. Berkeley: University of California Press, 2004.

Hyfler, Robert. *Prophets of the Left: American Socialist Thought in the Twentieth Century.* Westport, CT: Greenwood Press, 1984.

Isenberg, Andrew C. *The Destruction of the Bison: An Environmental History, 1750–1920.* Princeton: Princeton University Press, 2000.

Israel, Jonathan. *A Revolution of the Mind.* Princeton University Press, 2010.

———. *Revolutionary Ideas: An Intellectual History of the French Revolution from the Rights of Man to Robespierre*. Rev. ed. Princeton: Princeton University Press, 2015.

Jackson, Holly. *American Radicals: How Nineteenth-Century Protest Shaped the Nation*. New York: Crown, 2019.

Jameson, Frederic. *Representing* Capital: *A Commentary of Volume One*. London: Verso, 2011.

Janes, Lewis G., *Evolution of Morals*. Boston: The New Ideal Publishing Company, 1889.

Janet, Paul. *La Morale*. Paris: Librairie Ch. Delagrave, 1891.

Jaures, Jean. *Socialist History of the French Revolution*. Abridged and translated by Mitchell Abidor. Introduction by Henry Weller. New York: Pluto Press, 2015.

Jelley, S.M. *The Voice of Labor*. Philadelphia: H.J. Smith & Co., 1891.

Johnson, Oakley J. *Marxism in United States History Before the Russian Revolution (1876–1917)*. New York: Humanities Press, 1974.

Johnson, Paul. *A Shopkeeper's Millennium: Society and Revivals in Rochester, New York, 1815–1837.* New York: Hill and Wang, 2004.

Jones, Colin. *The Fall of Robespierre: 24 Hours in Revolutionary Paris*. Oxford: Oxford University Press, 2021.

Jones, Peter D'A. "Henry George and British Socialism." *The America Journal of Economics and Sociology* 47, no. 4 (October 1988): 473–491.

Jossa, Bruno. *Political Economy of Cooperatives and Socialism*. London: Routledge, 2021.

Juares, Jean. *A Socialist History of the French Revolution*. Translated by Mitchell Abidor. Introduction by Henry Weller. London: Pluto Press, 2015.

Judis, John. *The Socialist Awakening: What's Different Now About the Left*. New York: Columbia, 2020.

Kain, Philip J. "Marx's Theory of Ideas." *History and Theory* 20, no. 4 (December 1981).

Kallman, Theodore. *The Kingdom of God is at Hand: The Christian Commonwealth in Georgia, 1896–1901*. Athens: University of Georgia, 2021.

Kates, Gary, ed., *The French Revolution: Recent Debates and New Controversies*. London and New York: Routledge, 1998.

Katz, Jonathan. *Gangsters of Capitalism: Smedley Butler, the Marines, and the Making and Breaking of America's Empire*. New York: St. Martin's Press, 2022.

Kazin, Michael. *American Dreamers*. New York: Vintage, 2011.

Kencheyan, Razmig. *The Left Hemisphere: Mapping Critical Theory Today*. London: Verso, 2010.

Kipnis, Ira. *The American Socialism Movement, 1897–1912*. New York: Columbia University Press, 1952.

Kirk, Rudolf, and Clara Kirk. "Howells and the Church of the Carpenter." *New England Quarterly* 32, no. 2 (June 1959).

Kirkup, Thomas. *History of Socialism*. New York: Macmillan, 1909.

———. *Inquiry into Socialism*. Longmans, Green, and Co., 1907.

———. *A Primer of Socialism*. First edition 1908. London: A&C Black, 1908.

Klay, Robin, and John Lunn. "The Relationship of God's Providence to Market Economies." *Journal of Markets & Morality* 6, no. 2 (Fall 2003).

Kloppenberg, James T., *Uncertain Victory: Social Democracy and Progressivism in European and American Thought, 1870–1920*. New York: Oxford University Press, 1986.

Knight, Peter. *Reading the Market: Genres of Financial Capitalism in Gilded Age America*. Baltimore: Johns Hopkins University Press, 2016.

Kruger, Mark. *The St. Louis Commune of 1877: Communism in the Heartland*. Lincoln: University of Nebraska, 2021.

Kruse, Kevin, and Julian E. Zelizer, eds., *Myth America: Historians Take on the Biggest Legends and Lies about the Past*. New York: Basic Books, 2022.

Kuklick, Bruce. *A History of Philosophy in America, 1720–2000*. Oxford: Oxford University Press, 2002.

Lambert, Frank. *Religion in American Politics: A Short History*. Princeton: Princeton University Press, 2008.

Lamoreaux, Naomi R. *The Great Merger Movement in American Business, 1895–1904* Cambridge: Cambridge University Press, 1988.

Lasch, Christopher. *The Agony of the American Left*. New York: Vintage, 1968.

Lawday, David. *Danton: The Giant of the Revolution, A Life*. New York: Grove Press, 2009.

Lear, Jackson. *Rebirth of a Nation: The Making of Modern America, 1877–1920*. New York: HarperPerennial, 2009.

Lee, R. Alton, and Steven Cox, *When Sunflowers Bloomed Red: Kansas and the Rise of Socialism in America*. Lincoln: University of Nebraska Press, 2020.

Lefebvre, George. *The French Revolution from 1793 to 1799*. Translated by John Hall Stewart and James Friguglietti. New York: Columbia University, 1964.

Leikin, Steve. *The Practical Utopians: Cooperation and the American Labor Movement, 1860–1890*. Detroit: Wayne State University Press, 2005.

Lenin, Vladimir Ilyich. *Collected Works*. Moscow: Progress Publishers, 1977.

———. *Imperialism: The Highest Stage of Capitalism*. Chippendale, Australia: Resistance Books, 1999.

———. *What Is to Be Done?* New York: International Publishers, 1931.

Levy, Jonathan. *Ages of American Capitalism: A History of the United States*. New York: Random House, 2021.

———. *Freaks of Fortune: The Emerging World of Capitalism and Risk in America*. Cambridge: Harvard University Press, 2014.

Liedman, Sven-Eric. *A World to Win: The Life and Works of Karl Marx*. Translated by Jeffrey N. Skinner. London: Verso, 2018.

Linebaugh, Peter, and Marcus Rediker, *The Many-Headed Hydra: Sailors, Slaves, Commoners, and the Hidden History of the Revolutionary Atlantic*. London: Verso, 2000.

Linton, Marisa. *Choosing Terror: Virtue, Friendship, and Authenticity in the French Revolution*. Oxford: Oxford University Press, 2015.

Lipow, Arthur. *Authoritarian Socialism in America: Edward Bellamy and the Nationalist Movement*. Berkeley: University of California Press, 1982.

Lipset, Martin Seymour, and Gary Marks, *It Didn't Happen Here: Why Socialism Failed in the United States*. New York: W.W. Norton, 2000.

Lloyd, Henry Demarest Lloyd. *Wealth Against Commonwealth*. New York: Harper & Brothers Publishers, 1894.

Luxemburg, Rosa. "Social Reform or Revolution," *The Rosa Luxemburg Reader*. New York: Monthly Review Press, 2004.

Maggor, Noam. *Brahmin Capitalism: Frontiers of Wealth and Populism in America's First Gilded Age*. Cambridge: Harvard University Press, 2017.

Maher, Paul. "Laurence Gronlund: Contributions to American Socialism." *The Western Political Quarterly* 15, no. 4 (December 1962).

Mandel, Ernest. *Marxist Economic Theory*. Vol. 1. Translated by Brian Pearce. New York: Monthly Review Press, 1970.

Martin, Robert W. T. *Government by Dissent: Protest, Resistance, and Radical Democratic Thought in the Early American Republic*. New York: New York University Press, 2013.

Marx, Karl. *Capital*. Vol. 1. New York: Penguin Classics, 1976.

——. *Contributions to the Critique of Hegel's Philosophy of Right*. Translated by A. Jolin and Joseph O'Malley. Edited by Joseph O'Malley. Cambridge: Cambridge University Press, 1970.

——. *Dispatches for the New York Tribute: Selected Journalism of Karl Marx*. Edited by James Ledbetter. New York: Penguin Books, 2007.

——. *The 18th Brumaire of Louis Bonaparte*. New York: International Publishers, 1994.

——. *The Poverty Philosophy of Philosophy*. New York: International Publishers, 1963.

*Marx and Engels on the United States*. Moscow: Progress Publishers, 1979.

Marx, Karl, and Fredrich Engels. *Collected Works of Karl Marx and Frederick Engels*. Vol. 29. New York: International Publishers, 1975–2005.

Mason, Laura. *The Last Revolutionaries: The Conspiracy Trial of Gracchus Babeuf and the Equals*. New Haven: Yale, 2022.

Mathiez, Albert. *The French Revolution*. New York: Grosset & Dunlap, 1964.

Mattingly, Paul H. *American Academic Cultures: A History of Higher Education*. Chicago: University of Chicago Press, 2017.

May, Henry. *Protestant Churches and Industrial America.* New York: Harper and Brothers, 1949.

McCann, Charles R. "Apprehending the Social Philosophy of Henry George." *The American Journal of Economics and Sociology* 67, no. 1 (Jan. 2008).

McCarraher, Eugene. *The Enchantments of Mammon: How Capitalism Became the Religion of Modernity.* Cambridge, MA: Belknap/Harvard, 2019.

McCarthy, Timothy Patrick, and John McMillian, *The Radical Reader: A Documentary History of the American Radical Tradition.* New York: New Press, 2003.

McGerr, Michael. *A Fierce Discontent: The Rise and Fall of the Progressive Movement in America, 1870–1920.* New York: Oxford University Press, 2005.

McGirr, Lisa. *Suburban Warriors: The Origins of the New American Right* (Princeton: Princeton University Press, 2002.

McGrath, Alistair. *Reformation Thought: An Introduction.* Cambridge: Blackwell Publishers, 1995.

McKanan, Dan. "The Dialogue of Socialism: Common Interest in a Better World Led the Way for Religious Pluralism." *Harvard Divinity Bulletin* 38, no. 3 & 4 (Summer/ Autumn, 2010). https://bulletin.hds.harvard.edu/the-dialogue-of-socialism/.

———. *Prophetic Encounters: Religion and the American Radical Tradition.* Boston: Beacon, 2011.

McLellan, David, ed., *Karl Marx: Selected Writings.* New York: Oxford University Press, 1977.

McNeill, George Edwin. *The Labor Movement: The Problem of Today.* Wilkes-Barre, Pennsylvania: T.M. Moyles & Co., 1888.

McWilliams, Carey. *Factories in the Field: The Story of Migrating Farm Labor in California.* Berkeley: University of California Press, 2000.

Meister, Daniel. "The Biographical Turn and the Case for Historical Biography." *History Compass* 16, no. 1 (January 2018).

Menand, Louis. *The Metaphysical Club: A Story of Ideas in America.* New York: Farrar, Straus, and Giroux, 2001.

Messer-Kruse, Timothy. *The Yankee International: Marxism and the American Reform Tradition.* Chapel Hill: University of North Carolina Press, 1998.

Miller, Daegan. *This Radical Land: A Natural History of American Dissent.* Chicago: Chicago University Press, 2018.

Miller, Sally. *Victor Berger and the Promise of Constructive Socialism, 1910–1920.* Westport, CT: Praeger, 1973.

Montgomery, David. *Citizen Worker: The Experience of Workers in the United States with Democracy and the Free Market during the Nineteenth Century.* Cambridge University Press, 1994.

———. *The Fall of the House of Labor: The Workplace, the State, and American Labor Activism, 1865–1925.* Cambridge: Cambridge University Press, 1989.

Morgan, Arthur E. *Plagiarism in Utopia: A Study of the Continuity of the Utopian Tradition with Special Reference to Edward Bellamy's Looking Backward.* Yellow Springs, OH: Published by the author, 1944.

Moss, Laurence. *Henry George: Political Ideologue, Social Philosopher and Economic Theorist.* Wiley-Blackwell, 2008.

Mulford, Elisha. *The Republic of God: An Institute of Theology.* 4th ed. Boston: Houghton, Mifflin and Company, 1882.

Nelson, Robert Gabriel. "The People's Capital: The Politics of Popular Wealth in the Gilded Age." Ph.D., diss., UC Berkeley, 2019.

Nichols, John. *The "S" Word: A Short History of an American Tradition . . . Socialism.* Verso, 2015.

Norris, Stephen M. "A Biographical Turn? *Kritika: Explorations in Russian and Eurasian History* 17, no. 1 (Winter 2016).

Obermann, Karl. *Joseph Weydemeyer.* New York: International Publishers, 1947.

O'Connell, Jay. *Co-operative Dreams: A History of Kaweah Colony.* Northridge, CA: Raven River Press, 1999.

O'Donnell, Edward T. *Henry George and the Crisis of Inequality: Progress and Poverty in the Gilded Age.* New York: Columbia University Press, 2017.

Owen, A. K. *Integral Co-operation.* New York: John W. Lovell Company, 1889.

Owen, Robert. *Two Discourses on a New System of Society; as Delivered in the Hall of Representatives at Washington.* London: Whiting and Branston, 1825.

Patnaik, Utsa, and Prabhat Patnaik, *Capital and Imperialism: Theory, History, and the Present.* New York: Monthly Review Press, 2021.

Pearce, Trevor. *Pragmatism's Evolution: Organicism and Environment in American Philosophy.* Chicago: University of Chicago Press, 2020.

Peel, J. D. Y. *Herbert Spencer: The Evolution of a Sociologist.* New York: Basic Books, 1971.

Perez, Louis, Jr., *The War of 1898: The United States and Cuba in History and Historiography.* Chapel Hill: University of North Carolina Press, 1998.

Perry, Lewis. *Civil Disobedience: An American Tradition.* New Haven: Yale University Press, 2013.

———. *Radical Abolitionism: Anarchy and the Government of God in Antislavery Thought.* Ithaca: Cornell University Press, 1973.

Piketty, Thomas C. *Capital in the Twenty-First Century.* Translated by Arthur Goldhammer. Cambridge: Belknap/Harvard University Press, 2014.

Pinkard, Terry. *German Philosophy, 1760–1860: The Legacy of Idealism.* Cambridge: Cambridge University Press, 2002.

Pittenger, Mark. *American Socialists and Evolutionary Thought, 1870–1920*. Madison: University of Wisconsin Press, 1993.

Phelps, Christopher, and Robin Vandome, *Marxism & America: An Appraisal*. Manchester: Manchester University Press, 1824.

Pope, Daniel, ed., *American Radicalism*. Malden, MA: Blackwell, 2001.

Popkin, Jeremy D. *A New World Begins: The History of the French Revolution*. New York: Basic Books, 2019.

Porter, Theodore. *Trust in Numbers: The Pursuit of Objectivity in Science and Public Life*. Princeton: Princeton University Press, 1995.

Postel, Charles. *The Populist Vision: An American Dilemma, 1866–1896*. New York: Oxford, 2007.

Powderly, Terence. *Thirty Years of Labor 1859–1889*. New York: A.M. Kelley, 1967.

Quint, Howard, *Forging of American Socialism*. Columbia, SC: University of South Carolina Press, 1953.

Rader, Benjamin. "Richard T. Ely: Lay Spokesman for the Social Gospel." *Journal of American History* 53 (June 1966).

Raihani, Nichola. *The Social Instinct: How Cooperation Shaped the World*. New York: St. Martin's Press, 2021.

Ranis, Peter. *Cooperatives Confront Capitalism: Challenging the Neoliberal Economy*. London: Zed Books, 2016.

Ratner-Rosenhagen, Jennifer. *The Ideas that Made America: A Brief History*. New York: Oxford, 2019.

Rauschenbusch, Walter. *A Theology for the Gospel*. New York: Abingdon Press, 1917.

Restakis, John. *Humanizing the Economy: Co-operatives in the Age of Capital: Co-operatives in the Age of Capital*. Canada: New Society Publishers, 2010.

Reynolds, Larry. *European Revolutions and the American Literary Renaissance*. New Haven: Yale University Press, 1988.

Richards, Jay. *Money, Greed, and God: The Christian Case for Free Enterprise*. NY: HarperOne, 2010.

Robertson, Michael. *The Last Utopians: Four Late Nineteenth-Century Visionaries and their Legacy*. Princeton: Princeton University Press, 2018.

Rodgers, Daniel T. *Atlantic Crossings: Social Politics in a Progressive Age*. Cambridge: Harvard/Belknap Press, 1998.

Rorty, Richard. *Achieving Our Country: Leftist Thought in Twentieth-Century America*. Cambridge: Harvard University Press, 1999.

Ross, Jack. *The Socialist Party of America: A Complete History*. Nebraska: University of Nebraska Press, 2015.

Rossinow, Doug. *Visions of Progress: The Left-Liberal Tradition in America*. Philadelphia: University of Pennsylvania Press, 2007.

Salvatore, Nick. *Eugene V. Debs: Citizen and Socialist.* Urbana: University of Illinois Press, 2nd ed. 2007.

Schama, Simon. *Citizens: A Chronicle of the French Revolution.* New ed. New York: Penguin, 2004.

Schneider, Henry W. *A History of American Philosophy.* 2nd ed. New York: Columbia, 1963.

Schneirov, Richard. "Thoughts on Periodizating the Gilded Age: Capital Accumulation, Society, and Politics, 1873–1898." *Journal of the Gilded Age and Progressive Era* 5, no. 3 (2006).

Seretan, L. Glen. *Daniel De Leon: The Odyssey of an American Marxist.* Cambridge: Harvard University Press, 1979.

Shannon, David. *The Decline of American Communism: A History of Communist Party of the United States since 1945.* New York: Harcourt Brace, 1959.

———. *The Socialist Party of America: A History.* New York: Macmillan, 1955.

Shannon, Fred A. *The Farmer's Last Frontier: Agriculture 1860–1897.* New York: Farrar & Rinehart, Inc., 1945.

Shore, Elliott. *Talkin' Socialism: J.A. Wayland and the Role of the Press in American Radicalism, 1890–1912.* Lawrence: University Press of Kansas, 1988.

Simmel, Georg. "The Metropolis and Mental Life." In *The Sociology of Georg Simmel.* Translated and edited by Kurt H. Wolff. Introduction by Kurt H. Wolff. Glencoe, IL: Free Press, 1950.

Simons, A. M. *Single Tax Versus Socialism.* Chicago, 1899.

Sklar, Martin J. *The Corporate Reconstruction of American Capitalism: 1890–1916.* Cambridge: Cambridge University Press, 1988.

Smith, Carl. *Urban Disorder and the Shape of Belief: The Great Chicago Fire, the Haymarket Bomb, and the Model Town of Pullman.* Chicago: University of Chicago, 1995.

Smith, Neil. *American Empire: Roosevelt's Geography and the Prelude to Globalization.* Berkeley: University of California Press, 2003.

Soboul, Albert. *The French Revolution, 1787–1799: From the Storming of the Bastille to Napoleon.* New York: Vintage, 1975.

Sombart, Werner, *Why Is There No Socialism in the United States.* Translated by Patricia Hocking and C.T. Husbands. Foreword by Michael Harrington. London: Macmillan Press, 1976.

Spann, Edward. *Brotherly Tomorrows: Movements for a Cooperative Society in America, 1820–1920.* New York: Columbia University Press, 1989.

Spencer, Herbert. *First Principles.* London: Williams and Norgate, 1862.

———. *The Principles of Ethics.* Vol. 2. New York: D. Appleton and Company, 1897.

———. *The Study of Sociology.* New York: D. Appleton and Company, 1898.

Sproat, John G. *"The Best Men": Liberal Reformers in the Gilded Age.* Oxford: Oxford University Press, 1968.

Sreenivasan, Jyotsna. *Utopias in American History.* Santa Barbara: ABC-CLIO, 2008.

Stack, David. *The First Darwinian Left: Socialism and Darwinism, 1859–1914.* Cheltenham: New Clarion Press, 2003.

Stansell, Christine. *American Moderns: Bohemian New York and the Creation of a New Century.* New York: Metropolitan Books, 2000.

Staughton, Lynd. *Intellectual Origins of American Radicalism.* New York: Vintage, 1968.

Stevens, Errol Wayne. "Los Angeles: Harrison Gray Otis and Job Harriman," *California History* 86, no. 3 (2009).

Stromquist, Shelton. *Reinventing "The People": The Progressive Movement.* Urbana: University of Illinois Press, 2006.

Sumner, Helen. "Laurence Gronlund," *The Comrade* (February 1905).

Sumner, William Graham. *Social Darwinism: Selected Essays.* Edited by Albert Galloway Keller. Englewood Cliffs, NJ; Prentice Hall, 1963.

Sylvis, James, ed., *The Life, Speeches, Labors and Essays of William H. Sylvis.* Philadelphia: Claxton, Remsen & Haffelfinger, 1872.

Tackett, Timothy. *Becoming Revolution: The Deputies of the French National Assembly and the Emergence of a Revolutionary Culture (1789–1790).* Princeton: Princeton University Press, 1996.

———. *The Coming of the Terror in the French Revolution.* Cambridge: Harvard University Press, 2015.

———. *When the King Took Flight.* Cambridge: Harvard University Press, 2003.

Taylor, Michael. *The Philosophy of Herbert Spencer.* London: Continuum, 2007.

Tendler, Joseph. "Alphonse Aulard Revisited," *European Review of History—Revue europeenne d'histoire* 20, no. 4 (2013).

Thelin, John R. *A History of American Higher Education.* 3rd ed. Baltimore: Johns Hopkins University Press, 2019.

Thomas, John L. *Alternative Americas: Henry George, Edward Bellamy, Henry Demarest Lloyd and the Adversary Tradition.* Cambridge: Belknap/Harvard, 1983.

Tomlin, Christopher. *The State and the Unions: Labor Relations, Law, and the Organized Labor Movement in America, 1880–1960.* Cambridge: Cambridge University Press, 1985.

Trachtenberg, Alan. *The Incorporation of America: Culture and Society in the Gilded Age.* New York: Hill & Wang, 2007.

Traverso, Enzo. *Revolution: An Intellectual History.* London: Verso, 2021.

Trefousse, Hans L. *Carl Schurz: A Biography.* New York: Fordham University Press, 1998.

Tsuzuki, Chushichi. "Laurence Gronlund and American Socialism." *Hitotsubashi Journal of Social Studies* 4, no. 1 (January 1968).

Vail, Charles. *Modern Socialism.* New York: The Humboldt Library, 1897.

——. *National Ownership of Railways.* New York: Humboldt Library, 1897.

VanOverbeke, Marc A. *The Standardization of American Schooling: Linking Secondary and Higher Education, 1870–1910.* New York: Palgrave MacMillan, 2008.

Voss, Kim. *The Making of American Exceptionalism: The Knights of Labor and Class Formation in the Nineteenth Century.* Ithaca: Cornell University Press, 1993.

Vovelle, Michel. *The Fall of the French Monarchy, 1787–1791.* Cambridge: Cambridge University Press, 1984.

Wahnich, Sophia. *In Defense of the Terror: Liberty or Death in the French Revolution.* London: Verso, 2012.

Wallace, William. *The Logic of Hegel: Translated from the Encyclopedia of the Philosophical Sciences.* Oxford: Clarendon Press, 1892.

Wallerstein, Immanuel. *Historical Capitalism.* London: Verso, 2011.

Wasserstraum, Jeffrey. *Oxford Illustrated History of Modern China.* Oxford: Oxford University Press, 2016.

Wayland, J. A. *Leaves of My Life: A Story of Twenty Years of Socialist Agitation.* Girard, KS: Appeal to Reason, 1912.

Webb, Sidney. *Socialism in England.* London: Swan Sonnenschein & Co., 1890.

Weinstein, James. *Decline of Socialism in America, 1912–1925.* New York: Monthly Review Press, 1967.

White, Richard. *Railroaded: Transcontinentals and the Making of Modern America.* New York: W.W. Norton, 2011.

——. *The Republic for Which It Stands: The United States During Reconstruction and the Gilded Age, 1865–1896.* New York: Oxford, 2017.

Widdicombe, Toby, James M. Morris, and Andrea Kross. *Historical Dictionary of Utopianism.* 2nd ed. Lanham: Rowman & Littlefield, 2017.

Wienen, Mark W. Van. *American Socialist Triptych: The Literary-Political Work of Charlotte Perkins Gilman, Upton Sinclair, and W.E.B. Du Bois.* Ann Arbor: University of Michigan Press, 2012.

Williams, Richard C. *The Cooperative Movement: Globalization from Below.* London: Routledge, 2016.

Wirzbicki, Peter. *Fighting for the Higher Law: Black and White Transcendentalists Against Slavery.* Philadelphia: University of Pennsylvania Press, 2021.

Witt, John Fabian. *The Accidental Republic: Crippled Working, Destitute Widows, and the Remaking of American Law.* Cambridge: Harvard University Press, 2004.

Wittke, Carl. *The Utopian Communist: A Biography of Wilhelm Weitling, Nineteenth-Century Reformer.* Baton Rouge: LSU Press, 1950.

Wolin, Sheldon. *Democracy Incorporated: Managed Democracy and the Specter of Inverted Totalitarianism.* Princeton: Princeton University Press, 2017.

Young, Alfred, ed., *Dissent: Explorations in the History of American Radicalism*. Dekalb: Northern Illinois University Press, 1968.

Young, Ralph. *Dissent: The History of an Idea*. New York: New York University Press, 2015.

## PERIODICALS/JOURNALS

*American Fabian*

*Appeal to Reason*

*The Arena*

*Boston Globe*

*The Bulletin of the Social Reform Union*

*The Commonweal*

*Comrade*

*The Dawn*

*Evening Star*

*Harper's Monthly*

*Journal of United Labor*

*Lincoln Journal Star*

*Los Angeles Herald*

*The National Economist Almanac*

*The Nationalist*

*The New Ideal*

*The New Nation*

*Pittsburgh Daily Headlight*

*Progressive Thought*

*Sacramento Bee*

*Salt Lake Herald*

*Seattle Post-Intelligencer*

*The Southwestern Local*

*The Spokesman-Review*

*Twentieth Century*

# INDEX